THREE WAR MARINE HERO

General Raymond G. Davis

COLONEL RICHARD D. CAMP

CASEMATE

Philadelphia & Oxford

Dedicated to all Marines—past, present, and future—Semper Fi

Published in the United States of America and Great Britain in 2020 by
CASEMATE PUBLISHERS
1950 Lawrence Road, Havertown, PA 19083, USA
and
The Old Music Hall, 106–108 Cowley Road, Oxford OX4 1JE, UK

Copyright 2020 © Colonel Richard D. Camp

Hardback Edition: ISBN 978-1-61200-939-1
Digital Edition: ISBN 978-1-61200-940-7

A CIP record for this book is available from the British Library

Printed and bound in the United States of America by Sheridan

Typeset by Versatile PreMedia Services (P) Ltd

For a complete list of Casemate titles, please contact:

CASEMATE PUBLISHERS (US)
Telephone (610) 853-9131
Fax (610) 853-9146
Email: casemate@casematepublishers.com
www.casematepublishers.com

CASEMATE PUBLISHERS (UK)
Telephone (01865) 241249
Email: casemate-uk@casematepublishers.co.uk
www.casematepublishers.co.uk

Contents

Part Five: Korea (Land of the Morning Calm)

Part Six: Vietnam

Foreword

In May 2000, with the heat and humidity growing by the minute, thankfully the Peachtree, Georgia, Memorial Day ceremony was drawing to a close. The event's Grand Marshal was retired four-star General Raymond G. Davis. Wearing his woolen, choker-collared "dress blue" uniform, he rose to the position of attention, saluting as the flag was hoisted.

But the halyard jammed, the flag was "stuck" nowhere near its proper position on the pole. In the stifling heat the color guard worked feverishly to break it free. The 85-year-old general stood motionless, his firm salute unwavering. As the minutes and heat became wearisome, out of courtesy to the retired general wearing the Medal of Honor, an event organizer whispered that it would be acceptable if he resumed his seat. Yet stoically he stood at attention until, at last, the flag was freed and properly hoisted. Only then did General Davis lower his salute.

For those who knew his combat record, it was no surprise to see him stand fast that day. After all, hadn't he always been at his best when the times were at their worst? A warm day in Peachtree was nothing compared to what this old warrior had been through in the 60-odd years since he had left Georgia for the Marines.

***

Students of military history are familiar with once great militaries that forgot their raison d'être: to fight well and win in the most atavistic environment imaginable, or even unimaginable for those who have never faced the crucible of combat.

If there is one organization among the militaries of the western democracies that has no institutional confusion about the reason for its existence, it is the U.S. Marine Corps. On any battlefield the arrival of Marines breeds confidence among allies and despair among foes.

Yet, like all militaries, the U.S. Marines are a human organization. The Corps' traditions, combat record and adaptive ability in the face of exigencies reflect the Marines' individual devotion and competence: devotion to comrades-in-arms past and present; and the highest degree of soldierly competence in a grim trade, never permitting complacency to squelch adaptation.

Unflinchingly honest, Colonel Dick Camp has brought this legacy to life through the career of one great Marine. A tested combat leader who played an outsized role in establishing the Marines' reputation for courage, competence and adaptability, General Davis led Marines in tough fighting in three wars.

Today, whether at happy hours, around fighting holes or in classrooms, Marines are taught their history so they understand the legacy they are bound to uphold. World War II beach assaults like Guadalcanal and Peleliu, the Korean War breakout from the frozen Chosin Reservoir, and jungle fighting in Vietnam's "Leatherneck Square," are dissected for their enduring lessons because they show Marines proving equal to the worst that combat can throw at them. These were among the very battles where General Davis proved his mettle.

Ray Davis led his sailors and Marines with personal courage, tactical cunning and deep-seated empathy. During his 34 years of service in peace and war, the demands of the battlefield were foremost in his mind. He was a realist, and in the most daunting circumstances, he never took refuge in pessimism. He saw his role as a leader as giving his best, that problems were his responsibility to solve. From taking an island from a well dug-in enemy or securing an escape route out of the frozen Korean mountains for isolated Marines, he faced the toughest missions matter-of-factly—a duty to be done, so he got on with it.

His leadership built trust among his men, such that subordinates came to confidently embrace his tactics. At the same time his seniors realized that here was a good man, a steady Marine, one who could be counted on to accomplish missions when facing the toughest tests. In the worst circumstances he would not be deterred rather he would adapt and overcome all obstacles no matter how badly the chips were stacked against his lads. That can-do spirit permeated the ranks of his Marines. An implacable fighting leader on the battlefield, he never lost his humanity or the spiritual connection with his youngest, most junior Marines.

In this superb study of the life and times of General Davis, fighting men can see clearly what Hemingway explained in *Men at War*, "… that there are no worse things to be gone through than men have been through before." For those Americans who in future fights will face their own crucible of fire, and on whose courage our national survival will rest, Dick Camp has brought into sharp focus this essential example of an American fighting man in his prime: Raymond G. Davis, U.S. Marine.

James N. Mattis
General, U.S. Marines (ret.)
14 March 2020
Richland, Washington

Preface

I had just given up my company, Lima, 3rd Battalion, 26th Marines, and was assigned as the battalion assistant operations officer. I was walking back to the COC bunker after a short break when Major Joe Loughran,[1] the battalion executive officer, stopped me and asked, "How would you like to be an aide?" I replied, somewhat cavalierly, "Will the assignment get me out of here?" On 21 January, the siege of the Khe Sanh Combat Base had started and the base was being pounded daily by North Vietnamese mortars, rockets, and artillery. Joe laughed—we had become friends—and said he would put me in for the assignment.

I didn't think much more about it until several days later, when Joe informed me that I had been accepted for an interview at the Phu Bai headquarters of Provisional Corps, Vietnam, with the newly assigned Marine deputy, Major General Raymond G. Davis. He had just arrived in country having completed a three-year tour as the assistant chief of staff, G-1 at Headquarters Marine Corps.

I left the next day, and after a harrowing flight out of the besieged combat base—the NVA regularly shelled the airstrip—I reported to the adjutant at Provisional Corps Vietnam (later XXIV Corps) for the interview.

Minutes later I was ushered into Davis' office. I knew nothing about the trim, pleasant-looking man sitting behind the desk, except that he was a Marine general officer and that made me nervous as hell. Captains very seldom got to talk with anyone above the rank of lieutenant colonel.

He invited me to sit down in a soft-spoken, southern drawl and asked me questions about my experiences in Vietnam. I told him I had been an infantry company commander in the 3rd Marine Division for six months and what my current assignment was. He asked me where I had operated and I told him all over the Northern I Corps area; from Khe Sanh, to Con Thien, to Leatherneck Square. He seemed genuinely interested in my answers and encouraged me to expand on my knowledge of the Division's tactical area of operations.

After about 20 minutes he thanked me for coming—as if it was just a neighborly visit—and ushered me out of the office. I had no idea whether I had the assignment. The adjutant told me to wait around. The general was going to interview another candidate from the 1st Marine Division and would make a decision later that afternoon.

I was invited back to Davis' office sometime later and he told me that I had the assignment. Now all I had to do was figure out what an aide-de-camp did.

At the time I was a 25-year-old captain with six months' combat experience, while Ray Davis was a hardened combat veteran. This was brought home to me one day while visiting a remote Army firebase in the jungle south of Khe Sanh. As the two of us strode along the jungle pathway, Davis suddenly stopped and peered intently into the thick green foliage. I suspected danger, brought my rifle up, and slipped off the safety. After a few moments, the general turned and said, "Dick, this reminds me of a command post I had on Guadalcanal." I mumbled, "Yes, sir," and surreptitiously fingered the safety to the "on" position. "Christ," I thought in awe, "I was only two years old at the time of Guadalcanal. This is the old man's third war!"

I served as Davis' aide for only three months in Vietnam, but during that time I was fortunate to observe a true professional at the top of his game.

Part One

Formative Years, 1915–1941

CHAPTER I

A Youngster from Georgia

Raymond Gilbert Davis was born on 13 January 1915 in Fitzgerald, a small town in south central Georgia, 155 miles south of Atlanta. The town was founded in 1895 by a former drummer boy in the Union Army as a community for Civil War veterans from both sides of the conflict. However, the majority of its first citizens were 2,700 Union veterans, which seems bizarre given the lingering hard feelings about the war. However, in a show of magnanimity, the first two streets running north–south were named after Confederate generals Lee and Johnson, while the first two streets on the east were named after Union generals Grant and Sherman. After a year, the citizens planned a Thanksgiving harvest parade. Separate Union and Confederate parades were planned. However, when the band started to play, the Confederate veterans joined the Union veterans to march as one beneath the U.S. flag. The Davis family tree, like many in the South, notes that one ancestor fought for the Union and another for the Confederacy.

Ray's father, Raymond Roy, was in the grocery business, which caused the family to move frequently. Ray recalled, "Even though I began school in Fitzgerald, we moved to Atlanta after only the second grade, where I spent most of my young life. In Atlanta I attended Cascade Springs Grammar School, a two-mile walk from my home, Samuel Inman Elementary School, and Bass Junior High." The grammar school was a small two-room building, with six grades, and two teachers. Ray's third-grade room housed two other grades. He vividly recalled the teacher using a large switch on an unruly boy. "The next morning we were shocked to see the boy's woman [mother] enter the classroom and give the teacher three lashes with a similar switch."

One of the teachers owned an open Ford touring automobile. "It would quit on occasion, while en route to school, so we pushed it up the hills in exchange for a ride on the running board on the downhills. It was a great way to break up a dull day at school, and the teacher seemed to go easier on us on days when we pushed her to school."[1]

"When I was in the 3rd grade, my uncle came back from WWI and I sat on his knee for about a week and that's about as close to the military as I came. He challenged me to be best in my class and participate in everything and I think that started my career."[2]

A varsity wrestler at Atlanta Technical High School, Davis was not a star but kept at it, vying for the top spot with another boy in his weight class. In addition to wrestling, he ran cross-country. "In my senior year I started 'pumping iron' because my physical education teacher had a gym in downtown Atlanta. He was a big brute of a guy who had enormous physical proportions, including a 17.5-inch neck. I think that I stuck with him more for hunting trips made during the season than for gym work, but the resultant physical power served me well years later in the combat of World War II, Korea and Vietnam."

In 1933 Davis graduated from high school, having been selected to the National Honor Society and as the best drill cadet in the JROTC unit, and entered the Georgia School of Technology (now the Georgia Institute of Technology; commonly called Georgia Tech). He signed up for the full four-year program in the Army ROTC unit because of its small monetary allowance and free uniform.

Davis enjoyed success at "Tech," graduating with a Bachelor of Science degree in Chemical Engineering. He was awarded the college president's Gold Key for Scholarship and was designated as an ROTC honor graduate, eligible for a commission in the Army. "I was very fond of some of the instructors. They were great inspiration to me in everyday life. I just enjoyed and appreciated them."[3]

"The time came for graduation from Georgia Tech. I was a chemical engineer and I had been awarded a teaching fellowship at the University of Tennessee in some experimental work in elemental phosphorus and it was to pay me a small chunk of money and guaranteed me a master's degree in 18 months if I worked at it. I accepted this program just before graduation but then I got word from Knoxville that the money for the project had been cut back to half as much. Well, what they were originally paying me was starvation wages. Half that much I just couldn't take it. This was during the Depression and I just didn't have the funds."[4]

"I talked to the Army instructors about going into the service and they offered me the five-year Thompson Act, where reserve officers could serve on active duty for a 5-year period, but with no assurance at all that you could continue in the Army. This friendly lieutenant colonel told me the Navy had a commission in the Marine Corps that was a more permanent nature. So I went down to inquire and they described the program. After several candidates were interviewed, I was selected as the Marine candidate for the class of 1938 from Georgia Tech." At the time, the Marine Corps took advantage of the lean depression years and offered commissions to the top one or two graduates from the best ROTC colleges and universities.[5]

Davis was briefly commissioned as a second lieutenant in the U.S. Army Infantry Reserve, before resigning his commission to accept appointment as a second lieutenant in the U.S. Marine Corps on 27 June 1938. He once told a friend that he asked the recruiter if he could have some active duty time so he could eat. At the time, the military had some of the only jobs available.

"I told my family I wasn't even sure what it was that I was getting into ... except the Marines had a great reputation," Davis recalled. "The regular commission on active duty sounded good, so it was the Corps for me. I caught a bus to go over to Charleston Navy Yard for a physical. Somebody on the bus commented as we went in the gate about the Marine on the gate. That was the first time I ever got a serious look at a Marine."[6]

Second Lieutenant Raymond G. Davis

Second Lieutenant Raymond G. Davis received a train voucher and a set of orders from the Commandant of the Marine Corps to report for the 1938–1939 Marine Officers' Basic School class. He arrived at the Philadelphia & Reading Train and Bus Station on Broad Street and took a trolley to the Navy Yard, where a Marine sentry directed him to the Bachelor Officers' Quarters.

The Marine Officers' Basic School then, as now, took newly commissioned officers and taught them the basics of how to be an officer by focusing on small-unit fundamentals and weaponry. The ten-month course, a total of 1,200 hours, included a four-week block of instruction in the field centering on combat firing and small-unit tactics and a second phase at the Indiantown Gap Military Reservation in the rugged foothills of the Blue Ridge Mountains of central Pennsylvania. In the fall, the student officers spent a month at firing ranges at Cape May, New Jersey, learning everything from hand grenades to mortars. Davis found the curriculum "interesting and enjoyable."

"My classmates were a great group of people, enjoyable and smart," Davis recalled. "Among the 75 men in the class there were one or two from every college and university in the country, including 25 of the top graduates from the Naval Academy." Davis recalled one of his classmates, Second Lieutenant Gregory H. "Pappy" Boyington, later a Medal of Honor recipient and one of the leading fighter aces in World War II. "I believe anything anyone wants to say about him. He was the top character of all time and a great flyer. There were a few training planes at the Navy Yard and we'd fly up to New York for the weekend. I would always pick Pappy, if I could, because of his flying skills."[1]

Philadelphia's closeness to Washington, D.C., was made to order for young bachelor officers and Davis was one of those "Liberty Hounds." "Washington was an attractive liberty town," he admitted. One of his buddies drove a robin-egg-blue Chrysler convertible, "which became our headquarters in D.C." However, duty came before liberty. One night near-disaster struck because the "Hounds" ran out of gas and decided to sleep it off before returning to base. Unfortunately they arrived just in time to discover the battalion executive officer was conducting a surprise inspection. The miscreants slipped into formation ... but not quickly enough. Davis was "chewed out" and had his liberty curtailed, which ended his D.C. adventures.[2]

Lieutenant Colonel Gilder T. Jackson, a World War I hero, commanded the Basic School. Jackson was somewhat aloof, not really close to the students. "He never got in there and mixed it up with any of us," Davis said. "I recall his one appearance in our classroom. There had been some rumors which he did not like. He mounted the platform. We waited in great anticipation to hear our first words from this big boss. Very quickly he said, 'Some birds were in a horse barn eating manure when discovered by the farmer. They flew to a nearby fence as he loaded his gun. The farmer did not notice where they were until they started noisy chirping. Bang! They were shot off the fence. Remember, don't chirp when you are full of shit!' Out he walked."[3]

Davis thought the instructors were competent. However, the legendary Lewis B. "Chesty" Puller was a cut above. He was one of the most popular instructors at the school. "Lewie [friends called Puller Lewie, never Chesty] taught tactics, primarily small wars," Davis recalled. "He was the kind of instructor who would walk in with his lesson plan, put it on the lectern, and talk about the nitty gritty of wars that he had been in, without referring to the lesson plan. His lectures would cover topics that make and break officers."[4]

Puller was also responsible for a platoon of lieutenants. He encouraged them to maintain high standards of discipline, military bearing, and dress. "You had to pass the Puller uniform inspection," Davis recalled. "If you had room to breathe, it was too loose." One lieutenant had his uniform made by Jacob Reed, considered to be one of the finest uniform tailors in Philadelphia. Puller told the young officer that the uniform did not fit. The youngster tried to defend the tailor, which was a mistake. Puller told him in no uncertain terms, "This uniform is just not right. You go back there and tell old man Reed that this uniform is not going to pass."[5]

Davis recalled visiting the Puller's quarters. "Mrs. Puller was just as nice and gracious as she could be. If there was a dance at the club, the real gentleman in the whole crowd was Lewie Puller. He was a perfect host, dancer and conversationalist. He was gracious, a true Southern gentleman when he was required to be. Lewie was a great inspiration to me and one that had a significant influence on my career."[6]

Another officer that Davis remembered well was Lieutenant Colonel Frank Goettge, the executive officer of the school. "Outstanding fellow. He was a great football player and a hero in his own right, and one that really got down and communicated with the new lieutenants on an eyeball-to-eyeball basis."[7]

After graduation from the Basic School in May 1939, Davis was assigned to sea duty aboard the heavy cruiser USS *Portland* (CA-33), nicknamed "Sweet Pea." *Portland,* the sister ship of the ill-fated USS *Indianapolis* (CA-35), was home-ported in Long Beach, California, as part of Cruiser Division 5, Scouting Force. Davis reported aboard "fully prepared to assume my duties as the Marine Detachment's junior officer." The detachment consisted of two officers, three non-commissioned officers and 35 enlisted Marines. They served as an orderly for the ship's captain, guarding the brig (jail), security details, and ceremonial duties. But most importantly they "manned the ship's 5-inch antiaircraft battery," on the upper deck. These secondary batteries were designed for defense against surface and aircraft threats.[8]

Davis was one of those unfortunates who suffered "mal de mare." The Sweet Pea was an unstable ship that often rolled, even at anchor in a slight swell. It was reported that one time in heavy seas, the ship's inclinometer, a devise that measured rolls, reached 42 degrees. Since 45 degrees was marked as the danger point, the ship was in some peril. Davis' general quarters' station was high on the foremast where the pitch, sway and gut-wrenching plunges were most extreme. "I was cramped inside one of these directors to control the guns with assigned dials to watch and knobs to turn. The pitch and roll of the ship was greatly multiplied for those of us high up on the mast. I barely made it through the first drill. I was sick in my stateroom afterward and missed dinner. I could only crawl into my bunk and wish for death."[9]

In June 1939 the *Portland* deployed for the annual Fleet Problem (XXI), an eight-phase operation for the defense of the Hawaiian area and "in the far reaches of the Pacific," that lasted 47 days. It was the first Fleet Problem and the last that did not include virtually all the major units of the fleet because of the worsening world tensions. The exercises were designed to provide training of commanders in estimating the situation and planning, scouting and screening, communications, coordination and convoy escort, seizure of advanced bases, and finally, decisive engagements.

Upon completion of the exercise, the fleet remained at Pearl Harbor. As relations with Japan worsened in the summer of 1940, President Roosevelt was convinced that permanently transferring the Navy's Battle Force, which included the Scouting Force, to Pearl Harbor would be a restraining influence on Japan's aggressive ambitions in the Pacific. The fleet transfer was strongly opposed by Admiral James O. Richardson, its commander-in-chief, who took the opposite position; that the fleet was more vulnerable. Richardson argued against the president's decision so forcefully that he was relieved and replaced by Admiral Husband E. Kimmel. The Japanese attack on 7 December proved him correct.

Marine Major General Wilburt S. Brown was a captain aboard the USS *Pennsylvania* at the time of the fleet's transfer. "Roosevelt hit upon the idea of threatening Japan with an empty gun. For some reason he thought he was cowing the Japanese by keeping the fleet out there. The Japanese knew readiness for war much better than he did." Roosevelt's decision played right into their hands. In late summer 1940, Admiral Isoroku Yamamoto, commander-in-chief of the Japanese combined fleet, devised a plan to destroy the U.S. fleet in the Pacific at the onset of war—a surprise attack on Pearl Harbor.[10]

Davis developed a strong interest in gunnery and while aboard *Portland* he applied for the Base Defense Weapons School at Quantico, Virginia, in July 1940. "The school was touted as an antiaircraft and shore gun school which had some appeal to me. When you go to sea and live with the 5-inch guns in the AA battery and the detachment Marines for 15 months, you get interested in what you're doing." He worked with early mechanical computers and technical material, which was right up his alley because of his engineering background from Georgia Tech.[11]

"I really enjoyed the course, but as it progressed, we started doing base defense employment problems on far-flung islands in the Pacific. I discovered that all gunnery school graduates were promptly assigned to Defense Battalions and shipped to remote Pacific Islands for duty. The Defense Battalions at Guam and Wake were captured by the Japanese early in the war." The latter island fell after a heroic 18-day fight. "Such out-of-the-way coast defense positions did not appeal to me at all."

Davis avoided this assignment by "some luck and some design."[12] "Chesty [Lewie Puller] urged me to request duty with the newly formed 1st Marine Division. 'Well, I'll tell you Old Man (he always called me 'Old Man' throughout our long careers), there is a billet down in the 1st Marine Division at Guantanamo Bay Cuba where they need an antiaircraft officer. I think you would enjoy that.'" Davis took Puller at his word and requested assignment to the 1st Marine Division ("The Old Breed"). "And that's how I got out of the base defense battalions and into the Division."[13]

CHAPTER 3

The Old Breed: Special Weapons Battalion

Davis received orders to the 1st Marine Division at Guantanamo Bay, Cuba, in the summer of 1941. He boarded one of the Navy's transports at the Norfolk Navy Yard. In those days, traveling aboard one of the Navy's "finest" was a lesson in resilience. The Marines were crammed into suffocating troop compartments—gear jammed everywhere, racks stacked four and five high, no room, suffocating heat, no air circulation and the smell—stale sweat, faint vomit and the overwhelming odor of body odor and fuel oil—permeating everything. The general consensus among the Marines was that they were just human baggage in transit—looked down upon by the crew and barely tolerated except for the use of their muscle power to help maintain the ship.

One sea story that made the rounds concerned an unfortunate Leatherneck who was shanghaied to paint the side of the ship. He was lowered over the side in the hot sun, armed with gallons of paint and numerous brushes. After several hours, he was retrieved, but only after venting his frustration in true artistic fashion. Emblazoned on the hull, for all the world to see, was his rendition of the ship's name, *Chaumont*—"Christ Help All US Marines On Naval Transports." True or not, the story was accepted as gospel by the Marines.

Being an "Old Salt" and wise to the ways of naval transports, Davis got his unit settled and then scouted around until he found a "tiny stateroom with a porthole over the top bunk and climbed into the top bunk right under cool breeze from the porthole." He was awakened by two second lieutenants who demanded "seniority rights" to the bunk. "I played 'possum' for a spell," he said, "then I awoke slowly to rise up and say, 'Welcome! As Senior Officer, you two can move into my room if you like.'" Davis knew that he was two months their senior and won the good-natured argument. "We quickly became fast friends," he added.[1]

On the voyage, measles broke out on the troop ship and the passengers were quarantined in one of the vacant regimental camps on a finger of land well away from the main encampments. "To keep the men busy we organized a big working party to dig latrines for the encampment," Davis recalled. "It got to be a way to spend time during the quarantine period."[2]

At the end of the quarantine period, they were packing up ready to leave when the absent battalion whose camp they were in returned. Its commander, Lieutenant Colonel Julian N. "Bull" Frisbee, accused the quarantined men of stealing his troops' homemade furniture. "Frisbee made us assemble the men and stood us out in the sun for a while and bulldozed us right under," Davis grumbled. Frisbee had a violent temper. "I'm going to give you so much time to get all those things back in camp—or else!" Davis said, "He didn't have to explain what 'or else' meant."[3]

"We had no way of knowing what was missing," Davis recalled. "I turned it over to the NCOs and the next thing I knew they were going in all different directions." Within a couple of hours the "missing" furniture was replaced. "The NCOs had gone over to another vacant camp and brought all its stuff over, put it in Frisbee's camp, and off we went. I didn't hear any more about it because I received orders to return to the newly constructed Marine Barracks, New River, North Carolina."[4]

"I got there in time to join the 1st Antiaircraft Machine-Gun Battery that had just been organized under the command of Captain Victor H. 'Brute' Krulak [later Lieutenant General and a leading figure in keeping the Corps from being abolished after World War II]. It was a great lesson to watch the Brute in action with the Division staff where it was obvious that he was already a 'power' even as a captain … he had a great influence on me over the years." Davis, initially assigned as a platoon commander, later became the battery executive officer.[5]

While in New River, the battery was expanded into a Special Weapons Battalion with three batteries: antiaircraft, and two antitank (37mm and 75mm half-tracks) under Major Robert B. Luckey—"one of the finest gentleman I've ever been involved with. I really liked the man," Davis said. "Great sense of humor and very competent."[6]

Luckey recalled in a 1973 oral history interview, "'A' Battery was commanded by Ray Davis. It had .50-caliber machine guns [and] was labeled an antiaircraft battery. 'B' Battery had 12 37mm antitank guns and was designated an antitank battery and 'C' Battery had four half-tracks with a French 75mm mounted in the stern. They were known as tank destroyers. The half-tracks were not very efficient. The 75s weren't big enough to do any harm, and the .50-calibers weren't much of a threat to any airplane. But that's all we had, and that's what we went to Guadalcanal with." The mission of the battalion was to "support the Division from the point of view of antiaircraft and antitank service."[7]

The battalion stayed busy on maneuvers throughout the winter, which, even though North Carolina is considered to be in the south, from January through March can be extremely cold, especially for those in the field under canvas. Davis caught a break when he was assigned as an umpire for an Army training exercise at Fort Story, Virginia. "Because of this we were able to live in some warm Army barracks. They were old, but they were warm, with good chow and facilities." Davis was promoted to first lieutenant in August 1941 and captain six months later.[8]

Davis was designated the Division antiaircraft officer, an assignment that made him a special staff officer in the Division Operations Section where he got to know several key members of the staff—"Gerry Thomas, Wally Greene, Sammy Griffiths, Bill Buse, and Jim Masters, a battalion commander in the 1st Marines"—who would play a major role in the Division's future.[9] As an antiaircraft specialist, Davis contributed to the various operations plans and employment of the battalions weapons. He also administered antiaircraft training and ran the Division antiaircraft school. "We had airplanes pull target sleeves across Onslow Beach for all the truck drivers and others with machine guns to fire for practice. They all took a shot at the sleeves at least once so that when we went to war, they had some experience under their belts.[10]

As a commander, Davis was responsible for the well-being of the men in his battery, including their moral health. "In our tent camp we had some undue commotion late one night. One of my Marines coming off liberty smuggled his girlfriend into camp and into his tent at the far end of the street. She had so much fun that she moved to the next, and then the next. When the First Sergeant responded to all the excitement, she was halfway down the street and a line of men had formed outside the tent. She was escorted off the base. The First Sergeant told me that she had a pocketbook full of dollar bills, but when he accused her of prostitution, she objected, saying she only received a few 'tips!'"[11]

The incident was not uncommon at Camp Lejeune during those early hectic days when the Division was forming up and thousands of vibrant young men prowled the area during their free time. "Lejeune was at that time in a very isolated part of North Carolina, but girls came there from everywhere. They lived in attics, shanties, back rooms of roadside bars and restaurants and nearby motels. When liberty call went at camp, they seemed to appear from everywhere."[12]

In November, Brigadier General Alexander A. "Archie" Vandegrift was able to persuade the Commandant, General Thomas Holcomb, to allow him to leave Washington for field service. He was assigned as the 1st Marine Division's assistant commander and given responsibility for its training. He arrived at Camp Lejeune on 26 November, just a little over a week before Pearl Harbor. "My aide and I had gone down to Wilmington, which was on a Sunday, to have lunch at a restaurant we knew when the word came of Pearl Harbor and, of course, we lost no time in getting back to the base."[13]

Part Two

World War II: Central Pacific–Guadalcanal

CHAPTER 4

"War"

"Pipe down," an excited voice shouted, as an announcement blared from a short-wave radio. "We interrupt this program to bring you a special news broadcast. Pearl Harbor has been bombed!" The word went out. Men gathered around the few radios in the tent camp. Davis remembered, "Everybody stayed up all night listening to the news and thinking about getting ready to go [to war]." Shortly after Pearl Harbor, in February 1942, Davis was promoted to captain and then he was promoted "about once a year after that," because of the rapid growth of the Corps.[1]

Training at the huge New River, North Carolina, base took on a new importance. However, war scares were rampant and Davis' battery was called out to defend the base. "Reports of a hostile German dirigible coming across the Atlantic to drop bombs on us led to an organized AA defense around our camps. We had to dig pits all round Camp Lejeune and mount our machine guns and stand round the clock watches to shoot down this dirigible. I performed my only engineering project in the Corps ... I supervised the building of a low bridge so that we could move our guns wherever they were needed." The report soon proved to be false, and training continued until the following summer.[2]

While the airship rumor proved to be false, German U-boats operated off the North Carolina coast as early as mid-January 1942. On 19 January, the SS *City of Atlanta* was torpedoed by a U-123, killing all but three of her 47-man crew. The U-boat attacked three more ships just hours later. The Outer Banks of North Carolina soon earned the name "Torpedo Junction" because so many ships were sunk.

Thousands of men were ordered to Marine Barracks, New River, North Carolina, to bring the 1st Marine Division up to war strength—"Young recruits only recently out of boot training ... others were older; first sergeants yanked off 'planks' in Navy yards, sergeants from recruiting duty, gunnery sergeants who had fought in France, perennial privates with disciplinary records, a yard long."[3]

The expansion between 7 December 1941 and 1 May 1942 brought the Division from a small pre-war nucleus to a war-strength division. This buildup presented the serious problem of training, equipping, and quartering the men, which was further

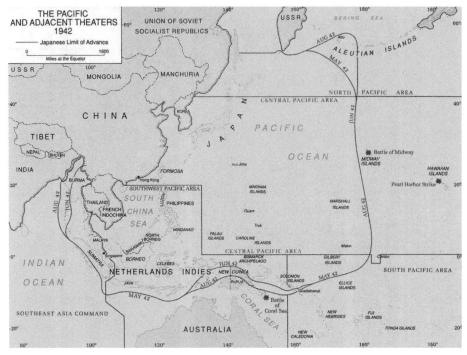

By the summer of 1942, Japan had expanded its conquest across a vast distance of the Pacific and threatened Australia. (U.S. Army, 'Western Pacific: The U.S. Army Campaigns of World War II')

complicated by the early detachment of a provisional brigade for immediate service in the South Pacific.

The formation of this brigade built around the 7th Marines (reinforced) withdrew a disproportionate number of officers, non-commissioned officers and men trained and experienced in amphibious warfare. "We were told at that time, and this affected our morale very badly, that no Marine division would participate as a division in World War II," Major William Twining said. "The division would exist only as a training cadre to spawn these defense contingents." The Division was also bled white to furnish men for the Raider and Parachute Battalions.[4]

These experienced men could not be replaced. As a result, the Division was reconstituted with two regiments—1st Marines and 5th Marines—and supporting units. The 1st Marines was a regiment in name only. It was just forming up at Parris Island with raw recruits, new inexperienced NCOs and old timers that hadn't been to the field in years. The Division remained a two-regiment organization until the arrival of the 7th Marines on Guadalcanal in September 1942 returned it to the original triangular organization.[5]

With the Japanese advance across the Pacific and the fall of the Marine garrisons on Guam and Wake, war preparations began at a hectic pace. Bob Luckey explained,

"I think everybody in the Division realized that it was only a question of time before we were going to leave and go somewhere."[6]

"We got the ranges set up to do realistic training with live ammunition, including getting the infantry used to having artillery fire over their heads," Vandegrift explained. The training continued up until the time that the Division left for New Zealand.[7]

Practical training included "one really fine field exercise in which we moved the whole Division back inland about 50 miles from the coast and then marched them into the reservation, deployed them, and set up a real defense of the beach line along there."[8]

In addition to the training at New River, each reinforced combat team of the 5th Marines and one of the 1st Marines engaged in a ten-day landing exercise on the Solomon Islands, Maryland, during March and April.[9]

The exercise did not go well. It was blamed on a lack of training but there was also an undercurrent of a lack of confidence in the Division commander, Major General Phillip H. Torrey. He did not get along with his boss, Major General Holland M. "Howlin' Mad" Smith, who according to Twining, "was entirely too old and irascible and extremely difficult to get along with."[10]

Vandegrift was observing the exercise when he was abruptly summoned to Washington by the Commandant, General Thomas Holcomb. "He came back that night and told me," Twining recalled, "'Bill, I am going to take over the Division from General Torrey. General Holcomb told me so today.'" On 23 March, Vandegrift was given a second star and took command of the Division "at a brief ceremony in front of the rehabilitated farmhouse that would serve as both his residence and as a temporary headquarters." Torrey received orders to Headquarters Marine Corps as Director of Marine Corps Reserve.[11]

Vandegrift immediately shook up the Division staff by either reassigning those he deemed unfit or replacing them with his own team. Twining, for example, was brought in by Vandegrift to be his assistant operations officer under LtCol Gerald C. Thomas; LtCol George E. Monson, the G-4 was replaced; LtCol Roy Hunt stepped down as the chief of staff to take over the 5th Marines; and Colonel W. Capers James became the chief of staff. According to Twining, "It was a loyal staff. People liked him [Vandegrift]. I believe it was the happiest staff you will ever find."[12]

Vandegrift instituted a vigorous training schedule and Ray Davis found himself right in the middle of the hectic training pace. He met himself coming and going. But despite it all, Ray found time to meet and fall in love with Ms. Willa Knox Heafner, a pert, outspoken young school teacher from Washington, North Carolina. Calling her the light of his life, Knox (the name she was known by) would become Davis' confidante for life. Courting was tough though. "Because of our war preparations, there was a fast, wild courtship and we secretly eloped." The new Mrs. Davis concealed her marriage until the end of the school year and then resigned. They were married for 62 years. Whenever they were apart, they wrote each other every day.[13]

CHAPTER 5

Operation *Watchtower*

"The Division had not attained a satisfactory state of readiness when in mid-April 1942, it received the details of 'Operation *Lone Wolf*,' a particularly prescient code name under which we were to ship out immediately for Wellington, New Zealand," Vandegrift explained. "Although we ultimately were to serve as the Landing Force of a newly established South Pacific Amphibious Force, we were to train in New Zealand for a minimum of six months prior to being committed. It was estimated that no combat mission would be required of the Division prior to 1 January, 1943."[1]

The first echelon (Division Headquarters, certain divisional units and 5th Marines Reinforced) reached New Zealand on 14 June; the second echelon (1st Marines, reinforced, 11th Marines, and remaining divisional units, including the 1st Antiaircraft Battalion) arrived on 11 July.[2] "We had no idea that our destination was Guadalcanal," Davis remarked.[3]

The Special Weapons Battalion was being re-equipped with new types of antiaircraft guns because "there was some concern about Japanese air threat," Davis recalled. "It was decided at the last minute that we would keep all of our .50-caliber heavy machine guns and take along a bunch of 20mm and 40mm antiaircraft automatic guns, which we received in crates from the factories in Sweden. Consequently we went in equipped with three complete sets of weapons. The antitank half-tracks were also just arriving."[4]

Davis was told to pack everything. "Where you're going, you'll need every stick of lumber you can take." He recalled making boxes out of scrap lumber and filling them with more scrap lumber. The added square feet played hell for the embarkation officers.[5]

Because the deployment orders indicated a lengthy period of time before entering combat, it helped to assuage General Vandegrift's concern because the Division had not "attained a satisfactory state of combat readiness." However, the orders impacted the Division's loading plan. There seemed to be no need for combat loading, so the Division's equipment and supplies were crammed into ship's spaces without regard for prioritizing offload, which is how civilian ships commercially load. The bulk of the men were organizationally loaded on two large passenger vessels—*Wakefield* and *Ericsson*—which had little cargo carrying capacity. Supplies and equipment were loaded aboard seven cargo ships.[6]

The 1st Special Weapons Battalion was shipped by train to San Francisco. Luckey recalled, "We [boarded] trains from a siding right there in Tent City. There were freight trains and day coaches and a few Pullmans. We went all the way across the country to San Francisco, where we embarked on the SS *Ericsson* (formerly *Kungsholm*), a Swedish-American liner for the month-long voyage to Wellington, New Zealand."[7]

Davis recalled, "This ship was not prepared for the load of troops and supplies. We had trouble with the food; some of it was bad. Everybody got sick. People were vomiting all over the ship, and there were inadequate head [toilet] facilities." The men were fed two inadequate, poorly prepared meals a day, less than 1,500 calories. The embarked troops lost between 16 to 23 pounds per man. The cooks used oil substitutes in place of cooking oil, causing a round of gastrointestinal problems. Just prior to sailing, the ship attempted to load rancid butter and condemned eggs. The crew also gouged the troops by selling items at exorbitant prices. "There were threats against the crew and even rumors that Marines were ready to throw them overboard," Davis recalled. "It was a long, long voyage."[8]

On 26 June, only 12 days after the arrival of the first echelon, Major General Vandegrift and key staff members met with Commander South Pacific (COMSOPAC), Vice Admiral Robert L. Ghormley, at a conference in Auckland. Ghormley handed the Marine general a dispatch from the Joint Chiefs of Staff that read: "Occupy and defend Tulagi and adjacent positions (Guadalcanal and Florida Islands and the Santa Cruz Islands) in order to deny these areas to the enemy and to provide United States bases in preparation for further offensive action."[9]

The Division was reinforced by the 2nd Marine Regiment, 1st Raider Battalion, and the 3rd Defense Battalion. However, the Commander, amphibious Force South Pacific, Admiral Richmond K. Turner, shanghaied the 2nd Marines to serve as the Division reserve with the proviso that it could only be used if the admiral authorized it. Nonetheless, Company B, 1st Battalion was released to capture Tanambogo, which was part of the Tulagi–Gavutu–Tanambogo island complex.

Gerry Thomas noted in his 1966 oral history that Ghormley and MacArthur were opposed to the operation because they thought it was too risky and that it would not be successful. They recommended to Washington that the operation be cancelled. Washington said, 'No, it's going to go through ... Well, that's not a very happy omen for the future!"[10]

Tulagi was selected as the primary objective because it had been the capital of the British Solomon Islands Protectorate. "Tulagi contained the commissioner's residence as well as several public buildings, including a hospital and prison, and was also the location of a radio station, golf course, and several other accessories of western civilization."[11]

Ghormley stunned Vandegrift by telling him that D-day was slated for 1 August, but eventually changed to 7 August after the admiral requested a delay from Washington. Considering that the second echelon would not arrive until 11 July, the Division had little less than a month to get ready for a major amphibious assault against a hostile beach. Vandegrift admitted being shocked. "Seldom had an operation been begun under more disadvantageous circumstances."[12]

Luckey remembered the first time he heard about the operation. "A conference was called for all the unit commanders—down to battalion level. General Vandegrift made a little speech about the fact that the Division was going to mount out and go into an operation. Jerry Thomas [G-3] stood up and said that the Division was ordered to attack, seize, and hold the island of Guadalcanal and Tulagi [Gavutu–Tanambogo] for further operations up the Solomon Islands chain. I can remember sitting there with two or three of my friends saying, 'Where the hell are the Solomon Islands? And I wonder what Guadalcanal looks like.' We didn't know anything about it. We didn't have the remotest idea. [But] at least we knew where we were going."[13]

Vandegrift returned to Wellington to begin operational planning. It was immediately apparent that intelligence was the weakest component of the process. "No one knew anything about the typography, the beaches, or anything else about the islands that we were supposed to land on," Vandegrift complained.[14]

The Division intelligence officer (G-2), Lieutenant Colonel Frank B. Goettge, a well-known football player for the Quantico Marines, was sent to Australia "to locate traders, planters, shipmasters, and a few miners who had visited or lived at Guadalcanal or Tulagi and to collect all available information, particularly maps, coastal charts, aerial photographs. He also arranged with MacArthur's Southwest Pacific Area Headquarters (SWPA) for maps to be made from a strip of aerial photographs and delivered prior to the sortie of the 1st Marine Division. The maps were not delivered in time because of oversights and confusion in mounting out the Division."[15] The lack of good maps was a deficiency that was never remedied throughout the campaign.[16]

On 17 July, the Division assistant operations officer, Lieutenant Colonel Merrill B. Twining and Major William B. McKean were sent to fly over the objective area in an Army B-17 to take pictures along the beach. "We had just about completed the first run when we were jumped by three [Japanese] Zero float planes ... the photographer naturally dropped his camera and grabbed his machine gun, and we were in a fight. We barely made it back."[17]

Two of the Japanese planes were shot down and the third driven off before the damaged B-17, which had been hit by 20mm cannon fire, reached the safety of cloud cover. After a 13-hour flight, they reached Port Moresby, Australia, with nearly empty gas tanks. The flight had been worth it because Twining's photographs substantiated what he saw from the air; advanced construction of the airfield and a landing beach on Guadalcanal that seemed to be perfect. The Tulagi beaches were surrounded by reefs, making them impractical except for small landing craft.

The Division staff did the best they could to complete the intelligence annex. "There was no time for a deliberate planning process, and in many instances irrevocable decisions had to be made even before the essential features of the naval plan of operations could be ascertained," Vandegrift explained. His plans were based upon the assumption that the Allies would firmly control the air and sea routes. By 29 June, the Division D-3 section (operations) had produced Operation Order 5-42, the combat organization of the Division into two reinforced regimental combat groups, each comprising a headquarters and support sub-group and three reinforced battalion combat teams.[18]

Ten days later, Operations Order 6-42, the first complete order for operations, was issued. It directed the force be embarked for a period of amphibious training or for employment in active operations. The plan called for the simultaneous landings on Tulagi and Guadalcanal:

- To land the First Marine Raider Battalion, followed by one infantry Battalion on Beach Blue on the southwest coast of Tulagi at H hour;
- To land the First Parachute Battalion on Gavutu at H plus 4 hours to seize Gavutu and Tanambogo;
- To protect the flanks of these major landings by landing small forces on Florida, in the vicinity of Halavo and Haleta respectively;
- To land the remainder of the Division on Beach Red (on Guadalcanal 6,000 yards east of airfield) beginning at H plus 30 minutes to seize a beach head and then attack to the west capturing the airfield.[19]

Frank Goettge returned from Australia on 13 July with "eight Guadalcanal 'experts,' some rough maps and charts, and mounting radio intelligence about the Japanese order of battle."[20] Thomas said, "Those people that Goettge brought back were very useful to us because they were familiar with the territory, but it's surprising how little they really knew about it."[21]

While in Australia, Goettge learned about the British and Australian stay-behind intelligence operatives called Coastwatchers. These men performed a valuable service by reporting on Japanese air raids, providing intelligence on enemy locations, rescuing downed airman, and assisting Marine patrols. Equipped with radio transmitters, and assisted by trained native scouts, they were in a position to communicate vital information concerning enemy activity.[22]

Goettge also returned with an estimate of Japanese strength on Guadalcanal to be 5,275, composed of an infantry regiment reinforced; an antiaircraft regiment; a heavy machine-gun battalion; two engineer units; air and service personnel; and a labor unit. The major part of these troops was believed to be concentrated between

Kukum, just west of Lunga Point and the mouth of the Tenaru River, with a small garrison at Tetere and other small detachments elsewhere.

Japanese installations consisted of docks at Kukum and Lunga Point, and stores, motor transport, and a radio station at Lunga. The airfield southeast of Lunga was believed to have been completed, with another at Tetere and possibly a third at Tenaru under construction. Artillery was believed to be confined to eight heavy antiaircraft guns between Kukum and the Lunga River, four on the hill in the rear of Kukum, and a few light guns at other points. Tulagi was believed to be defended by 1,850 Rikusentai, Japanese Special Naval Landing Forces, mistakenly referred to as Japanese marines.

With this information, Operations Order 7-42 was finally completed, spelling out specific task organizations and unit responsibilities.

The Division order specified that Davis' antiaircraft battery would:

(1) Land the AA elements on Beach Red. These pass to control CO Support Group on landing. Assist in AA defense of beach area.
(2) Land 1/3 AA elements on Tulagi and Gavutu, and provide AA defense in that area.
(3) Land 1st and 3rd Platoons Battery A, Special Weapons Battalion on flanks of Beach Red and furnish AA defense of beach area, 1st Platoon to right, 3rd Platoon to left. The two platoons will revert to battalion control upon landing of Headquarters, 1st Special Weapons battalion.

Davis was excited about the forthcoming operation. He believed that, "As a battery commander sailing for combat with the 1st Marine Division, I was launching the building of what I hoped would be a distinguished record during operations in the Pacific. At the same time, some of my less fortunate Quantico classmates sat out the war either as prisoners of the Japanese or in the drudgery of defending various pieces of real estate on small Pacific isles."[23]

With the operational planning and intelligence gathering under way, the Division was faced with a monumental logistical task. The ships had to be unloaded and reloaded because they had been commercially loaded—that is, equipment and supplies had been stowed to take maximum advantage of space, rather than the uneconomical combat-loading, where items are placed so as to be ready for unloading in accordance with the priority of their necessity in an assault landing.

Loading and unloading operations were centralized at Altea Quay, Wellington, New Zealand, "a beautiful facility with a paved area which extended the full length of the pier which was capable of berthing five vessels at once." Unfortunately labor difficulties and work ethic by the highly unionized stevedores resulted in the entire unloading and reloading being done by Marines. "The 'Wharfies' [dockworkers] knocked off at 10 o'clock in the morning for tea," Thomas complained. "They didn't come back for three quarters of an hour. Then they'd knock off in the middle of the afternoon for tea, and they'd work about a six-hour day. We brushed them aside [and] assigned 300 Marines to each vessel. They worked eight-hour shifts around the clock."[24]

Civilian labor was restricted to skilled equipment operators, because the Wharfies were found to be inadequate and unreliable. Very little equipment was unloaded because it rained steadily for ten days. There was no shelter and carton-packaged foodstuffs and other supplies deteriorated rapidly in the persistent cold windy rain.

Combat loading had to take place simultaneously with the discharge of incoming cargo. "The loading was a complete terror and uproar and got worse," Twining said. "We'd had to fire the Wharfies. I'll always remember the sign in the latrine where some Marine had scrawled in chalk right over the little boys' place, 'All Wharfies is bastards.' That summed up that operation."[25]

Davis was designated the transport quartermaster to combat load the battalion. "I got detailed as the ship's transport quartermaster. I lived aboard the ship for six days reloading it. It rained constantly and all the cardboard packing boxes and all the paper items on the dock got wet, melted down, and trampled over, just an awful mess," he remembered. Eyewitnesses described the scene: "The dock was covered with drifts of mushy cornflakes, thousands of rolling C ration cans, and cases of water-logged cigarettes and pogey [candy] bait." Davis emphasized that, "It was a rough task to get my unit spread throughout so many ships with the supplies and equipment they would need in combat."[26] The 1st Special Weapons Battalion was embarked on the USS *Heywood*, except for Battery A's 1st Platoon (USS *American Legion*) and 3rd Platoon (USS *Libra*).

Space aboard the transports was at a premium. Some Division units had to be left behind; all excess equipment and supplies were eliminated, and even normal supplies were radically reduced. Seabags, extra clothing, bedding rolls, and company property were stored in Wellington, and bulk supplies such as rations and fuel were reduced from a normal 90-day to a 60-day basis. Only ten units of fire were embarked, three on each attack transport (APAs) and seven on the supporting attack cargo ships (AKAs).

At 0900 on 22 July, the 17 transports and six cargo ships carrying 20,000 men of the 1st Marine Division left Wellington under naval escort bound for Koro Island in the Fiji group to rehearse the landing, codenamed "Dovetail." Four days later, 26 July, Vandegrift, Turner, and senior staff officers were requested to attend a council of war for senior officers aboard Vice Admiral Fletcher's flagship, USS *Saratoga* (CV-3). "It was the roughest darn sea that you have ever seen in your life," Vandegrift declared. "We couldn't come alongside, so we had to get in a small boat and climb up an accommodation ladder." Vandegrift pinched his leg between the ladder and the side of the ship and badly bruised it.[27]

Fletcher handed out the operation order to the group seated around a conference table. Turner and Vandegrift were stunned. "Fletcher announced the operation as a raid … and that the Navy would give us 48 hours, no later than the morning of Sunday, 9 August, to unload [the ships]." This was not what Vandegrift had been led to believe previously. "We were told that we would go there, occupy and hold, and the plan was laid out with that idea in mind. We would get our material ashore, consolidate the landing, and then build an airfield. It was sternly fixed in our minds that we should have air cover during the process of this landing. We knew that we could not expect the fleet to stay around until we could get an airfield built, but we did expect air cover for a period of landing, which we did not have."[28]

Twining recalled, "This was the first time anybody had heard of that. It was a real blow because all of our concepts had been based on that this was a sustained operation and it threw our logistics completely up in the air. General Vandegrift was deeply disturbed."[29]

Turner and Vandegrift protested. One of the participants, Captain Thomas G. Peyton, Turner's chief of staff, recollected that the conference was "stormy."

Despite their protests, Fletcher remained "hard over," and would not budge from his decision to withdraw his ships after 48 hours. The meeting broke up and the attendees returned to their respective ships.

Koro: Fiasco in the Fijis

The Division sent representatives to reconnoiter the Koro rehearsal area. After flying over the landing area and talking to the locals about the beaches, "They urged that we not put the rehearsal there." But Turner said, "It doesn't make any difference, we don't have any time, we're going to rehearse at Koro."[30]

General Vandegrift considered the four-day rehearsal—28–31 July—"to be a complete bust. The coral conditions on the beaches prevented boats from landing … and to that extent the rehearsal period was unsatisfactory. I shudder to think what would happen if those beaches turned out to have been defended in strength," but later he rationalized that "a poor rehearsal traditionally meant a good show." And history would prove him right.[31]

Vandegrift noted in the Final Report on the Guadalcanal Operation: "From the point of view of the landing force the Koro rehearsal provided nothing beyond a valuable period of debarkation training and, in view of the rapid increase of enemy activity in the Solomons, the wisdom of devoting priceless time to such limited advantage appeared dubious."[32]

Codenamed "Cactus," Guadalcanal's 90-mile length is serrated by three mountain ranges, rising in one place to 8,000 feet. The island is a jumbled carpet of green ridges, foothills, and thick jungle, intersected by streams that flow to the ocean. A wide belt of grassy plains runs along the northern coast. Most of the population lived here, in clusters of native huts. Copra plantations, with their well-ordered coconut groves, provided the population with a source of income. Heavy rainfall, coupled with temperatures in the high eighties, resulted in a humid, unhealthy climate. Malaria, dengue, catarrhal "cat" fever, and fevers "of unknown origins" sapped strength and vitality. Fungal infections grew rapidly, causing sores that refused to heal, further weakening immune systems.

The operation was designated *Watchtower*, but in view of the limited forces available and the formidable opposition expected, its baffled planners and participants began to refer to it as Operation *Shoestring*.[33]

On 6 August 1942, the 82 warships of Operation *Watchtower*, one of the largest invasion fleets ever assembled up to that time, slipped silently down the coast of Guadalcanal. "It was quite a sight to see all those ships that we thought were so many and so fine to cover our landing," Vandegrift voiced.[34]

The weather was with Task Force 62. Low clouds and mist concealed its progress all day on the 6th. During the night it cleared sufficiently to make navigation easier. Shortly after midnight on 7 August, while about 40 miles southwest of Guadalcanal, the transport group split; Transport Group X-Ray—15 transports and cargo transports—continued south of Savo Island to the waters off Guadalcanal, while Transport Group Yoke—four transports and four destroyer transports bearing the Tulagi assault force—turned to slightly northeast and began to venture around the north side of Savo Island.

"At 0133 Guadalcanal could be made out, broad on the starboard bow of the *Neville* in Squadron YOKE, at 0224 the thin crescent of the waning moon rose and the dark shadow of the shore line could be clearly seen. A little later Savo Island was visible by its pale light."[35]

At 0310, the X-Ray squadron turned to the east and entered the narrow passage between Savo and Guadalcanal, "a stretch of water that was later to be the scene of bitter surface engagements and where, a few hours later, four Allied cruisers were destroyed by a brilliant and daring strike by the enemy."[36]

"The two transport groups were escorted by eight cruisers and a destroyer screen. One hundred miles to the south lurked the Air Support Force: three carriers, a battleship, five heavy cruisers, fifteen destroyers and three oilers."[37]

CHAPTER 6

Starvation Island

Major Justice Chambers, who commanded one of the Raider companies scheduled to make the original landing on Tulagi, related, "I don't think that any of us will forget that last night before we landed. Officers and men realized that all their training for the last few months was finally going to be put to the test. I personally was worried to death and kept going over my notes for fear that I had forgotten some detail in the orders. As we headed up for Tulagi in the darkness of the night the men wrote their last letters home and I collected them knowing that for some of them it would probably be the last letters they would write."[1]

Reveille sounded at 0300 aboard the transports, rousing the troops in the cramped, steamy compartments for a hasty breakfast in the galley. For many it was an apple and two hard boiled eggs. A few had steak and eggs, much to the chagrin of the Division's medical officers, who did not relish sewing up bellies stuffed with food. After chow the men returned to the compartments to gather their equipment and weapons.

As the sky began to brighten, the ship's gun crews anxiously scanned the sky for Japanese aircraft. Fortunately luck was with them. An overcast sky and a mist limited visibility—less than ten miles with ceilings as low as 100 feet—rendering the three Tulagi-based float planes unable to spot the invasion fleet and forcing them to return to base. Surprise was complete. There was no challenge as the double column of ships slid through the haze at 12 knots.

The islands appeared. A Marine combat correspondent reported that Guadalcanal appeared to be an island of striking beauty. Its blue-green mountains towered into a brilliant tropical sky dominating the island. The dark green jungle growth blended into the softer greens and browns of coconut groves and grassy plains and ridges.

An observation aircraft off the heavy cruiser USS *Astoria* (CA-34) dropped a flare signaling the start of the naval bombardment. USS *Quincy* (CA-39) opened fire at 0613, quickly followed by 5- and 8-inch naval shells from cruisers and destroyers. The cruisers *Quincy* and *Astoria* pounded the shoreline of Beach Red, the 1st Marine Division's landing beach. Destroyers *Selfridge* (DD-357) and *Dewey* (DD-349) opened fire on a small interisland schooner loaded with gasoline which burst into flame. Suddenly a gasoline fuel dump west of Lunga Point exploded from *Quincy's* 8-inch salvo, sending flames and oily black smoke into the dawn sky.

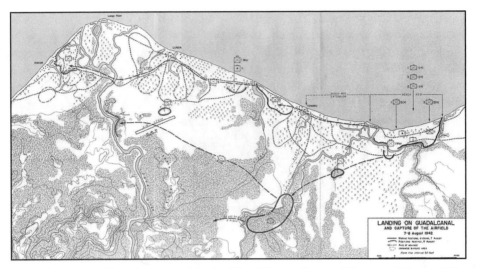

The landing on Guadalcanal represented the first United States offensive of the war and the first defeat of the Japanese in the Pacific. (U.S. Marine Corps)

As the shoreline erupted, 16 Grumman F4F-4 Wildcats from *Wasp*'s VF-72 swooped down to destroy all seven of the large four-engine Kawanishi H6K4 ("Mavis") flying boats and likewise torch all eight of the Nakajima A6M2-N float Zeros ("Rufes") of the Yokohama Air Group moored off Halavo.[2]

The ship's bombardment was "ineffective," Twining commented. "We knew so little about the targets. We had no teams on shore adjusting it. They were really just firing at the beach line."[3]

The Japanese radio station on Tulagi broadcast a plain-language emergency radio message at 0635 local time to the naval base at Rabaul. "Enemy surface force of 20 ships has entered Tulagi; air attacks are going on, and they are making preparation … the enemy is bombarding the shore … enemy troop strength is overwhelming … we will defend to the last man." That was the last message before the light cruiser *San Juan* (CL-54) knocked out the radio station.[4]

Rear Admiral Sadayoshi Yamada, commander of the Imperial Navy's land-based 25th Air Flotilla based on Rabaul, New Britain, immediately responded, dispatching a mixed force of 27 Mitsubishi G4M1s (Navy Type 1 Attack Bomber), known to the Allies as the "Betty," and 17 Mitsubishi A6M Type 0 (Zero or Zeke) fighters as escort. About an hour later, a second strike was launched consisting of 10 Aichi D3A Val dive bombers.

Eighty-five U.S. Navy carrier dive bombers and fighters attacked the airfield, wharves, enemy camps, and suspected Japanese encampments. Terrified Japanese and Korean workers of the 11th and 13th Naval Construction Battalions scurried into the jungle leaving behind food, supplies, intact construction equipment and vehicles. A few dead were found as a result of the aerial and naval bombardment, but upon examination of prisoners it appeared that the daybreak bombardment caught the

Japanese—430 sailors and 2,571 laborers—completely by surprise and that a state of panic ensued which was followed by a precipitate and disorderly flight to the west.

At 0700 boat teams lined the decks abreast their designated debarkation stations. Cargo nets hung over the side and on command a line of men started climbing down into the 36-man landing craft bobbing in the gentle swells below. On schedule the boats carrying Combat Group A (1st and 3rd Battalions, Fifth Marines) took their loads of men and equipment and circled the rendezvous area. The line of departure was marked by two destroyers lying 4,000 yards off the beach. On signal the first wave of landing craft crossed the line of departure and surged toward the beach. Two smoke bombs on either end defined its boundaries.

The first Higgins landing craft carrying the two battalions of the 5th Marines touched down on Beach Red, a strip of beach 1,600 yards in length between Lunga and Koli Points, at 0908 on 7 August 1942. Smoke marked Beach Red's extremities so the target area would be clearly visible for the landing crafts' coxswains.[5]

The Marines stormed ashore. A white rocket arched into the sky, indicating the beaches were undefended. Vandegrift heaved a sigh of relief. He remarked that the operation proceeded with smoothness and precision.

Ray Davis went ashore four hours after the initial landing just as 25 twin-engine Japanese bombers from Rabaul headed straight for the transports. "We loaded into the boats and were heading for shore when a formation of Japanese torpedo bombers attacked us. This was the first engagement for those American ships, and shot and shell were flying—it seemed like everybody was shooting at everything and everybody. The sky was full, just full of bullets." One of the transports, *Crescent City*, shot down five of the attackers, one of which was claimed by Marine Corporal Edward S. Stelloh, a gunner on the transport. Davis recalled "feeling very uneasy out there with the Japanese aircraft strafing and bombing, and our own ships firing machine guns and AA guns. I was happy to get ashore."[6]

A second attack on the transports came at about 1430 when the same area was struck by nine D3A Type 99 Aichi dive bombers. The bombers went after the transports instead of the supplies that jammed the landing beach. Their failure to destroy the critical supply dumps meant that the Division had just enough food and ammunition to carry them through until the Navy was able to bring in supplies. The afternoon raid was costly for the Japanese—five were shot down and four ditched during their return to Rabaul—for one hit on the destroyer USS *Mugford*, which suffered eight killed, 17 wounded and ten missing.

"We landed pretty much unopposed," Davis recalled. "They had work forces there building an airfield but very few armed forces."[7] Luckey said that, "Part of the Division area was a Japanese camp. I remember going into one tent, and the damned hibachi was still working with a bowl of rice sitting there, because they left in a hurry."[8] In addition to huge quantities of rice and other food stuffs, the Japanese also left engineer equipment—trucks, tractors, road rollers, and two gasoline locomotives—which were desperately needed to complete the airfield—and medical supplies.

"When we landed, my weapons [Swedish designed 20mm and 40mm Bofors automatic cannons] were still in factory crates," Davis recalled. The battalion had enough trucks to get the equipment off the beach, unlike the rest of the Division's supplies. The undermanned Shore Party Battalion was overwhelmed. The constant stream of material arriving at the little strip of sand beach could not be handled. At one time, 100 landing boats had been beached, while 50 more were waiting for an opportunity to land. The Shore Party commander reported that, "unloading was entirely out of hand."[9]

Davis quickly pushed his 1st and 3rd Platoons out to cover the flanks of the landing beach. The movement went well and within a couple of hours his antiaircraft guns were in position and prepared to defend the beachhead. He established his command post, a deep slit trench covered with crisscrossed coconut logs, alongside the upper end of the airstrip, just 100 feet off the edge in a coconut grove less than a quarter mile from the Lunga River. It was not a good location because his command post caught all the overs from the battleships and cruisers that came in to shell the airfield every night.

From his command post, Davis could see the "Pagoda," a crude Japanese-built one-story structure that served as both the control tower and air operations center (Air Ops) for the "Cactus Airforce," the name collectively given the Guadalcanal aircraft squadrons—Marine, Navy, and Army. The structure was located on a little coral ridge, known as Pagoda Hill or "the bull's eye," about 200 yards northwest of the middle of the airstrip. "You could see it 40 miles away," Major Albert D. Cooley, commanding officer of the Marine Air Group (MAG) remarked.[10]

The building was a target for Japanese bombing raids, which often resulted in errant bombs falling in and around Davis' position. According to Brigadier General Louis E. Woods, who served as chief of staff and then as commander of the Cactus Air Force, "Living in the pagoda on top of a hill, right in the middle of the flying field was probably … very stupid."[11]

The Pagoda also served as an early warning station. Initially, a captured siren was installed as an air-raid alert, but its wail often mingled with the sound of falling bombs, so it was augmented with a flag system. A black flag on the Pagoda's pole meant "Condition Red"—enemy planes were within two minutes of the field or overhead. The alert pennant was a white flag—"Condition Yellow"—bombers en route. The siren and flag system worked well, giving Davis' gunners time to prepare a warm reception. A Japanese report noted, "There was no way of charging into the airspace over the airfield because of the enemy's relentless wall of antiaircraft gunfire."[12]

By nightfall the Americans had carved out a mile-deep toehold on Guadalcanal. They halted for the night about 1,000 yards from the unfinished Japanese airfield near Lunga Point. By dusk on D-day, 11,000 Marines had landed on Guadalcanal without a single casualty.

The next day, 8 August, the 5th Marines, meeting only sporadic enemy resistance, advanced to the Lunga River and at 1600 captured the airdrome.

The Special Weapons Battalion spent the first night on Beach Red and the next day deployed around the newly captured Japanese airfield, soon to be named Henderson Field for Major Lofton R. Henderson, who had been shot down leading Marine Scout Bombing Squadron (VMSB) 241 at Midway. "We seized the airfield without opposition," Davis explained. "After that the Japanese started bringing forces down to drive us off. For the next six months we were bombarded from the sea and we were bombed from the air, and attacked from the ground, but we held them off."[13]

Davis recalled, "Some of my units were farmed out to the infantry regiments, forming special weapons units—a conglomerate antiaircraft and antitank units. One of our units used towed 37mm guns with anti-personnel shells during the battle of the Tenaru River, where a 700-man Japanese battalion was annihilated on 24 August. I was there the next day with my people. We took one or two wounded Japanese prisoners, almost all the rest were killed. I also had a unit near the airfield during the battle of Bloody Nose Ridge on 18 September." The battalion's impressive array of weapons—.50-caliber, 20mm, 40mm, and 90mm antiaircraft guns—greatly strengthened the defense of the perimeter.[14]

Davis' antiaircraft battery was placed under operational control of the 3rd Defense Battalion. "Initially my primary mission was to provide low-altitude antiaircraft defense of Henderson Field," Davis explained. "We had a mechanical fire-control computer for the 40s. However, for anything above 4,000 feet, we had no accuracy."[15]

The 3rd Defense Battalion, commanded by Colonel Robert H. Pepper, disembarked at 1100 and immediately deployed as per orders—a 1,000-yard strip along the beach—but finding there was no opposition, their defensive position was expanded to 7,000 yards. On D-day the battalion could mount only three .50-caliber machine guns. However, on D+2, they were able to land one 90mm antiaircraft gun, additional .50-caliber machine guns and dual 20mm machine guns.

The 3rd Defense Battalion emplaced their battery of 90mm antiaircraft guns north of the airfield and their antiaircraft machine guns throughout the Marine perimeter. "One of the most unsung units on Guadalcanal was the 3rd Defense Battalion under Colonel Pepper," Thomas acknowledged. "Before the 90s got in operation, the Japs came in at 10,000 feet, the first few days, and blasted us, but they learned pretty quickly when the 90s started to fire and they went up to 23,000 feet … and stayed there the rest of time." Thomas estimated the battalion shot down as many as "70 Jap planes."[16]

Two 90mm antiaircraft batteries landed on Guadalcanal and were set up in short order. When the air threat became obvious, "Pepper came over and brought the other 90mm battery, and we then had his full antiaircraft defense, including light weapons. These were all distributed around our airstrip on Guadalcanal, and they were, of course, right in the heart of it. As a matter of fact, our area was so small; our Division headquarters wasn't more than 100 yards from a 90mm battery."[17]

Guadalcanal's defense was further strengthened by the arrival of Captain Custis Burton's 5-inch coastal battery from Tulagi, where it had been initially posted to protect against an expected attack from Florida Island. The battery was landed without its trailers and sleds and had to be manhandled into positions on the beach east and

3rd Defense Battalion

The 3rd Defense Battalion was equipped with 90-mm antiaircraft guns, capable of firing to a height of 33,800 feet, and 5-inch guns for shore defense. The antiaircraft group also had 20mm and 40mm cannons and .50-caliber machine guns for defense against low altitude attack. Fire control was the responsibility of the various battery commanders in conjunction with the 1st Marine Air Wing's air operations officer. Battery E, on Guadalcanal, defended Henderson Field. Since there were so few guns, they fired from near the midpoint of the runway to concentrate their aim over the airfield. They were dug in so that the crews were not exposed to blast and shrapnel during Japanese attacks.

A 1939 table of organization and equipment (TOE) included:

- HQ Company
- Service battery
  - Six platoons, each with a searchlight and aircraft sound locator
- Coast Defense Group
  - Three batteries, each with two Mark 15 5"/51 caliber guns
- Antiaircraft Group
- Four AAA gun batteries, each with four mobile 3-inch M3 guns
  - Two AAA machine-gun companies, each with 24 Browning M2 water-cooled .50-caliber machine guns on AA mounts
  - Two beach protection machine-gun companies, each with 24 Browning M1917A1 water-cooled .30-caliber machine guns

west of the Lunga River to cover the channel. The positioning took ten days of hard effort before they were ready to respond to the Japanese naval threat. They were frequently in action, but lacked enough hitting power to be completely effective.[18]

The Division's defensive perimeter was manned by five rifle battalions—the entire 1st Marines and two battalions of the 5th Marines, with one of those battalions held in reserve. This defensive strategy was strengthened by intensive patrolling in the direction of an expected enemy attack.

Native scouts, under the guidance of Captain W. F. M. Martin Clemens of the British Solomon Islands Protectorate Defense Force assisted the Marine patrols. "My lads had been stalking the enemy on bare feet for some months so we were able to teach the Marines a thing or two …." Clemens was the former district officer commissioned for wartime service. In addition, a series of observation and listening posts were established to augment the perimeter defense.[19]

The perimeter, roughly a semicircle, measured nearly five and a half miles and was designed to envelop the plain around Lunga Point, with the airfield at the center and its defensive focus oriented toward the sea. The perimeter stretched for 9,600 yards from east to west and 5,000 yards from north to south.

Colonel Padro Del Valle's 11th Marines emplaced its 75mm and 105mm guns in positions on the center of the south side of the airfield from where they could provide supporting fires to any area of the perimeter. Infantry were posted in foxholes along the perimeter. One infantry battalion was designated as the Division reserve.

The perimeter was divided into five sectors:

- Sector One: A 7,000-yard stretch of beach on Lunga Point defended by the 3rd Defense Battalion. Davis' Company A antiaircraft battery was located on the airfield. Company C 1st Special Weapons Battalion's 75mm half-tracks were dug inland from the beach, but were on alert to move into prepared positions near the water in case of a Japanese landing attempt. The 3rd Defense Battalion had tactical command and coordinated the beach defense and the antiaircraft fire.
- Sector Two: A 6,600-yard line defended by the 164th Infantry Regiment and the 1st Special Weapons Battalion, extended along the beach from the 3rd Defense Battalion's right flank to the Ilu River, inland along the Ilu about 4,000 yards before swinging west through the jungle to the left flank of the 7th Marines.
- Sector Three: The 7th Marines (less one battalion), supported by elements of the 1st Special Weapons Battalion, occupied 2,500 yards of jungle between the 164th Infantry's right flank and the Lunga River, including the south slope of Bloody Ridge.
- Sector Four: The 1st Marines (less one battalion), supported two platoons of Company B, 1st Special Weapons Battalion (two 37mm antitank guns), under the command of Second Lieutenant James F. McClanahan. The 1st Marines occupied 3,500 yards of jungle between the Lunga River and the left flank of the 5th Marines, known as the Matanikau line.
- Sector Five: The 5th Marines held the western corner of the perimeter from the right flank of the 1st Marines north to the sea and then east along the beach to the left flank of the 3rd Defense Battalion.

On the evening of 8 August, Turner called for a conference aboard his flagship, USS *McCawley*, nicknamed "Wacky Mac." Vandegrift and Jerry Thomas finally found the flagship after three fruitless hours of cruising around from ship to ship in the dark. Turner welcomed them and then gave them startling news. "Fletcher has informed me that he's withdrawing his carriers tomorrow."[20] Vandegrift recalled, "Turner told me that Jack Fletcher had just notified him that he was leaving that night which was certainly startling because it was agreed that he would be at least three days in the area when we had our conference on the carrier flagship."[21] Fletcher's withdrawal would leave Turner without air cover, and therefore he decided to take his transports out at 0600 the next morning.

There was little Vandegrift could do. On the way back to shore he noted, "Flares covered the channel area to our stern. A constant boom of heavy naval guns penetrated the still air. Sailors on deck cheered at the sudden enormous explosions. We all felt elated—we were sure our forces were winning. We heard desultory firing all the way back, as well as in the early morning hours after arriving back at my headquarters."[22]

The next morning Vandegrift called a conference of the staff, the regimental and battalion commanders. By this time he had a good idea of the extent of the naval disaster and told them that, "we were on our own," and reminded them that "our mission was now to hold the airfield. Then I ordered them to relate these unsavory facts to their junior officers, NCOs and men." Vandegrift emphasized that his officers "must pound home that we anticipated no Bataan, no Wake Island."[23]

Vandegrift established three priorities: construction of the main line of resistance (MLR), completion of the airfield, and removal of supplies from the beaches. He also decided to "suspend ground operations temporarily in order to organize beach defenses on Lunga Point ...."[24] He directed that the Division would be limited to two meals a day to make the food supplies last longer. LtGen Woods recalled, "We had two meals a day, which was either 2/3 or 3/4 of a ration a day. We got an awful lot of Australian sheep tongue and an awful lot of Japanese rice. Food was pretty damn scarce ...."[25]

The Division's health deteriorated quickly in this "tropical paradise." Hundreds of men came down with malaria and dysentery. Davis was no exception. "We were overrun with malaria. With inadequate protection and an unbelievable mosquito population, the situation simply got out of hand. I had both types, plus a severe hepatitis jaundice attack ... Fortunately, I had a friendly surgeon who kept me out of the hospital and on my feet ...." The Division's medical log showed that in the three-month period just prior to leaving the island, 6,000 Marines were admitted to the hospital, most for contracting malaria. "In addition, we had dysentery following our first major ground battle with the Japanese. We killed over 700 of them in one small area and it took several days to get them buried. This delay brought a deluge of flies, which was overwhelming—really awful."[26]

The Goettge Patrol

A Japanese naval warrant officer was captured on 12 August. During interrogation he stated that "he came from the Matankiau area and that there were others in his particular group who might be willing to surrender. This information coincided with a patrol report that a large while flag had been seen displayed from the high ground beyond the Matanikau."[27]

Lieutenant Colonel Frank Goettge (G-2) decided to mount a 25-man reconnaissance patrol "for the purpose of contacting any groups wishing to surrender, or, failing in this, to obtain information of the terrain and defenses around the Matanikau."[28] The patrol landed after dark in an undetermined point west of Matanikau and was immediately attacked by a strong Japanese force. Goettge was one of the first Marines cut down and, "Shortly thereafter the patrol was ... overwhelmed." Only three men escaped to tell the tale.[29]

CHAPTER 7

Cactus Air Force

On 20 August, immediately after the noon Japanese air attack, Davis was summoned to the 3rd Defense Battalion's command post, where Colonel Pepper gave him the electrifying news that two Marine squadrons would fly in that afternoon. Davis immediately passed the word to his antiaircraft gun crews, with the admonition not to get "trigger happy."

After almost two weeks of unhindered Japanese air and naval bombardment, the escort carrier USS *Long Island* (ACV-1), one of the first "jeep" carriers, arrived with reinforcements: 19 F4F-4 Grumman Wildcat fighters of Marine Fighting Squadron (VMF) 223, led by Major John L. Smith, and Lieutenant Colonel Richard C. Mangrum's 12 SBD-3 Dauntless scout-dive bombers of VMSB-232.

"We were catapulted off the ship 200 miles off Guadalcanal in the middle of the afternoon to avoid the daily air raid and landed late in the afternoon," Mangrum related. By 1700, all 31 aircraft had landed safely. The Marine Wildcats and Dauntlesses were the first planes in the Cactus Air Force.[1]

Vandegrift was on hand to greet the Marine fliers. "I was close to tears and I was not alone when the first SBD taxied up and this handsome and dashing aviator jumped to the ground," the general admitted. "I told him, 'Thank God you have come.'"[2] Mangrum was surprised by the reception. "The Division had been 13 days with no protection from enemy aircraft or means to intercept enemy ships. So to put it mildly, they were glad to see us."[3] Lieutenant Herbert L. Merillat, the public relations officer at 1st Marine Division headquarters, reported, "A shout of relief and welcome went up from every Marine on the island."[4] Within eight hours of arriving, VMF-223 was supporting Marine defenders during the battle of Alligator Creek.

That same day, Marine Air Group 25, operating out of Espiritu Santo, began supply and evacuation flights in and out of Henderson Field in R-4D/C-47 transport aircraft. They brought in cargo loads of supplies and flew out 16 litter patients per trip.

The two Marine squadrons were followed on the 22nd and 27th by elements of the Army Air Force 67th Fighter Squadron. The squadron departed Espiritu Santo at 0725 on the 22nd and, "After flying a little less than four hours they reached Guadalcanal, broke formation into a landing pattern, and rolled their wheels on the rocky coral runway of Henderson Field. They were greeted with wild jumping and shouts of joy by the Marine ground troops, who lined the runway to watch the sleek shark-mouthed P400s touch down and taxi to an area near one of the ugly Japanese hangers."[5] The P-400 aircraft were relegated to close-air support of ground troops because they were inadequate to meet the demands of high-altitude aerial combat against the Japanese Zeros.

The buildup of the Cactus Air Force quickly turned the air and sea clashes around the island into battles of attrition. The Japanese were hell-bent on knocking out the airfield, and the Cactus Air Force was just as determined to prevent that from happening. The daily encounters turned into a deadly routine. The Japanese launched bombing raids from Rabaul, their route taking them over islands where the Coastwatchers were stationed. Most of the time the observers' reports would reach Cactus headquarters in time for the U.S. fighters to reach an advantageous altitude to meet the raids and for the antiaircraft gunners to break out ammunition and calibrate their guns.

Losses were heavy for both sides but particularly bad for the Japanese. The best estimate of their losses from 20 August through 15 November is 96 fighters, 92 Bettys, and 75 other types, mostly floatplanes. Cactus Air Force losses included 118 planes shot down and another 30 that were victims of operational accidents. Eighty-four Cactus pilots were killed from all causes, including 38 fighter pilots killed in aerial combat. For the Cactus Air Force, the struggle for Henderson Field was primarily over by mid-November. There would still be combat but not of the intensity of the first 88 days of the campaign.

There were so many Japanese air attacks that Davis got a little blasé. "We got so 'salty' that we would wait until the bomb bays opened at a certain point in the sky before we got into our shelters." He did not realize that a regimental command post had moved in across the runway. Lieutenant Colonel Clifton B. Cates, its commander and World War I hero, was a stickler for taking cover. "If people didn't get low enough in their holes during an air raid, he'd shoot toward them with his pistol." Davis played his usual game, but this time several pistol rounds cracked over his head. "I went tearing across that runway intent on straightening out whoever the hell it was shooting at me. I ran headlong into Cates for the first time. He told me exactly what was going on. In short, if I'd been in my hole, there would've been no chance of my getting shot. I said, 'Aye, Aye, sir!' to the future Commandant of the Marine Corps, and moved out smartly."[6]

The area around the airfield was a lethal location and not just because of the shelling and bombing. "Ammunition and bombs were haphazardly scattered throughout the area and then forgotten as the fast-growing Kunai grass covered the lethal piles. The first Japanese bombing attack set the grass on fire. Davis, as the local commander, had to put it out. "I would rush my troops out in order to extinguish the fires. On one occasion, I lost a boot while running. Minutes later I found myself standing with one shoe on and one bare foot, on top of a 500-pound bomb, beating out fire around it to keep the fire off the bomb! It's a good thing they weren't fused, but still it was a hairy way to spend an afternoon."[7]

CHAPTER 8

Japanese Ground and Air Counterattack

The 2nd Battalion, 1st Marines was dug in along the east bank of the Tenaru River, known as Alligator Creek, the Marine name for the confusing channels of the Tenaru. Company G, positioned at the mouth of the river, was able to string a band of rusty barbed wire salvaged from the island's plantation fences across the 50-foot-wide sandspit between the lagoon and the beach. The infantry company was reinforced by several machine guns and two 37mm antitank guns from 1st Platoon, Battery B, 1st Special Weapons Battalion, under the command of Second Lieutenant James F. McClanahan. The lieutenant instructed his men to dig in and sandbag the positions for the crew-served weapons.

Marine listening posts were positioned forward of the lines to provide warning of an approaching enemy. Sometime after midnight these forward elements began falling back to the main positions, bringing word that there appeared to be a rather large enemy force in the neighborhood of the Tenaru River. Flares and sounds of movement had been seen and heard, but no visual contact had been made.[1]

Unknown to the Marines at the time, Colonel Kiyono Ichiki was leading the reinforced 2nd Battalion, 28th Infantry, some 900 men through the jungle toward the Marine positions. The force halted just short of the mouth of Alligator Creek and prepared to assault across the sandspit.

About the time the listening posts were withdrawing, Sergeant Major Vouza, a retired member of the Native Constabulary, staggered into the command post of the 2nd Battalion. "He had been caught by the Japanese on 18 August in his village several miles to the east of the perimeter. When he refused to give them information, he was tortured and left for dead. He made his way, at night, through the enemy force and arrived at the mouth of Alligator Creek in time to tell Colonel Edwin A. Pollock, the battalion commander, of its presence."[2]

At about 0300, a sentry on the west bank of the river opened fire when he heard man-made sounds in the jungle. Ten minutes later a green flare's ghostly light lit up the sandspit and 200 Japanese in mass formation suddenly burst out of the foliage in a violent attack on the Marines' positions at the sandbar. One report noted, squad after squad, platoon after platoon, burst from the covering darkness of the coconut grave to dash against the line. The enemy soldiers were met by concentrated fire from rifles, machine guns and canister rounds from McClanahan's 37mm guns. The shotgun-like blasts scythed through the Japanese ranks. Despite heavy casualties, a number of the Japanese succeeded in overrunning a few emplacements on the left bank.[3]

McClanahan's Silver Star citation stated that he was "painfully wounded during the latter part of the engagement, [but] refused evacuation." Nevertheless, he was well enough to work on fixing numerous jammed automatic weapons. His second-in-command, Platoon Sergeant Nelson Braitmeyer, was shot to death when he launched a one-man assault against several Japanese who were setting up a machine gun which would be able to sweep the antitank emplacements. Private Elmer Fairchild, manning one of McClanahan's heavy .50-caliber air-cooled machine guns, had the three middle fingers of his right hand shot away. Nevertheless, and despite shrapnel wounds in both legs, Fairchild wrapped his bleeding right hand in his shirt and carried on.[4]

Another grenade knocked out Corporal Glenn Campbell's 37mm gun, incapacitating one more American gun aimed at the sandbar. Where the bar met the bank they were assaulting, several Japanese had entered Corporal Jim Oliff's 37mm emplacement—an 8-foot-by-6-foot bunker, 4-feet deep and covered with logs and dirt—Oliff's men killed them. More bayonet-wielding enemy soldiers fell on the west bank by the lagoon mouth, as Company E's third platoon emptied rifles and machine guns as fast as they could. Japanese gunners also were shooting at Slim Fairchild's .50-caliber and Jim Oliff's 37mm, whose crew had repositioned that antitank gun to fire canister rounds straight down the sandbar. In all 16 men from Battery B—two KIA and 14 WIA— became casualties.

Braitmeyer's Navy Cross Citation

The President of the United States of America takes pride in presenting the Navy Cross (Posthumously) to Platoon Sergeant Nelson Braitmeyer (MCSN: 248057), United States Marine Corps, for extraordinary heroism and conspicuous devotion to duty while serving as second in command of the First Platoon of Battery B, First Special Weapons Battalion, First Marine Division, during action against enemy Japanese forces on Guadalcanal, Solomon Islands, on the night of 20–21 August 1942. When a hostile attack penetrated his gun positions at several points and imperiled our lines, Platoon Sergeant Braitmeyer, with grim determination and complete disregard for his own personal safety, assisted his platoon commander in clearing Japanese gun positions at the mouth of the Tenaru River until he was killed in action. The conduct of Platoon Sergeant Braitmeyer throughout this action reflects great credit upon himself, and was in keeping with the highest traditions of the United States Naval Service. He gallantly gave up his life in the service of his country.

Major Bob Luckey rushed to the 1st Marines CP as soon as the attack started, to coordinate 2nd Battalion's supporting arms. Messages from the lines soon convinced Luckey that fire from 81mm mortars, and the 75mm pack howitzers of 3rd Battalion, 11th Marines, were falling on friendly troops. Luckey was about to order corrections when an icy calm Colonel Clifton Cates told him, "That's an old trick, Bob. Keep right where you are." Cates was right; the Japanese were firing their mortars in such a way as to give the illusion that friendly fire was falling short. A pair of half-track mounted 75mm antitank guns were rushed forward.[5]

The Marines held and at daybreak, the 1st Battalion, 1st Marines (LtCol Lenard B. Cresswell), moved upstream and came down on the Japanese flank. Caught between the two battalions and the sea, and with most of his 900 men dead or dying, Colonel Ichiki burned his colors and shot himself through the head.

Davis recalled, "One of our units used towed 37mm guns with anti-personnel shells during the battle of the Tenaru River, where a 700-man Japanese battalion was annihilated on 21 August. I was there the next day with my people. We took one or two wounded Japanese prisoners, almost all the rest were killed. The gunners fired canister rounds into the packed Japanese ranks, momentarily halting them as riflemen and machine gunners fought to recover from the shock of first contact."[6]

For the first time in the Pacific, Japanese soldiers had lost a major battle, breaking the "victory fever" that for years had emboldened Imperial Army forces. At the cost of 35 dead and 75 wounded, the Marines had nearly annihilated their attackers, killing 790 of the 875 men who had set out from Taivu Point. Vandegrift explained proudly, "This fight … did more to boost the morale of the Division than anything that happened, perhaps excluding the arrival of the air force, and it was an entirely different attitude the next day and for the rest of the time that we were on the canal."[7] Young Americans—mostly in their teens—who had been rushed through training and into combat, had shown that the empire's brave and battle-hardened soldiers, while willing to fight to the death, were not invincible after all.

On 3 September, BGen Roy S. Geiger and his 1st Marine Air Wing staff arrived to coordinate the island's air defense. Two weeks later, Vandegrift received a most welcome addition to his hard-pressed Division. Admiral Turner delivered the 4,262 men of the 7th Marine Regiment (reinforced) and its supporting artillery unit, the 1st Battalion, 11th Marines.

General Vandegrift noted in his Final Action Report:

> This accretion of force required us to re-examine and readjust our plans in accordance with improved circumstances and in the light of lessons learned from the bitter fighting of mid-September. Ten infantry battalions and one raider battalion were now available on Guadalcanal. These were supported by four battalions of artillery, a nearly complete defense battalion, a small provisional tank battalion, and a growing air force.[8]

Davis thought October was the toughest month. "At that point there was no food, and we had to eat captured rice. The cook said that the black spots in the rice were weevils, but some of us ate them, too, as a source of protein. The cook put in a few raisins to camouflage them. Fishing boats came in from the West Coast with food. We were sick with dengue, dysentery, and malaria. I had both types of malaria, and something else. I also had a jaundice attack, so much so that I can't give blood even today."[9]

They were bombed every day in October at noon, like clockwork. The bombing became known as "Tojo Time." One man said you could set your watch by them. The Japanese bombers would come in Vee formations of between 20 to 40 aircraft at 20,000 feet. "We could see the enemy bomb bays open and hear the clicks of the bomb release before we jumped into our holes," Davis explained. "At night, we absorbed fire from ships ... [that] were out of range of my guns, but we watched carefully to see the ships' gun flashes because they would signal the time to go for our holes."[10]

The historian of the 67th Fighter Squadron expressed the feelings of the men during the bombardments:

> There was a routine of noises at Tojo Time. First the red and white flag [a captured Japanese rising sun] would go up at the pagoda. That meant scramble. Every airplane that would fly would start up immediately and all would rush for the runway, dodging bomb craters. Often through the swirling dust the ground crews would see a wing drop. That meant another plane had taxied [into] a dud hole or a small crater, indistinct in the tall grass. The first planes to the runway took off first, and two at a time, whether ... Grummans, dive-bombers or P-400s.
>
> The formations would join later in the air. The P-400s and dive-bombers would fly away to work over the Jap territory. The Grummans would climb for altitude, test-firing their guns on the way. The whining of engines at high r.p.m., the chatter of machine guns, and settling dust.
>
> On the ground the men would put in a few more minutes' work, watching the pagoda all the while. Then the black flag would go up. It was amazing how fast the tired and hungry men could sprint ... In a moment the field would be deserted.
>
> Then the high, sing-song whine of the bombers would intrude as a new sound, separate from the noise of the climbing Grummans. Only a few moments now. The sing-song would grow louder. Then: swish, swish, swish. And the men would pull the chin straps of their helmets tighter and tense their muscles and press harder against the earth in their foxholes. And pray.
>
> Then: WHAM! (The first one hit) WHAM! (Closer) WHAM! (Walking right up to your foxhole) ... WHAAAMM! (Oh Christ) WHAM! (Thank God, they missed us!) WHAM! (the bombs were walking away) WHAM! (they still shook the earth, and dirt trickled in). WHAM!
>
> It was over. The men jumped out to see if their buddies in the surrounding fox holes had been hit. The antiaircraft still made a deafening racket. Grass fires were blazing. There was the pop-pop-pop of exploding ammunition in the burning airplanes on the ground. The reek of cordite. Overhead the Grummans dived with piercing screams. And the Jap bombers left smoke trails as they plummeted into [the] sea.
>
> In a little while the airplanes would return. The ground crews would count them as they landed. The ambulance would stand, engine running, ready for those who crashed, landed dead stick, or hit the bomb craters in the runway. Then the work of patching and repairing the battered fighters would start again.
>
> But naval shellings were much worse:

… A bombing is bad, because as the big planes drone overhead the whole field seems to shrink up to the size of your foxhole and when the bombs start to swish-swish-swish in their fall they seem to be aimed right at that tiny spot. But a bombing is over in a minute.

… A shelling, however, is unmitigated, indescribable hell. It can go on for a few minutes or four hours. When the shells scream overhead you cringe expecting a hit and when there is a let-up you tremble knowing that they are getting their range and the next one will be a hit.[11]

The 1st Special Weapons Battalion's gunners reverted to type—appropriating anything that was "lying around," and not "nailed down." Davis said, "The Division G-4 [supply and logistics] was upset and accused my outfit of 'stealing' jeeps. I wasn't aware of this, so I investigated. It seems that my troops had become so hardened to the bombers' air raids that after a while when others abandoned jeeps in the area in response to early warning to seek cover, my men would get the abandoned jeeps and haul them off to the nearby woods, where they would paint out their serial numbers and unit symbols. Not surprisingly we did have extras, but I noted they were always Army jeeps; Marines would not 'steal' from brother Marines. The variations in paint made it easy to spot the four extras and send them back to the Army."[12]

Occasionally, one of the Japanese fighter escorts would come down on the deck to strafe the airfield. "The Zeros would come around and every now and then they would swoop down over the strip just to see what was going on," Davis remembered. "Once, four or five Zeros came in to sweep the airfield, and all of them were shot down. We claimed them, but between the 3rd Defense Battalion and every Marine with a rifle, who knows who really got them."[13]

LtGen Charles H. "Fog" Hayes, then a major, played a key role in the completion and operation of Henderson Field. "The Japanese got mixed up somehow; they apparently had a plan by which their ground forces on Guadalcanal were supposed to take the airfield on a certain night and the aircraft would fly in the next day. Well, their ground attack failed, but that word apparently didn't get back to the Army and the Navy flyers, and they came in the next day and the automatic weapons people shot them down like ducks."[14]

The battalion deployed all the extra weapons—20mm, 40mm and .50-caliber— that had been issued just before leaving New River. "We had a mechanical fire-control computer for the 40s … but for anything above 4,000 feet, however, we had no accuracy." The 3rd Defense Battalion came in with 90mm guns. "Our weapons were responsive to the defense battalion commander, who was killed just across the runway from me," Davis recalled. "Fortunately, we had some Marine fighter squadrons to deal with the [Mitsubishi G4M] Betty bombers."[15]

Twining echoed Davis' comment about October. "I think the low point of the campaign undoubtedly was the time of the terrific [naval] bombardment. They [Japanese] chased the Navy out. The Japanese gave us this plastering which caused pretty heavy losses, including a lot of officers and especially aviators … and they got every plane we had. We didn't have anything operational."[16]

In preparation for a major offensive, the Japanese conducted a major attack on Henderson Field during the night of 13/14 October. The battleships *Kongo* and *Haruna* unleashed a brutal, 80-minute barrage with their 16 14-inch naval guns, raining 918 14-inch shells on the airfield. This barrage put Henderson Field temporarily out of order and damaged 48 of 90 aircraft on the field. Additionally, the barrage killed 41 and destroyed most of the aviation fuel. The Marines would remember that night as "The Bombardment." Heavy shells crashed into the gasoline storage and ammunition dump, while all over the field the aircraft went up in clouds of smoke and flame. In hundreds of foxholes and improvised bomb shelters, men clung to the ground, cursing, praying, and in some cases, going out of their minds.

"After the bombardment, pilot officer Imahashi Takeru led two other Zeros in a low-level attack at tree-top level in close column, flying the length of Henderson Field. Every gun that could opened an intense AA fire. Turning left, the Japanese shot the length of Henderson Field, their shells bouncing off the steel Marston matting. Imahashi plowed into the ground just west of the field; Shimizu took three hits, and Takahashi, his plane heavily smoking, departed with nine."[17]

The morning after the bombardment, Henderson Field was unusable. Only seven of 39 SBDs were flyable. Fortunately, the Cactus Air Force had Fighter One—which was not damaged by the shelling—and 24 Wildcats remained available along with six Army Air Force P-400s and P-39s.

On the night of 14/15 October, the cruiser *Chokai* unleashed another 752 8-inch shells onto the airfield. That night saw another 1,500 eight-inch shells hurtled onto the airfield by the cruisers *Myoko* and *Maya*. This series of naval bombardments was complemented by a series of significant Japanese air attacks. The Americans struck back when Guadalcanal-based airpower destroyed three of the six fast transports. U.S. submarines also sunk an additional three freighters and an aircraft ferry. This shelling was the final straw for Ghormley, who Nimitz replaced with Vice Admiral William "Bull" Halsey on 15 October. The U.S. Navy struggled to gain naval superiority in the Southern Solomons throughout the Henderson Field defense. Their record was mixed, but ultimately they helped the U.S. regain the offensive.

Vandegrift was visited by Vice Admiral Kelly Turner who gave him some very bad news. A huge Japanese amphibious force might launch an attack in the next two or three weeks. If this wasn't bad enough, "Vice Admiral Robert L. Ghormley said he had to withdraw the fleet and that we had his permission to surrender if we needed to," Davis recalled. The Navy could no longer support the Guadalcanal operation because of a shortage of ships, airplanes, and a lack of supplies.[18]

Vandegrift was taken aback but not unnerved. He told his operations officer, Colonel Jerry Thomas, "We're going to defend this airfield until we no longer can. If that happens, we'll take what's left to the hills and fight guerrilla warfare." He also talked with Roy Geiger. "If the time comes when we no longer can hold the perimeter, I expect you to fly out your planes." Geiger replied, "Archer, if we can't use the planes back in the hills, we'll fly them out. But whatever happens I'm staying here with you."[19]

By mid-November the 1st Marine Division was "no longer capable of offensive operations. The cumulative effect of long periods of fatigue and strain, endless labor by day and vigilance by night were aggravated to an alarming degree by the growing malarial rate."[20]

However, reinforcements were pouring into Guadalcanal—two reinforced regiments of the 2nd Marine Division, two Army regiments, Army artillery, the 2nd Raider Battalion, and elements of two Marine Defense Battalions, plus many other supporting elements—replacing the worn-out defenders. On 9 December, the 5th Marines sailed for Australia, followed at intervals by the Division troops, 1st Marines, and the 7th Marines. Major General Alexander M. Patch, commanding general of the Americal Division, took over command of the island from General Vandegrift.[21]

"The miracle of it [Guadalcanal] is that the operation came off at all," Twining said. "I am sure no successful operation of any magnitude has ever been staged under more unfavorable conditions. You just can't conceive of the conditions under which that operation came off—the greatest luck, the unbelievable lack of tactical perceptiveness by the Japanese, everything in the world conspired to make it succeed at all."[22]

"Guadalcanal changed a lot of minds," Davis declared. "It proved that our guys could defeat the Japanese." He remained on Guadalcanal until January 1943, when he sailed with the antiaircraft battery to Australia. "I liked Australia," Davis remarked, "but there was so much uncertainty. We arrived there with the idea of retraining and re-equipping, then getting back in the war in a few weeks. No one was prepared for the long, long, long stay that we had. We were there for eight to nine months recovering from both malaria and dysentery."[23]

The Division was rife with the disease. "We would have 5,000 to 6,000 Marines in the hospital for two or three weeks to recover from the initial attack; [then] get out of the hospital, spend all their time in the pubs and on the town in Melbourne, and in two weeks' time be back in the hospital. In between times another 5,000 men would take their place in the hospital in a never-ending rotation. The doctors didn't understand the problem. The men just couldn't get the malaria out of their system and it prolonged our stay there on and on and on."[24]

The Special Weapons Battalion was co-located in the city park at Ballarat with the 11th Marines and the tank battalion. "There was not too much in the way of training areas," Davis explained. "We did have some thin forest in the area where training could be done, but the Division needed to prepare for combat in heavy jungle in preparation for the next fight."[25]

The battalion had been sent control mechanisms for the Oerlikon 20mm and the Bofors 40mm antiaircraft guns but, "We had nobody trained," Davis explained. "We had a couple of kids out of school who knew how to work the things so we went into a great effort to get these complex weapons in hand."[26]

Part Three

World War II: Southwest Pacific– Cape Gloucester

CHAPTER 9

The Green Inferno

In early November the Division was back on its feet. Davis received word that the Division was scheduled to "seize, occupy and defend" Cape Gloucester on the western end of New Britain in the Bismarck Islands group, under the command of LtGen Walter Krueger's U.S. Sixth Army. Designated "Dexterity," the operation was a three-phased attack in MacArthur's Southwest Pacific Area (SWPA). It was scheduled to kick off on 26 December 1943.[1]

General Krueger inspected the Division prior to the operation. "He walked through the place with his staff," Davis recalled, "and gave us some instructions on how the Army wrote their SOPs."[2] The Sixth Army devised an operational plan which the Division considered unacceptable—too complicated and a dangerous dispersal of forces—and voiced their concerns directly to General Douglas MacArthur during a visit in mid-December. According to *The Old Breed*, "MacArthur asked, as if in politeness only, how the First liked the plan for the coming operation. 'Well, General,' spoke LtCol E. A. Pollock, Division D-3 (Operations officer), 'we don't like anything about it,'" which earned him the enmity of Krueger's staff. Subsequently the Cape Gloucester landing plan was changed; the Division's 1st and 7th Regiments would land in assault, with the 5th Regiment in reserve.[3]

Many of the senior Division officers were glad to be mounting out. "We'd been down there long enough," LtCol Luckey said. "It was getting to be on the verge of being there too long. You know, these boys can get entrenched in a place to the point where they begin to not worry about the war—having too good a time. I think it was time we got out of there."[4] The Special Weapons Battalion was ready. "We were in good shape and passed all inspections with flying colors before we left."[5]

Radio Tokyo got wind of the Division's movement: "This gang of degenerates, cutthroats and assorted jailbirds, it seemed, had been withdrawn from Melbourne because of their disgraceful conduct ... our soldiers are fully prepared to repulse this insolent attempt. The jungles will run red with the blood of the Guadalcanal butchers!"

"The Gloucester operation was very different from Guadalcanal," Luckey remarked. "We captured the airfield on the first day, with almost no opposition, except rain and mud. The weather in the damned jungle in New Britain contributed a large share of the operation being extremely difficult. It was a horrible place."[6]

LtCol Frank O. Hough and Major John A. Crown described Cape Gloucester's seasons in *The Campaign on New Britain* as "wet and less wet." "The area's hot, humid climate 'rain forest,'" they noted, "produced giant trees towering up to 200 feet into the sky above dense undergrowth lashed together by savage vines as thick as a man's arm and many times as tough, in the coastal area interspersed with occasional patches of kunai grass sometimes higher than a man's head, and hip-deep swamps."[7]

The Division's action report noted, "Water backed up in the swamps in rear of the shore line, making them impassible for wheeled and tracked vehicles. The many streams which emptied into the sea in the beachhead area became raging torrents. Some even changed their course. Troops were soaked to the skin and their clothes never dried out during the entire operation."[8]

The maps described one area as a "Damp Flat." One Disgusted Marine declared, "It was 'damp' up to your neck. Time and again members of our column would fall into waist-high sink holes and have to be pulled out. A slip meant a broken or wrenched leg." The rain-saturated ground caused trees to fall, which killed and injured at least 100 men during the campaign.[9]

A newly promoted Major Davis, now Special Weapons Battalion commander, found that his battalion was being split up. "My AA platoons were farmed out to the regiments." Battery C and 2nd Platoon, Battery A, were assigned to Combat Team B. Battery B and 1st Platoon, Battery A, were assigned to Combat Team A, while Battery D was assigned to Combat Team C. Initially the batteries were tasked to provide antiaircraft defense of the landing beaches, under the control of the 12th Defense Battalion.[10]

Davis was left behind with only his battalion headquarters and he was not happy about it. "I was walking along the beach where his men were embarking on ships to leave the island. I spotted LtCol Puller, who had moved from being commanding officer, 1/7, to serve as regimental executive officer. I complained to that pugnacious officer that all my units had been doled out and I was being left behind. Puller replied in his characteristic fashion: 'It's a hell of a note when a man wants to go to war and no one will let him. Get on that ship over there, and tell them I said to take you to Cape Gloucester.' I wasted no time asking silly questions about written orders or baggage. I complied with his oral directive and wound up commanding a battalion in the Cape Gloucester operation."[11]

"We were transported by LSTs [Landing Ship, Tanks] out of Melbourne to Goodenough Island, off eastern Papua, where I spent time ashore for a few days. Then off to Cape Gloucester," Davis recalled. The LSTs were able to run up on the beach where they dropped their ramps and the men literally walked ashore without getting their feet wet. Nobody was shooting at them … but as soon as they got off the ship, they ran head on into the jungle.[12]

After reaching Cape Gloucester on 27 December, Davis "started out initially just off the beach. We had sent along a package of maintenance and supplies and I just collected those up and built my command post around them. We found a little place near a swamp from which I could keep contact with my troops." The jungle terrain posed a problem for his antiaircraft batteries until they got off the beach and were able to set up on knobs that were free of trees that masked their fire. "It was easy shooting from there, particularly around the airfield." During the four months Davis was on the island, he said, "I don't think we had more than a half dozen enemy planes come over our operation."[13]

"I really didn't have a lot to do in terms of fighting," Davis explained. "Mine was in supporting my units, keeping then supplied and equipped and inspecting them for administrative matters. The time on the island seemed to stretch on and on—December to April. In about five or six weeks after we were there, things started to slow down." With time on his hands, Davis tried to keep morale high. "I had a little theater built for all the local [Marine] entities around so that they could have a place to see a movie."[14]

One day Davis happened to run into an old friend, LtCol Joseph F. Hankins. "I asked him how things were going. He said, 'Well, fine, but you know, the first battalion commander is going to become the regimental executive officer, and I don't see anybody in sight to take over that battalion. Why don't you do it?' I hotfooted over to Puller and told him that I had been in the special weapons business long enough, and I'd like to get in the infantry."[15]

"My motivation for infantry was a prolonged ongoing process," Davis explained. "Now that I was a battalion CO of Special Weapons, I became more and more concerned that my units were farmed out in support roles. The cohesive command enjoyed in the infantry appealed to me. Puller hired me on the spot. Thus, on 24 April 1944, I took off with the First Marine Regiment for Pavuvu, where I would re-equip and train my infantry battalion, 1/1, for one of the bloodiest battles in Marine Corps history: Peleliu!"[16]

CHAPTER 10

A Steamy Pest-Hole

"I think God has forgotten where Pavuvu is."
"God couldn't forget, because He made everything."
"Then I bet He wishes He could forget he made Pavuvu."

—ANONYMOUS MARINE

Pavuvu, a steamy pest-hole located approximately 60 miles north of Guadalcanal, was picked by General Geiger as a training and rest area. With its romantic-sounding name, it conjures up an image of beautiful coral beaches, hula-skirted bare-breasted women, good food, cold beer, and warm nights. Unfortunately Pavuvu had none of them. It was a rain-soaked, rat-infested hunk of real estate; a terrible location to recover from a debilitating jungle campaign. Lieutenant Colonel Lewis Fields thought that Pavuvu "was one of the great mistakes as far as I am concerned in the whole war, stationing a division in such a place."[1]

The Division camp was located in a 600-acre coconut grove that reeked of rotting coconuts and palm fronds. The stench permeated everything, clothing, equipment and even food. There was inadequate drainage, and the area soon turned into a sea of mud. Davis recalled distastefully, "We lined coconuts up and down the company streets and put coral and mud over the top of that, which gave us a raised walkway to get out of the deep mud. We made a mistake in building sidewalks out of coconuts and, of course, they not only rotted away but they also gave away."[2]

Rupertus complained to his old friend "Archer" Vandegrift, who responded, "Had I known prior to the arrival of the First [Division] that it was a virgin area, I certainly would have used every effort I could to have the rehabilitation area changed. Knowing the Russells [Islands], or part of them at least, to be a very pleasant place to be located, I assumed that the camp area was all laid out, which just shows that you can't go on assumptions." One disillusioned Marine groused, "If you were gonna give the world an enema, that's where you would put it."[3]

The men found deplorable conditions but there was little they could do about it. Colonel John T. Selden recalled "it was General Geiger's idea to base the Division in the Russells in order to avoid having to furnish large working details, as was the rule on Guadalcanal [average of 1,000 men a day], which would interfere seriously with the training program. Unfortunately, [Geiger's] reconnaissance was made by air and failed to disclose the more serious terrain difficulties."[4]

Instead of rest and relaxation, the men had to build a camp from scratch. There were no streets, no mess halls, no lights, no decks for tents—nothing but acres and acres of coconut palms. O. P. Smith, the assistant Division commander, complained that "decayed coral rock underlay the coconut groves and the abundant rainfall did not readily drain through it ... foot and vehicle traffic churned the turf into mud ... and the roads were hub-deep in mud most of the time. There was not surface water until we eventually dug seven wells with a daily output of 200,000 gallons, which did not provide much water for bathing."[5]

Abandoned coconut plantations covered the island, littering the ground with tons of rotting nuts. The stench was overpowering. Unenthusiastic Marines were dragooned into working parties to gather the rotted husks, which usually cracked when handled, drenching the unfortunates with rancid milk.

Uncounted multitudes of land crabs inhabited Pavuvu and hundreds of thousands of repulsive-looking rats also populated the island. Their numbers simply overwhelmed every effort to eradicate the filthy beasts—poison, explosives, even flamethrowers. "We killed upward of 400," a disheartened officer reported, "but the next night I saw we hadn't even dented Pavuvu's rat population. I got discouraged and forgot about the scheme." One Marine wag wrote about the island's ecology. "Land crabs ate rotted coconuts—rats ate the land crabs—Marines killed the rats. Everyone thrived in harmony!"[6]

The island was so small that it was impossible to hold large-scale field maneuvers. Even company-sized units were forced to skirmish through the streets of the tent camps and "found themselves dodging among heads [rest rooms] and mess halls and tripping over the guy ropes of their own tents." There was continuous congestion on the ranges because of the limited number that could be built.[7]

Devoid of beaches and overladen with palm groves, Pavuvu lacked the variety of terrain, as well as the space, to train a Marine Division efficiently. Russ Honsowetz remembered that "Puller would march us around and around [Pavuvu], up and down the few hills that were on it. The head of the column and the tail weren't very far apart when you get a 5,000-man regiment going."[8]

The Division suffered a shortage of critical equipment—flame throwers, demolitions, bazookas, engineering, signaling and water-proofing equipment—during its entire time at Pavuvu. Much of the equipment arrived barely in time to be loaded for the movement to Peleliu.

Despite the training limitations and terrible living conditions, Davis immediately started small-unit training. "There was an area where we could assault four or five positions with total freedom of action. We employed mortars overhead with live ammo, plus rockets and flame throwers in assault teams. It was the best assault team training I ever witnessed and totally realistic and very dangerous, but we were going into a pretty dangerous situation."[9]

Davis pushed his troops hard because captured Japanese documents described the heavy fortifications they would face on Peleliu. "We built Japanese-style bunkers, then assigned a squad of Marines, with satchel charges, flame throwers, and rocket/bazookas the task of taking the bunker. These were innovative tactics, because captured documents had given us an indication of the heavy fortifications we would face on Peleliu. The small-unit commanders knew the lives of their men were at stake and they really went at it to get ready for the assault. It developed superbly skilled and finely tuned assault teams."[10]

On 13 July, halfway through training, Lieutenant Colonel Jack M. Warner was given command of the battalion, bumping Davis to the number-two slot. On his first day in command, Davis took him on a tour of the training area. "He walked up on the assault training and started yelling, 'Stop it, stop it, somebody is going to get killed.' He had just come from teaching tactics at the Quantico Marine base in Virginia, with its extensive safety rules. He was pretty horrified to see this training. He just couldn't believe we'd turn an assault team loose to go at a bunker."[11]

"Unfortunately, he became a real pain for me from that day forward," Davis said. "Playing basketball with the battalion officers, he would trip them up, and do all kinds of dastardly things. He was a nut. He got drunk one night and decided to kill one of the tank battalion officers with his pistol. I got the magazine out of the weapon but couldn't check to see if there was a round in the chamber. My drunk commander sobered up somewhat and poured a pitcher of ice water over his head, and I was then able to get him back to his bunk."[12]

"Just two days later," Davis recalled, "he took a small boat over to another island ostensibly to check on supplies—and never came back [for several days]." Davis found out later that there was a Navy hospital on the island staffed with nurses. "Our new commander had joined up with the Nurse Corps," Davis remarked, tongue in cheek.[13]

Puller found out and threw a fit, reducing the lieutenant colonel to his permanent grade of first lieutenant on the spot when he returned. Davis was restored on 21 August, just in time for Operation *Stalemate*, the capture of Peleliu.

The 1st Division was not so isolated that the famous comedian Bob Hope could not find it. Hope was on a USO-sponsored trip to Banika, a short plane hop from Pavuvu, when he heard about the Marines next door. Hope prodded the Navy into allowing his troupe to do a morning performance. According to one Marine, "The fact that they'd come to a godforsaken place like Pavuvu really lifted our spirits. It made us feel like we weren't totally forgotten."

O. P. Smith remembered, "Because of their tight schedule, we brought the troupe over in eight small Cub planes. About 15,000 men were assembled in the open space back of the docks. The planes made their approach to a landing by flying over the heads of the crowd." The irrepressible Hope said that circling over the heads of his audience was one of the highlights of his Pacific tour. A road doubled as a makeshift runway. It was a tricky landing according to one of the Marine pilots. "You had to make a steep bank around a large grove of palms and then line up, come down, and hit the middle of the road. It had a high crown, and if you didn't hit it just right you'd ground-loop into the ditch.[14]

Hope's troupe put on an unforgettable 90-minute show that had the troops laughing, cheering, whistling and applauding. The highlight of the performance was scantily clad dancer Patti Thomas. Straight-laced O. P. Smith reminisced smilingly, "First Patti did different types of dances in pantomime and after each dance, men near the stage were asked to dance with Patti." The skit brought the house down. Bob Hope closed the performance with his theme song, "Thanks for the Memories." One Marine said, "Man, what a show! One show every day and we could fight this damned war with a smile!" George McMillan thought "it was one of the most pleasant memories of Pavuvu the men retained."[15]

The first stop for the invasion fleet was at Cape Esperance, Guadalcanal, for its final landing rehearsal. Davis' battalion landed on 27 August and re-embarked on the same day. "The troops were in good spirits and a fair state of health," Davis noted. The next evening the battalion "made another landing, this time with a fake bombing and preliminary naval gunfire support. The battalion re-embarked and sailed for Tetere, arriving there the same evening." From 30 August to 5 September the transports lay at anchor off Tetere, where the troops were allowed to go ashore to exercise and wash clothes.[16]

Part Four

World War II: Peleliu

CHAPTER 11

Breakwater of the Pacific

Following the landing rehearsals at Cape Esperance, a critique was held in the former movie area on Guadalcanal, four days before the transports sailed for Peleliu. General Rupertus hobbled to the stage—he had severely strained his ankle following a fall from an amtrac—and stood before the large assembly of Marine and Navy officers. He announced, "We're going to have some casualties, but let me assure you this is going to be a short one, a quickie. Rough but fast. We'll be through in three days. It might take only two."[1]

Major Gordon Gayle, commanding officer 2nd Battalion, 5th Marines, was among the attendees at the rehearsal critique. "I never understood why he said such a thing like that because it was pretty obvious from the terrain information that we had that while we might make the assault in 72 hours and might establish ourselves in a position so that there was no question about the outcome ... the terrain was such that inevitably there would be an awful lot of Japanese to dig out of that place."[2]

LtCol Russell Honsowetz, commanding officer 2nd Battalion, 1st Marines, was outspoken, calling Rupertus, "Rupe the dupe." "I didn't have much confidence in the briefing where he said it was going to be over in 72 hours. I was worried about [Rupertus]. I wondered what was making him tick at that stage of the game. None of us, among the people I talked to, was inspired one damn bit. In fact, we were all a little bit worried about the operation after listening to that speech." Davis was left with the impression that "we were expecting to go ashore, secure the airfield, upgrade it, get some exercise, and get back on the ship." In an interview years later for Fox News, Davis was asked about the Division commander. "Rupertus," he replied, "what a jackass!"[3]

Rupertus prepared a letter to all the troop commanders and newsmen that was to be opened on D-1:

MEN OF THE FIRST DIVISION:

Once again the eyes of the Marine Corps will be focused on you. In a few days you will prove that your selection to spearhead another and deeper thrust into enemy territory is an honor which you richly deserve.

At Guadalcanal, Cape Gloucester and Talasea, you demonstrated that you were superior to the best troops the enemy could place in the field. YOU ARE STILL SUPERIOR.

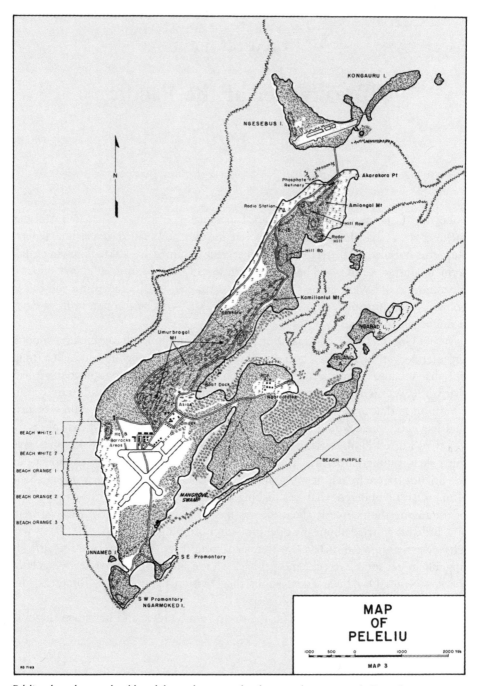

Peleliu, shaped somewhat like a lobster claw, proved to be a tough nut to crack. Davis lost 70 percent of his battalion in five days. (U.S. Marine Corps, Historical Monograph: *The Seizure of Peleliu*)

You will land after intensive naval bombardment and air bombing to meet the enemy with one idea upper-most in your minds—to carry out the mission entrusted to you.

Within 48 hours from the time that the first Marine puts foot on enemy soil, our country should have still another base from which to continue the march to Tokyo.

That each and every one will do his duty is well known. I am proud to command such a body of men and to be with you in your victory.

Good luck and God be with you.

William H. Rupertus
Major General, U.S. Marine Corps
Commanding

The message upset Gordon Gayle. "I think it had a very negative effect because some people believed it, and if you were in my position, you couldn't discredit the Division commander's statement, but neither could you believe it."[4]

The 1st Marine Division (reinforced) was 5 percent over its authorized strength and at the time of embarkation consisted of 26,995 enlisted men and 1,489 officers. The Peleliu operation was the third operation for approximately 264 Marine officers (Davis being one of them) and 5,700 enlisted Marines.

Davis' battalion, 1,478 officers and men of Landing Team 1-1, embarked aboard the USS *Warren* (APA-53), one of ten specially constructed assault transports. Lightly armed with one 5-inch .38-caliber gun and 20mm and 40mm antiaircraft mounts for defense, the APA carried 17 assorted landing craft. 1st Battalion would use the ship's wooden landing craft to get to the transfer line, where they would climb aboard amtracs for the final swim over the reef to the beach. *Warren* remained offshore as a floating hospital. Among those treated were Marines from the 1st Battalion, who only a short time before had been passengers.

At 0630 on 8 September, the *Warren* sailed for Peleliu, a 2,100-mile voyage. "Though their [berthing compartments] were crowded, all hands took a new interest in the care of their weapons. Many of the troops took their jungle hammocks out of their [bed] rolls and slept topside in preference to crowding into the holds."[5]

Shortly before sailing, Davis received a copy of the regimental operation order, which he used to plan the battalion's scheme of maneuver. He then briefed his company commanders, who, in turn, gathered their men by platoons and briefed them. They used special 1:10,000 and 1:5,000 scale tactical maps of the island to orient the men, using terrain features as points of reference. Unfortunately they did not take into account that many of the features they used would be obliterated by the naval and air bombardment. As the men gathered to "get the word," many of them took Rupertus' comments to heart and talked about a rough but short operation. The veterans remained skeptical after studying the tactical maps and noting that much of the island was jungle covered. No one could determine what lay under the dense growth.

By the summer of 1944, the United States was advancing on Japan's home islands in a two-pronged attack through the Central and Southwest Pacific Theaters. Japan's first line of defense in the Marshall and Mariana Islands had been shattered and the country was desperately pouring men, weapons and equipment into a second line. This absolute zone of national defense extended west of the Marianas–Carolines–Western New Guinea line, where each Japanese soldier was expected to fight to the death.

General MacArthur's southwestern forces had reached the western extremity of New Guinea and were preparing for a move into the Philippine island of Mindanao, to honor his "I shall return" promise. In the Central Pacific, Admiral Chester W. Nimitz's amphibious forces had seized Saipan in the Marianas and were planning to move toward Iwo Jima in the Volcano Island Group—only 800 miles from Tokyo.

First, however, MacArthur's advance had to be secured. Admiral Nimitz directed the seizure of the southern Palaus in the western Carolines to "remove a definite threat from MacArthur's right flank and to secure a base to support his operation into the southern Philippines." On 7 July he designated it Operation *Stalemate II* and assigned Phase I (Peleliu) a target date of 15 September 1944.

Peleliu

Peleliu (known as Periryu by the Japanese) is one of six large islands and numerous islets in the Palaus group, the westernmost extremity of the vast Caroline Islands chain spanning 33 degrees of longitude just north of the Equator. Palaus group's 100 to 200 separate islands lie along a generally northeast–southwest axis roughly 500 miles east of the Philippines and an equal distance from New Guinea. Covering some 175 square miles of ocean, they vary from flat atolls in the north, to volcanic central islands, to coral-limestone composition at the southern end. A great coral reef encircles them, forming a barrier reef on the west coast and a fringing reef on the east coast.

First discovered by the Spanish in the mid-1500s, the Palaus' remoteness kept them from being developed well into the 18th century, until they were sold to Germany in 1899 for four million dollars. The Germans promptly exploited the island's resources, mining phosphates and producing coconut oil. However, with its defeat in World War I, Germany surrendered them to Japan, a member of the victorious Allies. Japan quickly consolidated control by encouraging 20,000 mainland Japanese—three times the number of local Palauans—to emigrate. Emigre men were encouraged to marry the daughters of prominent Palauan families to further cement ties to the homeland. Japan kept its activities in the islands secret and attempted to exclude all foreigners.

The principal islands of pre-war interest to the American military were Bebelthuap, the largest and most heavily defended; Koror, the administrative, commercial and communication hub of the islands with a deep-water lagoon, anchorage and sea plane facilities; Angaur, suitable for the development of air facilities; and Peleliu, with its two-strip, hard-packed coral surface airfield, complete with taxiways, dispersal areas and turning circles. A second airfield was under construction on Ngesebus Island off the northern tip of Peleliu.

It was the airfield development that attracted the attention of American planners and intelligence experts in early 1944. Aircraft launched from Peleliu posed a threat to MacArthur's imminent return to the Philippines. The airfield, located on the only flat ground in the southern sector of the island, was a branch air arsenal and the home of Japan's depleted 26th Air Flotilla. It was well developed, complete with barracks, hangars, large water cisterns, maintenance shops, a power plant, a radio station and a large two-story administrative building. The main runway was over 1,675-meters long, with a shorter fighter strip of 1,220 meters intersecting it at a 90-degree angle. Revetments and trenches lined the runways, with concrete reinforced air-raid shelters positioned near the administrative area.

Photo interpreters identified more than 20 dual-purpose (air and ground) antiaircraft guns in and around the airfield complex. Their tell-tale circular and semi-circular revetments arranged in a triangular pattern made them readily identifiable from the air. The aerial photographs also showed numerous machine-gun positions interspersed among the heavy guns to provide defense against both high- and low-level attack.

The Joint Army-Navy Intelligence Service (JANIS) erroneously described Peleliu's terrain as "low and flat," except for the high ground along the upper half of its western pincer. This ridge system took its name from the almost-unpronounceable Umurbrogol Mountain, a 550-foot irregular series of broken coral ridges, narrow valleys and rugged peaks. Erosion wore away the rock formations, leaving a razor edge to its jagged crags.

It was this nightmare of crags, pinnacles and coral rubble honeycombed with natural caves that the Japanese used to bolster their defense. A Marine wounded in the fighting described the Umurbrogol, nicknamed "Bloody Nose Ridge," as "a place that might have been designed by a maniacal artist given to painting mathematical abstractions—all slants, jagged, straights, steeps, and sheers with no curve to soften or relieve. The Umurbrogol was a monster Swiss cheese of hard coral limestone pocked beyond imagining with caves and crevices. They were to be found at every level, in every size—crevices small enough for a lonely sniper, eerie caverns big enough to station a battalion among its stalactites and stalagmites."[6]

Thick jungle scrub cloaked the slopes, masking the Umurbrogol's rugged contours from aerial observation. Colonel Merwin Silverthorn, chief of Staff, III Amphibious Corps, thought "They looked like a normal ridge. But when we denuded it through gunfire and aerial bombardment, we found that there were these funny-shaped ridges that were as steep as the roof of a house. And instead of one ridge as it appeared under the foliage, there might be three or four parallel ridges with deep ravines in between." Brigadier General O. P. Smith declared, "There was never any question in the minds of the 1st Division planners but that the high ground was the key terrain feature of the island."[7]

Davis was convinced that Peleliu intelligence had failed. "The Japanese had chiseled out five levels of caves in the hillsides. They had apertures for firing machine guns and our intelligence had not discovered this, so when we landed we were fired at from all directions."[8]

Silverthorn noted that, "The island had been mined for many years for phosphate deposits. So, the situation actually existed where the Marines would capture the ground and be in possession of the ground, and the Japanese would be underneath. There would be no way to get at them, and they would come out at night ... sometimes with swords, and attack the Marines with these medieval weapons—very sharp swords capable of cutting a man's body in two."[9]

Because of American successes at Saipan, Bougainville, and Guam, the Japanese changed their tactics. Instead of attempting to annihilate invaders at the water's edge, they constructed a defense in depth, for a war of attrition (*jikyusen*) to play for time and bleed the invaders dry. Peleliu was organized into four defensive sectors that utilized the rugged terrain to construct mutually supporting positions. The main line of resistance was prepared far enough inland to minimize the effectiveness of the pre-invasion bombardment. This was backed up by defense in depth to wear down the American attackers combined with the hoarding of sufficient reserves to mount counterattacks. Davis noted that the island commander, "Lieutenant General Sadae Inoue ordered his troops to fortify the island, no more suicide attacks; stay in their positions; kill the enemy until they themselves die for the Emperor!"[10]

The Plan

On 15 August 1944, the Division issued Operation Plan No. 1-44. The plan called for a landing of three regiments—1st, 5th, and 7th—abreast on a 2,200-yard beachhead on the southwest coast of Peleliu at 0830, 15 September. The landing would be made in LVTs (Landing Vehicle, Tracked) preceded by a wave of LVT (A)s (LVTs armed with 37mm cannons).[11]

The 1st Marines, under the legendary Lewie Puller, was to land two battalions abreast, with one battalion in reserve (Davis 1/1), over the White Beaches on the left (north) flank of the beachhead to drive up the western shore and clear the Japanese from the ridges overlooking the airfield. The 5th Marines, under the scholarly Colonel Harold D. "Bucky" Harris, was to land in the center over Orange Beach 1 and 2, secure the airfield, and divide the island in half. The 7th Marines, led by Medal of Honor recipient Herman H. Hanneken, would land over Orange Beach 3 on the Division right flank abreast of the 5th Marines and drive across to the eastern shore. It would then wheel right to clear the isolated southern tip of the island from where the Japanese could enfilade the entire beach. One battalion of the 7th Marines and the Division Reconnaissance Company were designated the Division reserve.[12]

Naval and air bombardment would commence on D-3 and continue until the troops were established on the beach.

Naval Gunfire Support

In early August, the III Amphibious Corps commander, MajGen Roy S. Geiger and his staff flew to the Russell Islands to discuss naval gunfire support for the operation with the Western Attack Group commander, Rear Admiral George H. Fort. The meeting did not go well. The admiral started off the meeting with, "You're not going to get all the gunfire support here … I don't have the ships, and we don't have the ammunition." He announced there would be two days preliminary bombardment. Geiger found this unacceptable and argued forcefully for at least one more day, which was grudgingly accepted. Fort remarked acidly that, "The idea which some people seem to have of just firing at an island is an inexcusable waste of ammunition."[13]

The third day did not mean that a larger number of shells were fired; instead, the extra day merely allowed the same amount of ammunition to be expended with greater deliberation over a longer period of time. Admiral Oldendorf stated that, "the best that can be done is to blast away at suspected positions and hope for the best."[14]

The pre-assault air and naval gunfire plan called for two hours of ship bombardment followed by two hours of bombing by aircraft flying from escort carriers. Following this aerial bombardment, the heavy naval guns resumed their deliberate fire. This alternating naval gunfire and aerial bombardment was followed throughout D-3 to D-day.

At 0530 on 12 September, Rear Admiral Jesse B. Oldendorf's Peleliu Fire Support Unit—four old battleships, armed with 14-inch main battery, three heavy cruisers, one light cruiser and nine destroyers—commenced bombarding the most obvious targets with 2,255 tons of ammunition. Special attention was directed to known or suspected Japanese artillery and mortar positions. The shelling knocked down vegetation along Peleliu's central ridge (Umurbrogol Mountain), revealing numerous caves which had not been known to exist prior to the bombardment.[15]

With the bombardment well along, two high-speed transports, USS *Stringham* (APD-6) and USS *Clemson* (APD-31), lowered their Higgins boats, with frogmen from Underwater Demolition Teams 6 and 7 aboard. Their mission was to clear the beach approaches of underwater obstacles and make pathways through the coral reef for the shallow draft landing craft. After the landing, they also cleared boulders from roadways, and placed buoys and markers.

The night before the assault, frogmen crawled ashore to demolish rock cribs, posts, barbed wire, concrete cubes, and set buoys off the reef to mark the newly blasted passageways. Clad only in swimming trunks, these underwater experts were constantly fired at by Japanese machine guns and snipers.[16]

Air Support

The pre-H hour air support plan called for a heavy strike by 24 F6F Hellcat fighters (VF), 18 Navy scout-bombers (VSB) and 8 Navy torpedo bombers (VT) to support the landings on White Beach and Orange Beaches. Primary attack considerations were given to gun positions and beach installations. At H-hour the Strafing Group of 12 four-plane divisions would provide continuous attack from the time the landing craft were 800 yards off shore until the first wave hit the beach. The first two divisions would attack White Beach 1 and 2 and Orange Beach 1 and 2. The aircraft would make their runs on a heading parallel to the beach line from south to north. The air support plan dictated that eight planes should always be attacking to keep the beaches under constant fire. Commencing at 1045, 12 VFs and eight VTs would provide direct support for the troops ashore.

On D+11, 24 Marine white-nosed Corsairs from Major Robert F. "Cowboy" Stout's VMF-114 ("Death Dealers") began close air support (CAS) from the captured airfield. "When we landed at the air base on Peleliu the Japs had snipers shooting at us from the hills. It was just something we had to put up with. They flew some of the shortest close air support missions on record. Corsairs took off from the airstrip to drop napalm on the ridges 15 seconds beyond the runway. So close were these missions that the planes' wheels were never retracted, allowing them to return immediately to the airfield to quickly rearm. We had to be very careful where we dropped our bombs because we dropped them so close to our guys."[17]

Oldendorf ended the bombardment early. He sent a dispatch reporting that all known targets had been silenced and no more were available. Ammunition expenditure figures showed that fewer projectiles were fired than bombs. The Navy's gunfire recalcitrance would have deadly consequences for the Marine assault force.

Historians Jeter A. Isely and Philip A. Crowl in *U.S. Marines and Amphibious War*, wrote "… the conclusion cannot be avoided that preliminary naval gunfire on Peleliu was inadequate, and that the lessons learned at Guam were overlooked … Peleliu, like Tarawa and to a lesser extent Saipan, demonstrated that the only substitute for such prolonged bombardment was costly expenditure of the lives of the assault troops.[18]

CHAPTER 12

Death at the High-Water Line

Reveille was sounded at 0215 on 15 September and the troops headed for the mess decks for breakfast. Landing craft, vehicle and personnel (LCVP) boats were lowered into the water at 0655. The troops climbed down the sides of the transports on cargo nets hung from the sides and into the ship's boats. The carefully choreographed maneuver involved each boat team lined up on deck in four or five ranks. On signal that the landing craft was in position, the front rank straddled the rail and stepped down on a horizontal strand, grasping the verticals and then climbing down to the boat. As one file of men cleared the rail, another rank started down.

The maneuver seemed fairly simple, but in a heavy sea, carrying a weapon, full pack and ammunition, accidents were bound to happen. More than one man lost his grip and fell between ship and landing craft. The men were trained to keep their helmet chin straps buckled—to keep the two-pound steel pot from braining those below—and to unbuckle their cartridge belt in case they went into the drink and had to ditch it. Unfortunately the pack, heavy boondockers and waterlogged clothing were not so easy to shrug out of.

Lieutenant Robert W. Fisher, Communications Platoon, Headquarter Company, 1st Battalion, 1st Regiment, was crowded into one of the landing craft. "The constant rolling motion made life miserable for the boys with weak stomachs. Breakfast had consisted of a bountiful helping of fried potatoes plus a small fried steak, and while at the time this heavy meal seemed an excellent choice, many had reason to regret having eaten it ...."[1]

Davis watched from the ship as "the dive bombers peeled off and dove onto targets and receiving virtually no return fire that [he] could see. Only one plane, a Vought OS2U, was straddled by black puffs of heavy AA fire over Ngesebus Island to the north of our objective, but it twisted out unharmed. Apparently some of the smaller enemy antiaircraft found a target, though, for at about 0800 a speck directly above the island burst into flame and flashed downward at a slight angle, trailing a banner of flame behind it."[2]

"At 0800 columns of smoke spiraled up from various spots on the island, and the entire beach to our front and southward to the end of the island became obscured by smoke, through which occasional flashes from shell bursts could be seen. We felt complete confidence in ourselves and in our supporting arms."[3]

Rupertus' prediction of a quick operation infected the troops with a cockiness that did not survive the ride to the beach. The Japanese fought back from the beginning with a vengeance.[4]

As the first wave of LVT (A)s (Armored Amphibian tractors) from the 3rd Armored Amphibian Battalion (Provisional), mounting a 37mm cannon and several machine guns, approached the edge of the reef they came under Japanese antiboat guns … casualties were severe from the fire of high-caliber automatic weapons located on the headlands north and south of the beach. The enfilade fire from these weapons caused heavy casualties among the amphibian tractors, particularly at White Beach 1 and Orange Beach 3. An aerial observer reported excitedly, "There are amtracs burning on the reef. Repeat: There are amtracs burning on the reef."[5]

One particularly effective 47mm antiboat gun played havoc with the first waves. It was sited to fire the entire length of White Beach 1 and was located on a point of high ground, which projected about 25 yards to seaward just beyond 3/1's left boundary. The reinforced concrete casemate was built at the base of a coral mound and was protected by four pillboxes mounting heavy machine guns, surrounded by a series of trenches and spider traps containing dozens of diehard Japanese infantry. The expertly camouflaged emplacements had not even been scratched by the pre-landing bombardment, despite repeated requests from Colonel Puller. In 2009, the author explored the exiting casemates and found them intact. The surrounding trenches were still in evidence. Expended American .30-caliber cartridge cases littered the ground and in the shallow water. The badly rusted hulk of an amtrac lay in the water in front of the casemate, which still retained much of its coral rock camouflage. Even today the casemate was difficult to spot.

At 0850 the 1st Battalion began transferring from wooden landing craft into LVTs for the run to White Beach 1. "At about this time several large fires were seen on White Beach 2 at the left boundary, and at the same time geysers of water began to spring up in the water in closely knit lines exactly like troops at close order drill."[6] Twenty minutes later the battalion had completed the transfer to LVTs and started the run in to the beach.

Davis and several members of his CP group were in a "free boat"—an LVT that had not been assigned a specific wave. As he peered over the side of the lurching amtrac he saw a scene of utter destruction. Oily black smoke rose into the sky, marking the funeral pyre of more than 20 burning tractors off White Beach 1 and 2. Colonel Puller's plan to land Davis' battalion behind 3/1, to reinforce the left flank, was thwarted by the H-hour losses in LVTs. Davis' battalion was committed piecemeal, companies landed singly to the action.[7]

The bright flashes of exploding mortar and artillery fire marked the landing beaches that were wreathed in a heavy pall of dust and smoke. "Mortar shells began falling all around the LVTs; the Japs had apparently sited their heavy weapons to cover the area between the reef and the shore," Davis said. "Three tractors of our wave were hit going in, with great loss of life and the fires we had seen raging on the beach turned out to be numerous LVTs and DUKWs.[8] The ammunition which had been aboard them was exploding, and occasionally one of the tractors would blow up, scattering debris over the beach."[9] Japanese antiboat obstacles, posts strung with barbed wire, formed irregular patterns in the shallow water. Small Japanese flags marked artillery and mortar registration points.

Sergeant James Moll hunched down in one of the lead amtracs. "As we got closer to the beach, we could see the enemy's shells dropping and some of our landing craft being hit. I could hear the machine-gun bullets hitting the armor plate in front of me. As we got closer, my heart was beating like a jackhammer."[10]

Davis was knocked off his feet when the heavy vehicle slammed into the edge of the fringing reef. The driver gunned the engine, and the powerful machine easily lifted itself up and over the coral. Splashes from Japanese artillery and mortar fire erupted to the right and left. Dead Marines floated lifelessly in the water, the suction of the passing LVT drawing them in its wake. There was no stopping to pick them up. Many of the dead drifted out to sea and were never recovered. They were listed as missing in action. Other remains were not identified and buried as Unknowns. Specially trained graves-registrations teams had to wait until after the fighting moved inland to gather the dead. Theirs was a grisly task—decomposition, ghastly wounds and traumatic amputations complicated the job of identifying the remains.

The amtrac crossed the 600–700-yard reef and ground to a stop, the aft ramp came down fast, and Davis scrambled out into the maelstrom. "My battalion landed in reserve," Davis explained, "which was meaningless, because the Japanese defenses were so thick and so sturdy that when I got off the amphibian tractor on the beach, my run for cover was not quick enough, a mortar round splashed nearby and ran a long sliver into my knee. Fortunately it was not a critical wound. It bled a lot, but they got it out, doctored me up, and I went back to work."[11]

Later Puller, who was being carried on a stretcher because of a flare-up of a bad wound he sustained on Guadalcanal, saw the bandage on Davis' knee and pulled it off, telling Davis that, "it was not bad enough to be evacuated. I was aware that 'they' [battalion surgeon] had wanted to hand me off to a hospital ship, but that I wouldn't go. I was always convinced that Lewie Puller wouldn't have survived if he hadn't been crippled. His old wound from Guadalcanal flared up to the point that he couldn't walk. They carried him around on a stretcher. I was convinced that if he could have walked around as he was prone to do, he would have been killed."[12]

"The lead elements were bogged down on the beach," Davis recalled, "and the men had to fight their way off the beach." They suffered heavy casualties from the murderous Japanese fire. The cries of "Corpsman" and "Stretcher bearers," were nerve-wracking. "The beachhead was extremely shallow and the Japs were pouring in small arms fire from our front and flanks," the battalion after-action report said. "About 70 yards in from the shore was a low coral cliff which was offering protection to individual enemy riflemen; mortars and artillery were shelling the beach." To make matters worse, a steel-reinforced blockhouse in Company C's sector was giving them fits until an assault squad knocked it out.[13]

Davis had a hard time gathering his battalion together after hitting the beach. Lieutenant Robert W. Fisher, one of his Marines, explained why. "There were several factors which prevented us from quickly reorganizing. The terrific pounding ... had leveled everything along the beach. Landmarks had disappeared. In addition, some of the troops had landed several hundred yards from where they had been briefed ... and consequently they were temporarily lost. Finally, we could not go into our assembly area—300-yards inland—because the assault battalions were pinned down on the beach." Fisher found out the hard way when he walked toward the designated assembly area. A Marine yelled out, "Hey, Mac, you'd better get down; this is the front line."[14]

Major Nikolai S. Stevenson, Davis' second in command, was responsible for the rear CP: "As executive officer it was my job to be sure that communications kept us in touch with the rifle companies struggling to advance. Also involved was the need to keep food and ammunition flowing forward and to evacuate the wounded." Major Stevenson was also there in case Davis was incapacitated. On D-day, the forward CP was immediately behind the front lines, "a little more than a hundred yards in front of the rear command post, which had barely cleared the water line." The two CPs remained separate so that one shell did not get them both.[15]

General Smith described the terrain: "Particularly back of the northern end of the beach, the ground was rugged and well wooded. About 200 yards inland from the beach was a 30-foot coral ridge. Eight-hundred- to 1,000-yards inland from White 1 were the southern noses of the high rugged ground in the central part of the island. This high ground dominated the beaches and the airfield."[16]

Conditions ashore were chaotic. Japanese fire had decimated unit leaders, disrupting the normal flow of information up the chain of command. Those leaders still alive were trying to get the decimated assault units off the beach and to stay alive in the hurricane of fire. The 1st Battalion lost Lieutenant Mueller of Company C, who was shot through the head as he stepped ashore; Lieutenant Buss of Company A was wounded in the chest by a sniper and died later as a result. Later in the day, Captain George Dawes of Company B was wounded and evacuated.

Davis committed two companies, A and B, to close a gap on the regiment's left flank, where Captain George P. Hunt's Company K, 3rd Battalion, had been badly shot up trying to storm the cave-pocked coral ridge to their front. "I went up to join Hunt to get him inside our lines and this is where [we] got all mixed up," Davis recalled. "We had companies interlaced in between one another in a way that had to be sorted out."[17]

Sometime in late afternoon, Puller learned of Company K's desperate straits. He ordered Davis to commit one of his companies to reinforce it. "Company A moved into positions trying to take advantage of a Jap antitank ditch," the battalion after-action report stated. "It was apparent that the Japs had sited antitank weapons from the left flank and mortars from the ridges to the front to cover this ditch well, and his riflemen and mortars made the ground untenable. It is only natural that our Marines, lying in all the attitudes of death, should have sought shelter in this defiladed trench."[18]

The company was stopped cold; casualties were severe. Davis recalled, "The enemy had tunneled back under the coral ridge lines, sometimes 100 to 200 feet, and they would lay a machine gun to shoot out of a distant hole, with deadly crossfire from well dug-in and fight-to-the-death defensive positions."[19]

The Japanese counterattacked and cut off a squad. "Sergeant [Robert W.] Riley noticed two amphibious tractors and a Sherman tank that had been knocked out on his left," the after-action report noted. "He ordered his men to form a skirmish line to the right of the tank … took its machine gun and brought fire to bear, inflicting heavy casualties on the enemy and pinning them down. The squad was rescued when the company executive officer sent out another tank. Upon Riley's return, he was elevated to platoon commander after all its leaders had either been killed or wounded. Riley led the 2nd Platoon through some of the fiercest fighting of the campaign until wounded by grenade fragments. The platoon was turned over to the ranking Marine, PFC G. E. Hogan."[20]

"While Sgt. Riley and his men were occupied with the Japs in their sector, Sgt. Aubertin with the 2nd Squad of the 1st Platoon under command of Cpl. McQuade, succeeded in storming the coral ridge to their front and moved down the other side. They contacted Company I on their right and refused the left flank, bending it back to the ridge behind them. Since there was a distance of 200 yards to cover, Sgt. Aubertin organized four separate fire groups, with visual contact, and successfully held the ground he had taken until noon the following day. During the night they repulsed all efforts of the Japs to dislodge them."[21]

With Company A pinned down, Company B was committed to the attack but suffered the same fate. Corporal Herbert B. Goff "boldly faced the withering barrage in a determined effort to outflank the Japanese opposing troops and, skillfully disposing his men for maximum effectiveness, fearlessly led them in a determined attack," as recounted in his Navy Cross citation. "Aware that the fire of his squad was insufficient to neutralize the heavily fortified emplacement, he pressed forward alone and, armed only with grenades and a submachine gun, succeeded in silencing the hostile weapon and annihilating the crew before he was fatally struck down by enemy fire." His effort was not enough, and Company B was forced to go to ground.

At 1700, Davis received a "flash" message; "Japanese Tanks!" Stevenson was close to the edge of the airfield when he saw to his horror three Japanese tanks moving directly toward the center of the line. He had never encountered tanks in his previous campaigns and wanted desperately to stop them.

What Stevenson was seeing was an attempt by the Japanese island commander to throw the Marines back into the sea. The counterattack force consisted of an estimated 13 to 15 light tanks, supported by several hundred infantry. The tanks advanced in two echelon formations headed for the center of the 1st Battalion, 5th Marines. About half of the enemy tanks had eight to a dozen Japanese soldiers tied on the outside.

Davis directed Major Stevenson to set up a tank defense using the battalion's organic weapons—37mm antitank guns, bazookas, and rifle grenades. "The attack came across the airfield but it was stopped by front-line units. Sherman tanks knocked out three, dive bombers got two with rockets, and Corporal Edwards and PFC Vittera of Company C blew up one with bazooka fire. The infantry accompanying the tanks were repulsed."[22]

After the firing died down, Lieutenant Fisher inspected one of the disabled tanks. "[We] were amazed at its small size and lack of effective armor. It was considerably smaller than our own light tanks and certainly no match for a Sherman."[23]

After the tank attack, the battalion was stopped cold and pinned down by the heavy Japanese fire in a vicious, no-holds-barred slugfest. Davis rallied his men and partially closed the gap. He threw in Company C, his last fresh infantry, against a 30-foot coral ridge 200-yards inland from the beach. However, Japanese small arms, mortar and artillery fire was just too great. The advance was stalled, leaving a dangerous gap in the lines. If the Japanese exploited the gap, the entire beachhead would be in jeopardy. "It was possible," according to the 1st Marines report, "that a coordinated counterattack in force along the corridor between the coral ridge and the sea could roll up the line and sweep down on the beaches." Utterly spent, the battalion dug in for the night.[24]

Davis took stock of what his battalion had come up against. "The Japs we fought were not the wild, attacking hordes of the early stages of the war. These Japs were from a Manchurian Division, well equipped, well fed, well trained and well disciplined. Those of us who followed the Matsuda Division of Cape Gloucester as they floundered through the jungles of New Britain in abject defeat, were unaccustomed to the ferocious and wily foe in front of us who had never before tasted defeat, but were too cautious and tactical to waste their efforts in a few Banzai charges and then turn tail and run. As they were forced to withdraw they retired in good order, taking their dead and wounded with them."[25]

The 1st Marine Regiment now had all three battalions in line. General Smith reported, "The Division's casualties had reached the 1,000 mark. It was a heavy price to pay for a beachhead only 300 yards in depth, but the capture of a fortified beach is never cheap." He established communications with Colonel Puller. "I got Lewie on the telephone and asked him how he was coming," Smith recalled. "All right," Puller replied. "Do you need any help?" Smith asked. "No, I can manage," Puller responded in typical fashion. "What about casualties?" "Maybe as many as forty killed and wounded," was Puller's response. "[I] thought Puller seemed confident that he could hold his own," Smith wrote. "He'd been taking a beating all day, but that's Lewie; he wouldn't ask for help. He had as yet no definite idea as to the number of casualties he had suffered."[26]

Puller's idea of the number of casualties was grossly underestimated. At the time of the conversation with Smith, hundreds of men had been lost. "When the tide went out that night," one Marine reported, "you could have walked 300 yards across the beach on the bodies of dead Marines." Much later, as Puller learned more about the situation, he sent a message to Division indicating that the enemy was well dug in and were opposing strongly; little damage had been done by the preliminary naval gunfire; and he estimated that his casualties were over 20 percent. Men were starting to suffer battle fatigue and he ordered that no one was to be evacuated unless it was from bullet or shell wounds.

As Davis' utterly spent battalion dug in for the night, urgently needed supplies were brought forward and the wounded evacuated. The after-action report noted, "A Seabee unit landed in our area in the afternoon and immediately began doing valuable work, carrying stretchers loaded with ammunition and taking the wounded out." The battalion daily situation report included a footnote, "One unarmed Seabee was credited with killing a Jap sniper with his bare hands." Battalion casualties for the day were: 14 killed in action, 67 wounded in action, one missing in action, fit for duty 845.[27]

As darkness fell, exhausted Marines peered out into a nightmarish no-man's-land of shattered trees and blasted coral rock. Parachute flares turned this broken landscape into an eerie patchwork of green light and shadow. Japanese infiltrators skillfully exploited the cover to advance toward the American positions. "Suddenly the Marine lines were blanketed with grenades and knee mortar fire. Japanese infantry rose out of the darkness. With screaming battle cries—*banzai, banzai*—they ran forward—to be met by the concentrated fire of the 1st Battalion's automatic weapons and small arms fire. The fighting became hand-to-hand, but the Japanese attack faltered, beaten back by superior firepower. A few enemy managed to infiltrate during the night but were killed behind our lines the next morning."[28]

The Division had gained a beachhead of 3,000 yards in length and averaged 500 yards in depth. One-and-a-half battalions of 75mm pack howitzers and one-and-a-third battalions of 155mm howitzers were in position and registered. D-Day casualties numbered 209 killed in action, 902 wounded in action, and 58 missing in action. Most of the 1,119 casualties had been suffered in eight of the Division's nine infantry battalions.[29]

The Japanese defense was well coordinated, tenacious, and in depth. The beach defenses took into consideration natural obstacles, augmented with tetrahedrons, mines, wire, antitank ditches, mortars, antiboat machine-gun, and small arms fire. The gun emplacements were located on promontories (enabling enfilade fire to be placed on the beach) and in reinforced concrete blockhouses. The Japanese 40mm antiboat guns were particularly effective and their 150mm mortars were able to place heavy and costly fire on the beach and the reef.[30]

Japanese artillery and mortar fire began almost immediately after the first assault wave landed on the beach. Heavy concentrations were laid down from the outer edge of the reef to about 100 yards inland from the waterline. Their fire was particularly effective in the immediate beach area.[31]

Enemy mortars ranged from the small grenade discharger up to huge 150mm mortars measuring well over six feet in length. These indirect fire weapons were very difficult to knock out. Their positions were skillfully camouflaged and were located near large caves to which they were withdrawn in the event of counter battery fire or air strikes.[32]

The Japanese had abandoned their previous all-out *Banzai* attacks in favor of numerous small-scale night attacks involving 40 to 50 men. The only large counter-attack occurred in the late afternoon of D-day. Japanese infantry, covered by a mortar and artillery bombardment and preceded by a Type 94 tankette, attacked across the north portion of the airfield. The attack was beaten back by Marine tanks, bazookas, and antitank guns.[33]

CHAPTER 13

A Ferocious and Wily Foe

The second day ashore, Davis' battalion was ordered to attack, straight into the teeth of the enemy defenses. The pattern of the attack for each day was set. Usually the attack jumped off at 0700, preceded by an artillery, air and naval gunfire preparation. Normally, the fighting was broken off at 1700 and the troops dug in for the night. "Our mission the next morning was to go through the lead battalion to seize the regimental objective, some coral ridges," Davis explained. "We jumped off very early and got off in good order heading north. We went some 200 to 300 yards and ran into the beginnings of a fortified area … right into the heart of it. We couldn't move without getting shot at from two or three directions." Companies B and C continued the attack, taking heavy casualties as they mopped up Japanese emplacements.[1]

The battalion report singled out one NCO. "Sergeant [Charles] Monarch, with the Company C assault team, took and destroyed numerous dug-outs constructed in the coral ridge." Four months later the Indiana native was formally recognized in his Navy Cross citation: "When the advance of his unit was held up by a deep zone of strong enemy emplacements consisting of a series of concealed concrete pillboxes and rifle pits, and the cross-firing of heavy weapons swept the front of his company, Sergeant Monarch skillfully maneuvered his men into advantageous positions to deliver accurate covering flamethrower and rifle fire against the Japanese strong point … [He] personally placed heavy explosive charges into the embrasures … destroying ten of the strongholds."[2]

Company B fought its way through the Japanese defenses and made contact with Hunt's beleaguered remnants. Company C managed to fight its way alongside and tied in. The battalion report stated that, "The area though which B and C Companies worked [was] rutted with antitank ditches and a network of camouflaged pillboxes connected by trenches on the low and flat ground. The coral ridge was honeycombed with rifle pits and machine-gun nests. In particular, a pillbox with a pair of twin-mounted machine guns gave us a great deal of difficulty."[3]

The battalion OP group moved up behind the assault units. "We passed near a deep antitank ditch," Davis reported. "Dead Marines from the preceding day lay scattered about. It was apparent that the Japs had sited antitank weapons from the left flank and mortars from the ridges to the front to cover this ditch well." A battalion report noted that, "The few dead [Japanese] up to this point were all clean, well fed and equipped and rather large in stature—most were 6 feet in height. One of those killed had a dog tag indicating that he was a member of the 9th Company, 2nd Infantry Regiment of the 14th Infantry Division. Later intelligence identified members of the 3rd and 7th Companies, indicating that at least two battalions of enemy confronted the Marines."

An exhausted, weaponless Japanese NCO was captured by a patrol after it discovered him hiding in a cave that had been bypassed. One of only half-a-dozen Japanese soldiers captured during the battle, he verified the 2nd Infantry Regiment as the main enemy unit on the island. He freely admitted to a Japanese-speaking Nisei (a Japanese-American) interpreter that he was a message center chief in the 2nd Regiment's 6th Company. His company had been overrun and only he and three others escaped. During an attempt to locate the regimental commander's headquarters, his three companions were killed, and he had been trapped in the cave. So far as he knew, he was the only survivor of the 6th Company. He was shown a captured sketch map and he traced the defensive positions of the regiment and pointed out the location of 60 to 70 holdouts. He estimated that the preliminary bombardment killed half of the 2nd Battalion; the remainder fought on. Those who were wounded and couldn't walk committed suicide with hand grenades. Throughout the interrogation, he vehemently opposed the release of his name to the Red Cross because it would shame his family.

At 0950 on D+1, General Rupertus hobbled down the ramp of an amtrac and assumed command ashore. His game leg—the one he injured on Pavuvu—still bothered him, and he leaned heavily on a Malacca cane. O. P. Smith quickly brought him up to speed on the tactical situation and then reverted to his usual subordinate role. Rupertus, who had followed the action from the command ship, was not happy with the progress of the attack on the Umurbrogol. He picked up a field telephone and angrily called Puller. "Can't they move any faster?" he snapped. "Goddammit, Lewie, you've gotta kick ass to get results. You know that, goddammnit!" By this time, the 1st Marines had already suffered 1,000 casualties and had now hit the Japanese main line of resistance. Rupertus just did not understand what the regiment was up against.[4]

Davis quickly reformed his unit and launched them in an assault against the coral bluffs to the east and west of a coast road. Casualties among the officers and NCOs forced Davis to halt the attack and reorganize. Company A had been hit so hard that two platoons were combined under Lieutenant Hanson, the sole surviving lieutenant. As the unit moved through some dense brush, a Japanese officer armed with a pistol and a sword suddenly charged the veteran officer. He casually turned to the BAR man on his lift and muttered, "Well, why don't you shoot him?" The Marine obliged by emptying half a magazine into the enemy officer and the two moved on. If that wasn't enough, a Rikusentai (so-called Japanese Marine) machine-gun squad tried to set up their gun to shoot them in the back. An alert rifleman spotted the groups, and the combined platoon opened fire, killing all but one, who managed to throw a hand grenade that slightly wounded one of their number. Despite the wound, the Marine sharpshooter hit the Japanese soldier in the head with a single rifle shot. The platoon continued to blaze away at the Japanese in the brush. Their heavy fire kept the enemy pinned down, making it impossible for them to escape. At the end of a short firefight, the lieutenant reported "at least 40 dead Japanese were counted along a 300-yard stretch of road."[5]

As the attack continued toward the Umurbrogol's outpost hills, "The Japanese turned their fire on it," McMillan recorded, "cutting our exposed front lines to ribbons under perfect observation. The 1st [Regiment] was forced to push on, to seek desperately for some of that high ground to storm the Japanese out of their emplacements on the bluff." Infantry could not do the job alone. Davis called up Sherman tanks, which fired point-blank into the mouths of caves, while his riflemen inched forward in the 112-degree heat.[6]

According to General Smith, "For the assault, 18 medium tanks were assigned to the 1st Marines. Of these, 17 were hit by HE shells either while en route to the beach or on the beach. Three were knocked out before they reached the beach. The depth of water off the beach saved others from serious damage by absorbing the shock of the explosion. Within a few hours, six tanks were knocked out in addition to those lost on the beach. These tanks, although absorbing a lot of punishment, did considerable damage to the Japanese."[7]

Men clawed upward. McMillan noted, "The pock-marked surface offered no secure footing even in the few level places. It was impossible to dig in; the best the men could do was pile a little coral or wood debris around their positions. The jagged rocks slashed their shoes and clothes, and tore their bodies every time they hit the deck for safety." O. P. Smith wrote, "Many men were wounded by rock fragments thrown up by the blast of the Japanese mortar and artillery shells."[8]

Davis watched his men as they fought and died along the faint paths. "We would fight for hours, losing men every step of the way, along one of these ledges, only to find it ended abruptly in a sheer cliff and have to fight our way back. It was terrible!" Stevenson recalled, "All the jungle foliage had long since been blasted away; the landscape seemed like the mountains of the moon." One of Davis' men described the enemy positions. "When we hit them on top, they popped out of the bottom; when we hit them in the middle, they popped out of both ends."[9]

George McMillan explained that, "Each blast hurled chunks of coral in all directions, multiplying many times the fragmentation effect of every shell." The Marines received heavy shelling from enemy caves as well as deadly accurate small arms fire. The men were pinned down and suffered heavy losses. O. P. Smith remembered,

"There were dozens of caves and pillboxes worked into the noses of the ridges and up the ravines. It was difficult to find blind spots as the caves and pillboxes were mutually supporting. We found out later that some of the caves consisted of galleries of more than one level with several exits."[10]

As the battalion scrambled forward, Stevenson worried about adjacent units: "It became clear to me that there were no friendly troops on the right flank. It was completely open, entirely vulnerable to a Japanese counter-attack which could surge all the way to the beach. I called Colonel Puller to warn him of the peril and the urgent need for reinforcements. When I reached him on the field telephone he was true to form. First, he confused me with Steve Sabol (CO, 3rd Battalion) and when this was cleared up, his gruff voice spoke its usual formula, 'Just keep pushing, old man.' I stood transfixed, with my runner beside me as we heard Japanese voices and the clink of weapons on the far side of the vital road. Unbelieving, I called again. This time I got Lieutenant Colonel 'Buddy' Ross [regimental executive officer], who instantly perceived the urgency. 'Stay right there, Steve, don't move; I'm sending up a unit from the 7th. Tie them into the line as soon as they get there.' Within what seemed like minutes, they appeared and immediately took up firing positions to plug the gap. No sooner was this done when there came wild shouts of 'banzai' as the Japanese poured across the road into the devastating but crucially effective fire of the newly arrived Marines."[11]

By late afternoon, Davis' men were able to climb the steep slopes of Hill 160 and establish themselves on the commanding ridge but at a huge cost: 250 casualties. A company commander reported, "We're up here, but we're knee-deep in Purple Hearts." The units on its flanks could not maintain contact, so Davis had to order him back down the hill. The men of Company A who had struggled all day to take the hill were not comforted by the rationale in the report. Morale among the survivors reached a low point. Davis reported that "Company A depleted itself on the bare ridge on the right as Company C became seriously overextended on the left and was faltering. Everything we had was thrown in to fill the gaps. Remnants of Companies A and C, engineer and pioneer units and headquarters personnel were formed into a meager reserve as darkness fell."[12]

At 1700, the battalion dug in for the night, while engineers demolished caves and pillboxes to prevent them from being used by Japanese infiltrators. Sporadic mortar and small arms fire continued to plague the exhausted men, but they were cheered when the battalion S-4 (logistics officer) was able to bring up ammunition, chow and something to drink other than the foul-tasting water. "This was the first day the men found fruit and tomato juice in the front lines," it was reported. "A great many stomachs are constricted because of the effort, fear, and battle fatigue; it is of great value to be able to derive nourishment and energy from the stomach for digestion that the heavy, solid, or greasy foods do." The men were also supplied with "C" rations, which they considered "the equivalent of a steak dinner" after trying to wolf down Australian rations that were "too greasy and unappetizing for a stomach that has contracted from shell blast and fear."[13]

Davis tried to soften up the Japanese for the inevitable nighttime attack. Stevenson recalled that "a forward observer, a young ensign from the battleship *Mississippi*, appeared and declared himself ready to direct fire from its big guns on the enemy positions. For the rest of the night he called in salvo after salvo, hour after hour, on the honeycombed ridges facing the fast dwindling strength of our companies. There was continuous firing during the night and hand grenades were exchanged by both sides; the Japs tried fire crackers to draw our automatic fire but were unsuccessful as the men were seasoned troops by this time and fired only when distinct targets were available. The Navy and the mortars fired illuminating shells most of the night, but a star shell illuminates friendly, as well as, enemy terrain."[14]

During the night a Japanese sniper was killed a few feet in front of the Company C machine guns. The code numbers from his dog tag indicated he was a member of the 9th Company, 2nd Infantry Regiment, 14th Infantry Division. The tag verified advance intelligence data on the enemy order of battle.[15]

Movement at night was dangerous. A dog handler for the 4th War Dog Platoon was stabbed by a Marine when he failed to give the password. His wound was not life threatening but he had to be evacuated. The incident reinforced the need to emphasize and use passwords that contained the letter "L," as most Japanese have trouble pronouncing the letter. Words with double "Ls" like "Lollypop" and "Honolulu" were used.

CHAPTER 14

Bloody Nose Ridge

As morning came the fire increased as Japanese machine guns and mortars resumed their lethal chorus. Davis and his command group huddled together to plan the attack for the following morning. "Clearly it was to be the battalion's last throw of the dice," Stevenson reported. "If Bloody Nose Ridge could be taken, our fire from its height into the enemy-held crevices below would eventually dislodge them and Peleliu [would be] won at last." His assessment was more wishful then prophetic.[1]

The battalion reported that to date it had captured or destroyed "one large block-house, 37 pillboxes, 24 caves, and two antitank 47mm guns, two 70mm mountain guns, one six-inch naval gun and numerous machine guns. Over 300 enemy dead were counted." A footnote at the end of the report stated: "At the point where the battalion OP was set up, three enemy carrier pigeons were shot and the attached messages were sent to R-2 [regimental intelligence]. The battalion's losses for the day were 14 men killed in action, 81 wounded and two missing. Many more were victims of the 112-degree heat and combat fatigue. The battalion total strength at this time was 18 officers and 474 enlisted men."[2]

An officer of the battalion tried to explain the term "combat fatigue," commonly known as "shell shock": "To those who have never seen it occur, combat fatigue is hardly understandable. But who have experienced the constriction of the blood vessels in the stomach and the sudden whirling of the brain that occurs when a large shell bursts nearby or a friend has his eyes or entrails torn out by shrapnel can easily understand the man who cannot control his muscles and who stares wildly. It isn't fear alone that causes shock to the system. Often it is the knowledge of his impotence, his inability to help his shipmate who is whistling through a hole in his chest, that momentarily snaps a man's brain. Quite often, under the stress of combat fatigue, a man will perform acts of heroism that a reasoning mind would call foolhardy."[3]

Davis recalled an instance where a young highly decorated officer succumbed to fatigue. "I noticed [Second] Lieutenant [Gordon] Maples was in a state bordering on war-psychosis. He led his men forward into withering fire, exposing himself to assist his men. He was suffering from fatigue and the shock of seeing his men fall—but he never relaxed and kept moving in an entranced way. Finally one day he was shot in the abdomen and died just before reaching the hospital ship. This was his third campaign and he had distinguished himself in each [Navy Cross, Guadalcanal, Silver Star, Peleliu]."[4]

The Japanese, however, were not the only enemy the Marines had to face. O. P. Smith noted, "Beginning with the second day the troops had to contend with an additional enemy, the extreme heat. The thermometer went up to 105 degrees. In the intense fighting over rugged ground, the men soon exhausted the water in their canteens. Resupply was difficult. We began to have a good many cases of heat exhaustion."[5]

Japanese Tactics

Inland from the beach, the flat terrain gave the Japanese the opportunity for direct fire from pillboxes and blockhouses on the advancing Marines. These positions were constructed of concrete, reinforced with steel, and they were well camouflaged. Some blockhouses contained as many as 16 mutually supporting automatic weapons. Japanese small arms fire was particularly accurate and indicated thorough training in rifle marksmanship. Marine casualties often occurred at ranges from 200 to 400 yards distant.[6]

Historian George McMillan wrote, "The 1st Battalion (Lieutenant Colonel R. G. Davis) started out fine, moved with surprising ease for about an hour, but then was brought up sharp by fire from a concrete blockhouse the size of a small office building which stood directly in its path. Its reinforced walls were four-feet thick, and as if that was not enough protection it was also supported by 12 pillboxes all connected by a maze of tunnels."[7] The blockhouse is still in existence and is being used as a battlefield museum on Peleliu. The gaping hole caused by the USS *Mississippi* clearly shows the exposed steel reinforcing rods and the damage caused by her 14-inch shell.

Admiral Oldendorf had been badly mistaken. There were plenty of targets. "I took 25 casualties, including three dead," Davis recalled, "trying to take that objective. It could be called a fortress because of all the pillboxes surrounding it." Major Stevenson recalled that, "Dawn came and with it the fiercest fighting yet, centering on a squat concrete building with three-foot thick walls, impervious to 37mm and 75mm shells firing at point-blank range."[8]

Admiral Oldendorf commented that this blockhouse was not shown on the maps furnished to him and that during "the preliminary bombardment and until several days after the landing, my entire staff was on the sick list, only my flag lieutenant remaining on his feet. This threw a heavy load on me, as I not only had to supervise the details of the daytime operations but also operate tactically at night during withdrawals."[9]

Davis pulled the troops back and directed First Lieutenant N. R. K. Stanford, his naval gunfire forward observer, to knock it out. "I was lying in the coral rubble of the shattered bunker in front of the blockhouse with the Nambu fire going high to my left and the Jap mortars bursting in the ripped and twisted coconut grove behind me." The outline of the emplacement was blurred by the haze of coral dust, which hung in the air from muzzle blasts and mortar fire. "I set up my SCR-284 [radio] nearly at the top of an abandoned Jap bunker and crawled through the loose coral to look over a broken timber revetment at the top of the bunker." His radio operator handed him the handset and he established contact with "Ironsides," the code name for the old battleship USS *Mississippi* (BB-41). "Ironsides, this is Charlie Nine. Target is … reinforced concrete blockhouse … AP [armor piercing] one round. Main Battery … commence firing."[10]

The 14-inch shell passed low over his head with a heart-stopping crack and landed beyond the target. Stanford requested an adjustment. "Down 200, one salvo." The salvo roared past, smashing into the bunker. "I was numb from the concussion and it took my eyes a few seconds to focus, but I could see the camouflage had been stripped away and the shape of the blockhouse altered." An eyewitness reported, "The blockhouse began disintegrating, the big armor-piercing and high-capacity shells crumbled the walls, and their terrific concussion killed those Japanese missed by the fragmentation."[11]

The assault units moved past the blockhouse and the battalion command post moved into it. At the doorway lay a Japanese hand severed from its arm. The nearest body was fully 30-feet away. Inside this blockhouse lay some 15 to 20 dead Japanese not marked by a scratch, but dead from the terrific concussion. The battalion aid station moved in and began treating and evacuating the wounded. Davis set up his command post across the road in a large shell hole and covered it with a piece of tin and an abandoned shelter half.

Lieutenant Fisher took up residence in the shattered structure. He marveled at the number of men the battalion surgeon handled and evacuated from the blockhouse. Fisher saw PFC Thorval Pattee severely wounded by a mortar round. "Suddenly a shell landed squarely beside him and mangled his left forearm so badly that it hung to the elbow by only a few tendons and obviously was lost. Despite the severity of the wound, Pattee walked unaided for 500 yards to the battalion aid station, where the doctor immediately amputated the arm and sent him to the rear. The sight of Pattee walking into the aid station with his mutilated arm will never be forgotten by those of us who knew him. He even had the guts to wave his good arm and shake his fist at us as he was carried away."[12]

Davis stopped to reorganize prior to assaulting the high ground. While reorganizing, at about 1030 a Japanese 70mm mountain gun opened fire from one of the numerous caves on the steep slope to the front at point-blank range. The gun continued firing for about 45 minutes, inflicting terrible casualties on both Companies A and C and the 81mm mortar observation post. Three machine gunners from Company A were killed and three seriously wounded. An entire machine-gun squad of Company C was knocked out. The Japanese gun was finally destroyed by tank and bazooka fire. Heavy Japanese mortar and artillery fire continued to pound the exposed Marines. Casualties mounted.

Because of the heavy casualties, it was difficult to maintain contact and it was necessary to call on the USS *Mississippi* for illumination in order to place the lines properly. For seven hours the ship fired harassing fire to keep the Japanese from launching an attack.[13]

At the end of the second day, Puller's regiment was in somewhat better tactical shape then after the initial landing, but it had taken heavy casualties, and the toughest fight was yet to come—the jagged hill mass, Bloody Nose Ridge.

"After the first move north, everything just totally bogged down. Casualties were just unbelievable, so they pulled us out and moved us around to relieve Gordon Gayle [Major, CO 2/5] in the islands on the other side of the island," Davis explained.[14]

In his nightly report to the Division, Puller stated that "Front-line units have been decimated." The 1st Marines had lost 1,236 men. Puller called Colonel John T. Selden, the Division chief of staff, and asked for replacements.

"Johnny, half my regiment is gone. I've got to have replacements if I'm to carry out division orders tomorrow morning."

"You know we have no replacements, Lewie," Sheldon responded.

"I told you before we came ashore that we should have at least one regiment in reserve. We're not fighting a third of the men we brought in … all those damn specialists you brought."

"Anything wrong with your orders, Lewie?"

"Give me some of those 17,000 men on the beach," Puller retorted.

"You can't have them, they're not trained infantry."

"Give 'em to me and by nightfall tomorrow they'll be trained infantry," Puller replied grimly.[15]

A staff officer at Division thought that Rupertus, despite the heavy losses, still believed it would be a quick victory. "The overall feeling seemed to be that a break-through was imminent. Enemy resistance would collapse, or at worst, disintegrate as had happened on Saipan, Tinian, and Guam after a certain point had passed. The trouble with this reasoning was that on the other islands the collapse had occurred when U.S. troops reached favorable terrain and had been assaulted by at least one suicidal *banzai* charge. But there were no *banzai* charges on Peleliu, and the terrain was becoming worse instead of better.

Cumulative Division casualties to date amounted to 268 killed in action, 1,736 wounded in action, and 73 missing in action.

Japanese Tactics

The Japanese blasted a series of interlocking caves into the almost perpendicular coral ridges. They varied from simple holes large enough to accommodate two men to large tunnels with passageways on either side which were large enough to contain artillery or 150mm mortars and ammunition. Some of these caves were equipped with steel doors. Neutralizing them was difficult and costly.[16]

The great majority of the caves were natural, formed by the dissolving of limestone by underground streams and seepage. In one-third of these the Japanese had improved on nature by cutting fire ports and secondary entrances and escape routes, enlarging the inside, and concreting the walls both with a rough mix of rock and concrete and with a finished cement. Entrances were narrow and, in many cases multiple so that they could not be trapped inside once one had been closed. Blast walls had been constructed in front of the entrances with coral rock, barrels filled with stone and concrete. The author noticed on a visit to the island that the presence of barrels often marked the entrances to caves that otherwise would have extremely difficult to locate. In addition, all caves were either naturally twisting or were so constructed as to protect the occupants from the concussion effect of bombing and shelling and to provide cover from direct fire.[17]

The 1st Marine Division Special Action Report noted, "Several extremely large caves up to 500 feet in length were observed and inspected. In virtually all of these the rooms and passageways had been constructed at staggered levels, one of them having nine decks. Many were equipped with electric lighting systems, ventilation systems, and wooden decks, some with radio and telephone systems, and wooden decks. Stairways had been built of wood or cut from stone. Food and ammunition were stored in every nook and crevice as well as in storage rooms, and troughs had been built to collect water from the stalactite drippings and seepage."[18] The author explored the "Thousand Man Cave" on the northwest coast of the island. The cave was carved into the side of a hill and was large enough to shelter several hundred men. It was several hundred yards long with several laterals running off to the sides. The roof of the cave was high enough to allow one to walk without bending over.

The Japanese were experts in using the terrain to their advantage and using natural camouflage, cover, and concealment for their emplacements. Their defensive plan provided for a defense in depth. All pillboxes and casemates were in commanding positions, and all linked in a system of mutual cover and support. When their defensive position were overrun, they were able to withdraw to secondary positions and maintain organized resistance.[19]

The general scheme of the Japanese defense seemed to be of making the capture of Peleliu as costly as possible. The planning and execution of the defenses indicated that the enemy were first-line troops, capably led, who knew their mission and carried it out with fanatical devotion to duty. Of the over 10,000 Japanese defenders, only 92 became prisoners of war—seven Army, 12 Navy, and 73 laborers. Almost all of the military prisoners claimed they had not intended to surrender. They also agreed that those who were left would never surrender.[20]

In order to continue the attack, Puller put all available headquarters personnel in the front lines. "Regiment sent forward several officers and men," according to Stevenson, "a dozen or two cooks, bakers and truck drivers, converted overnight into riflemen … and a 37mm gun." The Division also furnished 100 men from the Short Party battalion. More importantly, Rupertus released the Division's reserve, Lieutenant Colonel Spencer Berger's 2nd Battalion, 7th Marines, to the 1st Marines. Upon receipt of the authorization, Puller sent a warning order to Berger to "relieve the 1st Battalion at daybreak the morning of the 18th and to be in position to attack at 0700."

Under sporadic mortar and small arms fire, Berger and his operations officer, Major John F. Weber, carefully worked their way forward to the 1st Battalion's command post. Davis' number two man, Major Nikolai S. Stevenson, quickly briefed them on the tactical situation. Stevenson painted a pretty dim picture. The Japanese had carved their defenses into the noses of the ridge and up the ravines so that it was extremely difficult to find blind spots. Many of the positions were at the base of the cliffs, others were partway up, and some were on top. He pointed out that a particularly effective Japanese tactic was to run a field piece out of a cave, fire, and then run it back inside before we could react. Finally, Stevenson gave him a summary of casualties, which were shockingly extreme—over half the battalion was gone!

After receiving the sobering brief, Berger, Weber and a 1st Battalion guide made a very hazardous reconnaissance around the lines. Berger and Weber then met Davis at his advance OP, where Berger attempted to get the lay of the land. He had trouble orienting himself on the ground because of the incredibly broken terrain. "There was no such thing as a continuous attacking line. Elements of the same company, even platoons, were attacking in every direction of the compass, with large gaps in between. When companies were asked for front lines they were apt to give points where the company commander knew or thought he had some men … There were countless little salients and counter-salients existing." At one point, Berger called for prep fires on an objective and found that "some of the target areas lay behind or squarely upon positions shown on some unit overlays as having been occupied the previous day."[21]

The two men worked out the details of the relief—a very difficult maneuver because the entire area was under Japanese observation and fire. At 0600 the remnants of Davis' battalion started withdrawing from their exposed positions as Berger's men replaced them. "Slowly we rose, [and] formed two files on each side of the cart track leading back," Stevenson recalled, thankful to be alive. "The relief took place in full view of the Japs atop Bloody Nose Ridge. If they had opened up, it would have been the final and apocalyptic carnage. Inexplicably, they didn't. We marched slowly away, some of the men contorted with the dry heaves, brought on by the salt tablets given to lessen the dehydration of the murderous heat." Sometime later, the Japanese "welcomed" Berger by shelling his CP for ten minutes with heavy mortar fire, causing ten casualties.[22]

About this time, Puller moved his OP to a small quarry, within easy rifle shot of Hill 210. Berger was embarrassed to find Puller operating behind some outcropping of coral, closer to the enemy than his command post. In fact, it was difficult to get out an operations map to read it without exposing himself.

The 2nd Battalion, 1st Marines, attacked Hill 200 and quickly became pinned down. The battalion commander urgently requested reinforcements. The only men at hand were the remnants of the 1st Battalion. Puller told Davis to send a company. It was the fate of 1st Battalion to be piecemealed into the fight. "With a heavy heart I watched them go," Stevenson remarked sadly, "knowing so well that in combat any supporting unit is always given the dirtiest, the most dangerous assignment."[23]

An hour later, Lieutenant Francis D. "Bonzai" Rineer of Company B reported to a dugout that served as the 2nd Battalion's CP. The battalion commander gave Rineer a quick brief and then personally led him to the edge of a wood, where he pointed out Hill 205, slightly forward and to the right of Hill 210. He ordered Rineer to seize it. The commander promised two machine-gun sections to support the attack. Rineer moved his men forward and spread them out in an attack formation, using a road as a line of departure. At his signal the company moved out and cautiously advanced up the hill. Surprisingly, there was little resistance and the company seized the high ground with only 12 casualties.

Rineer found that the captured ground was only an isolated point on a larger ridge system and decided to continue the attack. "Their charge to the top of the hill was one of the bravest and yet most disastrous acts of the campaign," according to Robert Fisher.[24]

O. P. Smith noted that, "In desperate fighting, progress was made on both sides … but the enemy continued to lay down heavy mortar and artillery barrages, accompanied by vicious counterattacks and withering small arms fire, all along the lines, particularly on the forward nose of Hill 200."[25]

At the end of the third day, the 1st Marines had suffered 1,500 casualties, half its total strength. Lieutenant Colonel Lewis W. Walt talked to Puller at a command conference. "He was absolutely sick over the loss of his men; he thought we were getting them killed for nothing."[26]

Lieutenant Francis D. Rineer's Navy Cross Citation

The President of the United States of America takes pleasure in presenting the Navy Cross to First Lieutenant Francis D. Rineer, United States Marine Corps Reserve, for extraordinary heroism as Commanding Officer of Company B, First Battalion, First Marines, First Marine Division, in action against enemy Japanese forces at Peleliu, Palau Islands, on 20 September 1944. Assuming command after his Commanding Officer had become a casualty during the initial fighting, First Lieutenant Rineer boldly led his company in repeated attacks against the enemy entrenched in dense jungle concealing a network of pillboxes. With only forty men left in his company on the morning of 20 September, he assaulted the steep coral slopes of Hill 200 in the face of intense fire emanating from hostile machine guns entrenched in coral caves and personally remained in the midst of the furious fighting to urge his men forward until seriously wounded in both legs. Steadfastly refusing evacuation, First Lieutenant Rineer courageously struggled forward to commanding ground and calmly organized his twenty-four remaining men into a defensive position from which they succeeded in accomplishing their mission. His cool gallantry, daring initiative and intrepid devotion to duty throughout were in keeping with the highest traditions of the United States Naval Service.

CHAPTER 15

Pope's Hill

At 0630 on D+4 Japanese mortars and artillery began falling in Company B's lines, concentrating on the 3rd Platoon, which lost 15 men. At 0800 Company B was pulled back to an open field to the right of the 2nd Battalion observation post. The Japanese spotted the movement and opened fire with a large caliber gun with an extremely high velocity and large bursting radius. The shells screamed in with the sound of ripping silk and exploded with a blast that sent shrapnel for 100 yards.

Several Marines took cover behind a small steam engine in the middle of the field. A dozen shells landed near the equipment, killing three enlisted men and wounding five. Second Lieutenant A. A. Hover, 3rd Platoon commander, left his covered position to go to their aid, and was killed.[1]

At 1800, Company B was relieved and moved off the line. Its effective strength at this time was 35 men and two officers; the mortar section consisted of ten men and one officer; the rifle platoons totaled 25 men and the company commander.

By the 19th, Davis' battalion had all but disappeared. "I lost all my platoon leaders and our casualties amounted to about 71 percent in four days." Despite the heavy losses, Company C was attached to the 2nd Battalion and ordered to seize Hill 100, a vital piece of terrain that in Marine hands would allow them to attack Bloody Nose Ridge from the rear. Captain Everett Pope, the 25-year-old Massachusetts native who commanded Company C, noted in his oral history:

> When we got to the foot of that hill [Hill 100] there were 90 of us left [out of 235]. We first tried to reach the foot of the hill through one of the swamps but there were guns firing on us from across the swamp and we couldn't get through. We had to have smoke shells cover us so we could pull back. We were again ordered to take the hill.
>
> It was still daylight when we moved up again as best we could. We received terrible fire from across the canyon from our rear. As we came around the hill we were exposed to fire from another direction [but] we got to the top.
>
> We were quite startled when we realized that we were not on top of the hill, we were on a plateau with high ground dominating it from the south. The Japanese were able to fire down on us.
>
> We ran out of ammunition and no one could get up to supply us. We had a few grenades and we had bayonets and we had some great Marines.

We held the hill overnight but it turned into a brawl. We'd roll a hunk of rock amidst the enemy and they'd stop for a minute to see if it was a grenade bouncing among them. It slowed them down a little bit. After you'd down that two or three times you'd throw a real grenade, one of the few we had left.

As daylight came, the Japanese formed up. We could see that it was going to be a heavy attack, 50 or 100 men. As that point we were ordered to withdraw. I had already decided we were going to get out of there anyhow. So we came tumbling down the hill. There were only eight of us at that point.

The hill was not taken for about eleven or twelve days. It took that long for my dead on the hill to be buried. A lot of brave Marines died on that hill I can never forget it.

Early the next morning, Puller ordered Pope to take the hill again. "It was a suicide mission," Pope said angrily. "The trouble is, it was our suicide, not Puller's, you see." Reluctantly he gathered his men together—12 men and two officers—and reported to battalion. "As we made ready to go, the lieutenant was needlessly killed. I then received orders to abort the attack. Why Puller wanted us all dead on the top of that hill has never been clear to me." (In a *St. Petersburg Times* interview with Pope dated 28 August 2005, Christopher Goffard reported that "Pope wants it understood, up front, that he has small regard for Puller, whom he thinks recklessly fed so many good men into Peleliu's death traps.") "Puller had a poor grasp of the island's terrain," Pope said, "Send enough men to their slaughter up the hill, Puller's strategy went, and a few are bound to make it. The adulation paid to him these days sickens me."[2]

For this heroic action, Pope was awarded the Medal of Honor.

The regiment's gains for the day were negligible—400 yards on the left and 500 yards on the right, but the middle had been stopped cold. By D+4, the 1st Marines was a regiment in name only, having suffered 1,500 casualties. Division casualties to date amounted to 490 killed in action, 2,567 wounded in action and 302 missing in action. Enemy dead totaled 6,035.

Pope's Medal of Honor Citation

For conspicuous gallantry and intrepidity at the risk of his life above and beyond the call of duty while serving as Commanding Officer of Company C, First Battalion, First Marines, First Marine Division, during action against enemy Japanese forces on Peleliu Island, Palau Group, on 19–20 September 1944. Subjected to point-blank cannon fire which caused heavy casualties and badly disorganized his company while assaulting a steep coral hill, Captain Pope rallied his men and gallantly led them to the summit in the face of machine-gun, mortar and sniper fire. Forced by widespread hostile attack to deploy the remnants of his company thinly in order to hold the ground won, and with his machine guns out of order and insufficient water and ammunition, he remained on the exposed hill with 12 men and one wounded officer, determined to hold through the night. Attacked continuously with grenades, machine guns and rifles from three sides, he and his valiant men fiercely beat back or destroyed the enemy, resorting to hand-to-hand combat as the supply of ammunition dwindled, and still maintaining his line with his eight remaining riflemen when daylight brought more deadly fire and he was ordered to withdraw, His valiant leadership against devastating odds, while protecting the units below from heavy Japanese attack, reflects the highest credit upon Captain Pope and the United States Naval Service.

CHAPTER 16

Shot to Pieces

Despite the horrendous casualties, Puller's orders stood: "Resume the attack with maximum effort." One of his battalion commanders privately said that Puller's "failure to recognize soon enough that we were a shot-to-pieces outfit—while still ordering us to do impossible things with the worn-out, pitifully few men we still had—was as sign that he was no longer in touch with the realities of the situation ... we were a remnant rather than a regiment."[1]

O. P. Smith outlined the day's objective. "The attack jumped off in an all-out effort to regain Hill 100. The 1st and 2nd Battalions [the two had been combined] reinforced by the Division Reconnaissance Company were used. Men from headquarters were fed into the battalions. A provisional machine-gun group ... was formed from cooks, communication personnel and quartermaster personnel." Every available man in the regiment went into the lines. Additional tanks, LVT(A)s, half-tracks, 37mm guns and mortars were brought up to support the attack.[2]

The combined 1st and 2nd Battalions jumped off on schedule at 0700. They were immediately taken under intense mortar fire. One company reported that it was pinned down, taking heavy casualties and had to withdraw. It only had ten men left in the line. There were only 150 effectives left in both battalions.

O. P. Smith noted sadly that, "Although some gains were made, the ground was untenable. The attack lost its drive and bogged down." Casualties increased. "The exhausted survivors fell back."[3]

By D+5 the 1st Marines had suffered 1,749 casualties. It reported an estimated 3,942 enemy were killed, while capturing ten defended coral ridges, destroying three blockhouses, 22 pillboxes, 13 antitank guns, and 144 defended caves. Division casualties amounted to 529 killed in action, 2,667 wounded in action, and 325 missing in action. The Division reported enemy dead totaled 6,445.

Shortly before noon on D+6, Geiger appeared at Puller's advanced command post. As usual, it was so close to the front lines that the sound of the action could plainly be heard. Small arms and machine-gun fire cracked just ahead—and the crump of mortars and grenades sounded loud in the sweltering heat. The regimental commander was on a field telephone barking orders to the 2nd Battalion commander. He looked drained, "very tired," according to one of Geiger's small escort. Puller was shirtless, bareheaded, boots unlaced and barely able to walk. He finished the conversation and noticed Geiger for the first time. "What can I do for you, general?" he asked. "Just thought I'd drop in and see how things were going," Geiger replied. In typical Puller fashion, he shot back, "We're still going in but some of the companies are damn small."[4]

Geiger pulled him aside for a private conversation. A witness recounted that the discussion was brief and heated. "It became rapidly apparent that the regimental commander was very tired; he was unable to give a clear picture of what his situation was and when asked by the Corps Commander what he needed in the way of help, he stated that he was doing all right with what he had." Geiger believed that he had lost all touch with reality. Within minutes of arriving, he was on his way to the Division command post and a showdown with Rupertus.[5]

Lieutenant Colonel Harold O. Deakin was present at the confrontation. "It wasn't what you'd call a really stormy session, although it had some very tense moments. The staff was going over the situation map when Geiger showed up and asked to see the latest casualty reports from Lewie Puller's outfit." They were appalling: over 1,700 men had been lost—more casualties than any regiment in Marine Corps history. Geiger told Rupertus, "The 1st Marines are finished"; he wanted to relieve it with an Army regiment. General Rupertus didn't want the Army regiment, so of course he said no. The Division operations officer, risking Rupertus' wrath, disagreed:

> The 1st Marines are pretty well shot up. They aren't fire eaters anymore. They need to be replaced. We could get more impetus if we had fresh troops. I told General Geiger and General Rupertus, we had to take them [Army's 81st Division], and let them pass through the 1st Marines and move to the north. Without further discussion General Geiger turned to Rupertus and ordered him to act immediately.[6]

Davis received the word. "We began wearily to gather up what gear we had left and waited for the arrival of the fresh troops." Davis led the pitiful remnants of his battalion back behind the lines. The thin ranks attested to the week of hard fighting. The battalion was no longer recognizable as the same highly trained outfit that landed on White Beach 1. The men were grimy, bearded and visibly emaciated. Many had not had a meal, other than a combat ration, since landing. Their faces were sunburned, eyes bloodshot and lips cracked and bleeding. Salt from sweat crusted their uniforms, leaving white circles under their arms, "like the rings on a tree," according to one veteran. The heavy herringbone twill of their uniforms was torn and frayed at the knees and elbows from the rough-edged coral. Blouses hung open from missing buttons. Their sturdy cord-soled field shoes were falling apart from the seams, and their combat gear bore mute testimony to hard service—helmets dented, cartridge belts torn, the non-essential thrown away or lost. An observer seeing the condition of the men would characterize them more as skid-row bums than an elite combat troops.[7]

There were so few men left that Davis had to form the battalion into two rifle companies and a small headquarters detachment. He disbanded Company D and assigned the pitifully few men to Companies A and C. Even with this drastic step, Company A mustered only 122 enlisted and four officers, while Company C numbered 117 enlisted and four officers. Everett Pope was the only original company commander left. The line companies consisted of clerks, cooks, mess sergeants, jeep drivers, mail orderlies and communicators. Stevenson compared the final muster role with the 930 enlisted men and 37 officers who made the initial landing.

Company C's heroic fight marked the end of the battle for the 1st Battalion. After 197.5 hours of combat, Davis' battalion had suffered 70 percent casualties and was virtually destroyed. Of the nine infantry platoons in the 1st Battalion, not one platoon commander survived the battle. Private Russell Davis, a rifleman in the 1st Marines, put it more succinctly: "The whole motley outfit—a fighting outfit only in the minds of a few officers in the 1st Regiment and in the 1st Marine Division—started up the hill. I have never understood why. Not one of them refused. They were the hard core—the men who couldn't or wouldn't quit. They would go up a thousand blazing hills and through a hundred blasted valleys, as long as their legs would carry them. They were Marine riflemen."[8]

Major Raymond G. Davis' Navy Cross citation

The Navy Cross is presented to Major Raymond G. Davis for extraordinary heroism as Commanding Officer of the First Battalion, First Marines, First Marine Division, in action against enemy Japanese forces on Peleliu, Palau Islands, from 15 to 22 September 1944. Although wounded during the first hour of landing, Major Davis refused evacuation to remain with his battalion's assault elements in many hazardous missions. On one occasion, when large gaps occurred in our front lines as the result of heavy casualties, and his right flank company was disorganized by point-blank enemy cannon fire following a successful 900-yard penetration through heavily defended line, he rallied and personally led combined troops into these gaps to establish contact and maintain hasty defensive positions for the remainder of the night. Despite many casualties from close-range sniper fire, he remained in the vicinity of the front lines, coordinating artillery and naval gunfire support with such effect that several determined counterattacks were repulsed. His outstanding courage, devotion to duty and leadership were in keeping with the highest traditions of the United States Naval Service.

O. P. Smith reported a truly staggering butcher's bill: "In this six-day assault against the high ground north of the airfield the 1st Marines engaged in one of the bitterest fights in the Pacific War. Out of a strength of approximately 3,000 men, the regiment had suffered 1,737 casualties (299 killed in action and 1,438 wounded in action). It had killed an estimated 3,700 Japanese in the eight days it had been in the lines. Losses in the rifle units had been so heavy, particularly among the officers and non-commissioned officers, that the units were no longer effective."

Division casualties amounted to 586 killed in action, 2,910 wounded in action, and 343 missing in action. Enemy dead totaled 6,792.

Brigadier General Merwin Silverthorn, the III Amphibious Corps chief of staff, remarked after the battle, "everything about Peleliu left a bad taste in my mouth. The fighting, the casualties, the difficulties at Peleliu were never properly explained." Davis thought it was "the most hotly contested and brutal campaign of World War II." First Lieutenant William Sellers wrote, "Japs, Japs, Japs, and ... trying to stay alive in all that confusion, but we did manage to stop'em. My God, though, so many of our men paid a dreadful price." The 10,000 Japanese defenders expected to make Peleliu the "Breakwater of the Pacific" for the invaders.[9]

On D+7 the 1st Battalion was ordered into reserve on flat ground facing the coral ridge, which hid Japanese snipers that kept up intermittent small arms fire. Dead Marines still lay along the ridge. The casualty collection teams were overwhelmed and there had been no time to bury them. Company A spent the day cleaning out and sealing caves. During the night there was a great deal of firing as the Japanese attempted to infiltrate the lines.

At 1600, the 361 men of the battalion were relieved by the 321st Regiment, 81st Army "Wildcat" Division and out-posted the strip of land between the swamp and the sea. The following day was spent recuperating. Bedding rolls and knapsacks were brought up and the men were able to bathe in the ocean and put on clean clothes. On D+10 the battalion relieved the 2nd Battalion and garrisoned two small islands off Peleliu. The men were able to wade across to occupy them.

On 1 October the battalion boarded ships for Pavuvu. Davis commented after leaving the island, "We could have saved a lot of lives by not trying to take the whole island. After we secured the airfield, we should have pulled back, got into a siege stage, got our guns up, and just pounded the place."[10]

Harry Gailey in his 1983 book, *Peleliu 1944,* noted, "In terms of sheer heroism, every man who fought at Peleliu deserved the highest awards his country could bestow. Their courage transformed Peleliu from a questionable operation to one which should always be remembered with pride."[11]

CHAPTER 17

Homeward Bound

Soon after the 1st Battalion returned to Pavuvu, Davis received orders home. "We came back on the USS [General William] *Billy Mitchell* (AP-114). It turned out to be a very eventful trip, in that a day or two before we sailed the Division officer's mess had received an enormous ration of whiskey for everybody. Since all the officers were going, they had put in their share and they carried it on board with them. They had one big stateroom down there just full of officers who spent much of their time playing cards and getting rid of their booze rations!"[1]

"I turned out to be the CO of troops for the trip, and it was an amazing collection. They had been by India and picked up some missionaries and students and a bunch of Army troops. It was a hodge-podge of people. It was run by an Army Transportation officer and they were operating under Army rules. It generated some interesting problems. Captain Coyle, Coast Guard, was the skipper and he had a Navy reserve commander as his exec, and this Army Transport fellow had set up some strange rules. For example, for every meal in the mess, a field grade officer would be in charge of each mess line. That was totally un-Marine like and I just told him that that wouldn't happen. It would be an embarrassment to my Marines to have a field officer standing around watching them eat, when they were accustomed to having a sergeant in charge of the mess line. He was considerably put out and went to the ship's exec and got him to agree with him. I got Captain Coyle to instruct them that we'd act like Marines on his ship. I got my officers together to ensure that nothing would happen down there that could prove him right. They got good NCOs in charge and so there was never any trouble."[2]

A week after the 1st Marines pulled out, Harold Deakin recounted how he and Rupertus were sitting on his bunk, alone. He had his head in his hands and he said something to the effect that this thing has just about got me beat. Deakin had not been one of Rupertus' friends but he tried to comfort the dispirited officer. He put his arm around the general's shoulder and told him that everything was going to be all right. Deakin considered that at that moment he was half staff officer, half chaplain, and deacon.

The Marine Corps Historical Division monograph, *The Assault on Peleliu*, noted, "The official casualty figure for the 1st Marine Division was 6,526 of whom 1,252 were killed in action—1st Marines, 1,749; 5th Marines, 1,378; 7th Marines 1,497. It was reported that the 1st Marines killed an estimated 3,942 Japanese and reduced the following enemy positions and installations: ten defended coral ridges, three large blockhouses, 22 pillboxes, 13 antitank guns and 144 defended caves."

Davis took a train across country directly to Atlanta for a homecoming with Knox. "We were married when Ray was captain," she explained. "We weren't married but a few months; Ray went off to war; Ray was gone two long years!" Davis met his 21-month-old son, Gilbert, who he had never seen. "He was a very bright little boy, of course, he objected to my first night in the bedroom because he'd been displaced a little bit. He cut up a little."[3]

Following a brief leave near St. Petersburg, Florida, the Davis family headed to Quantico for duty as Chief of the Infantry Section, Marine Air-Infantry School. "We arrived about dark. There was deep snow; it was cold, but a bachelor friend allowed us to use his BOQ room, while he was away." After spending several weeks in a motel, the family was lucky to be assigned to Quarters 138, "a nice home, well-maintained, perfectly furnished, manicured grounds, beautiful garden out back, quarters for a maid—a dream move for us. It was sited at the foot of the commanding general's driveway."[4]

Knox immediately became involved with the Girl Scouts, while Ray became Pack master for the Cub Scouts and a "reporter" for the Boy Scouts. Shortly after arriving, Knox gave birth to a second son, Miles. The Davis' splurged and hired a

---

1st Marine Division's Presidential Unit Citation

For extraordinary heroism in action against enemy Japanese forces at Peleliu and Negesbus from September 15 to 29, 1944. Landing over a treacherous coral reef against hostile mortar and artillery fire, the First Marine Division, Reinforced, seized a narrow, heavily mined beachhead and advanced foot by foot in the face of relentless enfilade fire through rain-forests and mangrove swamps toward the air strip, the key to the enemy defenses of the southern Palau's. Opposed all the way by thoroughly disciplined, veteran Japanese troops heavily entrenched in caves and in reinforced concrete pillboxes which honeycombed the high ground throughout the island, the officers and men of the Division fought with undiminished spirit and courage despite heavy losses, exhausting heat and difficult terrain, seizing and holding a highly strategic air and land base for future operations in the Western Pacific. By their individual acts of heroism, their aggressiveness and their fortitude, the men of the First Marine Division, Reinforced, upheld the highest traditions of the United States Naval Service.

live-in young woman to help with the children. Davis recalled, "This proved to be full of pluses and minuses—she worked hard, but was soon caught up in the heavy dating and night life enjoyed by young girls at Quantico."[5]

Chief of the Infantry Section

Ray was initially assigned as a Tactical Instructor but this position only lasted a short time before taking the position as Chief of the Infantry Section at the Marine Air-Ground school. "It was a period of transition in all of the Marine Corps Schools. The war was still in high gear, new classes were coming on board and overlapped in such a way that we couldn't stop and revise the instruction. We had to change piecemeal as the courses progressed … but it all soon straightened out. It was a great challenge, but rewarding."[6]

The family thrived at "The Crossroads of the Corps," as Quantico became known because all officers and many SNCOs passed through many of its professional schools. However, Knox was having second thoughts about staying in the Marine Corps. "When the massive release began after World War II ended, most of our friends were reservists who were being released. Many good friends that we really liked were departing." She told Ray that he needed to get out and get a job, "that's all there is to it. I'll go back to teaching school, if necessary."[7]

"So Ray sat me down and said: 'Well, you couldn't teach school, because we have our sons' … then he reviewed many reasons why the Marine Corps was his chosen profession. And I told him: 'All right. I will stay in with you, and you'll never hear that from me again …' I never one time after that complained about being in the Marine Corps."[8]

CHAPTER 18

1st Provisional Brigade: Guam

In July 1947, after two years at Quantico, Davis received orders to join the 1st Provisional Brigade in Guam, under the command of Brigadier General Edward A. "Eddie" Craig, a distinguished combat leader who led the 9th Marines on Bougainville and Guam and served as the Corps operations officer for Iwo Jima.

General Craig was ordered to Guam to organize a reinforced brigade, with the 5th Marines as a nucleus. "I arrived on 19 May 1947 and reported to the Naval Governor." The basic mission of the brigade was to train Marines for contingency operations in China during the Communist takeover of the country. "I had top secret orders at the time to be prepared to move out with the brigade prepared for combat on a few hours' notice to reinforce the garrison at Tsingtao. This situation required that I keep up an intensive troops training program and at the same time build up the cantonment."[1]

The Brigade's personnel arrived shortly thereafter by naval transport and was allotted an area that had been used by the 3rd Marine Division during the war. The unfinished camp was located on the high ground in an overgrown jungle area above Ylig Bay on the east side of the island.

The Brigade comprised two Battalion Landing Teams (BLT), each with its own artillery battery, tank platoon, antitank platoon, and support units. The Brigade's cantonment was named Camp Witek, in honor of Private First Class Frank P. Witek, who was posthumously awarded the Medal of Honor in the recapture of the island.

"Camp Witek was a new Marine Corps installation," Davis recalled. "Troops were housed in Quonset huts and tents. There were no quarters available for married officers and SNCOs. As a result the assignment was designated as an 'unaccompanied tour,' meaning families could not accompany their sponsors."[2]

Craig's immediate priority was to house the Brigade's several thousand Marines. "I was informed that in the jungle were 900 new Quonset huts in crates, plus a large number of large jumbo Quonset huts that could be used as storage. This was all World War II surplus." Craig was able to secure $300,000 for construction materials, but it had to be shipped from the United States.[3]

Davis was initially assigned as the Assistant Chief of Staff, G-3 (Operations and Training) and then Assistant Chief of Staff, G-4 (Logistics). "My basic function was to get the cantonment built," he said. One of his first tasks had nothing to do with building a camp. He was assigned to inventory and organize "a massive junkyard of World War II gear." "During the Pacific War, the Guam jungle was filled with supplies. No one knew precisely just what we had, and we didn't have an adequate staff to find out." It was finally decided to conduct a wall-to-wall, block-to-block inventory, using troops to do it.[4]

The 5th Service Depot, under a senior colonel, depended on the Brigade for manpower to sort the supplies so an inventory could be conducted. The Depot commander pushed Davis to furnish the working parties, while Craig pushed for training. "It was a most interesting task—treading water between General Craig and Colonel Thompson to get the work done without stepping on anybody's toes."[5]

Davis recalled, "We did not find much useable stuff and had to write it off by the ton and by the yard. So much of it was totally surplus to our needs. It would have been better if we had turned the whole thing over to a contractor."[6]

General Craig was determined to provide quarters for the members of his command. "My first priority was to finish barracks, mess halls and battalion clubs for the enlisted men. My second priority was to construct bachelor officers and SNCO quarters, and my last priority would of necessity be quarters for married officers and non-commissioned officers."[7]

The Marine Corps, in its infinite wisdom, declared that when quarters were available, families could join their sponsors. However, there was a catch. "We had to build our own quarters," Davis emphasized. "I was issued a vacant lot and a knocked-down Quonset hut. The hut consisted of a half-moon structure built with semi-circular metal frames; 3 feet by 6 feet pieces of tin for a roof; and 4 feet by 6 feet plywood slabs for the floor. Pieces of tarpaulin were attached to the outside walls to serve as screen-covered 'windows' during the heavy intermittent rains that swept Guam almost daily. No glass was allowed, since strong gusts of wind would have broken them out. We also had to personally order other essentials, such as commodes, stoves, and refrigerators from the States."[8]

"Because there were a number of officers awaiting families, the whole thing was kind of a do-it-yourself community. I was a pretty good plumber, so I put plumbing in four or five houses. Somebody else was an electrician, another was a carpenter—so it was a trade-off effort.[9] I do not know of any other time in the Corps when officers had to get out and build their own quarters. Many of them would work late at night under floodlights, after a long hard day of training."[10]

"It should be noted," Davis commented dryly, "that after building these Quonsets, along with the spending of substantial amounts of personal funds, the Marines had to give up their full quarters allowances in order to live in them!"[11]

Davis recalled that Japanese holdouts would occasionally surrender. On 12 May 1948, two Japanese soldiers surrendered to civilian police. "They were picked up and hauled off to be repatriated," Davis recalled. "There were also several war criminals incarcerated on the island and, after the war crimes trials, some were executed." In 1947 and 1949, 13 Japanese Army or Navy officers were found guilty of torturing and murdering American servicemen, including nine Marine Raiders captured on Makin. The men were hanged inside a Quonset hut and buried in unmarked graves on U.S. military land on Guam.[12,13]

***

The Davis family, Knox and two boys, Miles and Gilbert, arrived by ship before Ray had quite finished their new home. The jungle environment with its varied insect and animal life proved to be somewhat of a shock for the family. "The first night we discovered after we went to bed that the place was overrun with coconut rats—big ones. We cured the problem by placing food near the door, waiting in the dark until we could hear them at the food. We opened the door, turned on the lights and thrashed around over the house with brooms and sticks as they ran out."

On one of the first nights, Knox was treated to a disquieting welcome by a common house gecko. "One especially hot night we were asleep sans pajamas when a screech shocked me awake. In the dark I couldn't find Knox. Flipping on the light, I saw her terror-distorted face. A lizard had fallen from his ceiling perch onto her bare stomach. She must have levitated at least a foot off the bed when it hit! Needless to say, we declared war on all lizards."[14]

Part Five

Korea (Land of the Morning Calm)

CHAPTER 19

Reserve Infantry Battalion

In the spring of 1949, Davis received orders to be the Inspector Instructor (I & I) of the 9th Marine Corps Reserve Infantry Battalion in Chicago, Illinois. "We left Guam on short notice amid a lot of confusion. An early announcement stated that troop units would embark and leave dependents in the primitive camp. Since there was no known urgency, this seemed totally foolish." Several of the men, Davis included, threatened to send messages to their Congressmen asking for help. The threat forced the "powers that be" to back off. Next, they were told that the homes they had so beautifully constructed were to be abandoned and to leave their furnishings behind for personnel from the 5th Service Depot to pack up and forward—when they could get to it. Davis refused to sign a certificate relieving the government of any responsibility for damage or loss. This plan was also withdrawn. Finally, the family packed up their own household goods and embarked aboard a civilian liner. "The trip home was pleasant," Davis recalled. "[We] were quartered in an upper stateroom and dined with the captain. It was really first-class travel."[1]

The change from living on a relatively small island in the middle of the Pacific to a major metropolitan city in America's heartland brought about unexpected situations. The family moved to Deerfield, a small town just north of the city, and far away from any military medical facilities. Three-year-old Miles became ill with what appeared to be appendicitis. Because they were so new in the area, none of the civilian doctors would treat him. Knox was furious. "We could not get a local doctor to take care of him. They said, 'Well, you're not a patient of mine.'"[2]

Miles was quickly bundled into the car and driven to the Great Lakes Naval Hospital by his parents, arriving just before midnight. The medical duty officer quickly verified the illness and called in a surgeon. Within a short time several other medical officers arrived and the sick boy was taken in for surgery. Knox recalled, "We came back the next morning and when we saw him, we were almost in a state of shock." Miles had developed peritonitis and the doctors had to clean his stomach cavity. Ray said, "This incident built in me a great confidence in the Navy medical system."[3]

School started two or three days after their arrival and there was not an opportunity to shop for clothing so Gilbert was sent off to school in his shorts and a t-shirt. The weather had been hot when the family arrived but the first day of school it turned chilly. His teacher reminded them that "his clothing is just not appropriate for this weather." The boys were quickly outfitted for Chicago's cold weather.[4]

CHAPTER 20

North Korea Strikes

The predawn darkness was broken by the sharp flash and crump of exploding mortar and artillery fire. The detonations spewed jagged metal in a lethal arc of death and destruction. These deadly orchestrations began in the early morning hours of Sunday, 25 June 1950 (1700, June 24, in Washington, D.C.). Seven Russian-trained infantry divisions and an armored brigade of the 35-ton Russian-made T-34 medium tanks of the North Korean People's Army (NKPA) stormed across the 38th parallel. The main attack, two divisions and most of the tank brigade, struck south, through the Uijongbu Corridor, the historic invasion route that led straight to the South Korean capital of Seoul. Soviet records indicate that in January 1950 Kim Il Sung visited Moscow to argue his case for invading South Korea. Immediately after the visit, Russia provided military advisers and huge amounts of weapons and supplies.

In a coast-to-coast coordinated attack, the NKPA brushed aside the ineffective resistance of the Republic of Korea (ROK) frontier force. Within three days the invaders seized Seoul, the capital, 35 miles south of the 38th Parallel, forcing the government to flee and turning its citizens into fugitives desperate to escape the fighting. The North Korean Army was executing its operational plan, which called for advances of 15 to 20 kilometers a day with main military operations completed within 22 to 27 days.

In that summer of 1950, North Korea fielded an army of more than 100,000 men. Almost one-third were seasoned veterans who had served in the Chinese Communist Eighth Route Army in World War II and in the civil war against Chiang Kai-Shek's Nationalists. Three of the front-line divisions were almost entirely composed of veterans. The technical branches were largely staffed by Koreans who had served in the Soviet armies or had received a military education in the Soviet Union. All political officers and lower-level cadres were Soviet-trained. The senior commanders were graduates of the Whampoa Military Academy, China's West Point, and many had held commissions in the Soviet army during World War II.

Facing them were four poorly trained ROK divisions, armed primarily with light infantry weapons. They did not have any tanks, medium artillery, or effective antitank weapons. Most of their equipment was cast-off American World War II material. Their senior leadership was not professionally qualified. Many were political appointees, with little military experience. Junior officer and NCO leadership left a great deal to be desired, although many were tough and courageous, as would be seen in the first weeks of the war. Unfortunately, bravery alone could not stand up against the well-trained, ruthless NKPA.

Call for Help

Captain Joseph Darrigo U.S. Army, of the Korean Military Aid Group (KMAG), and the only American near the onslaught, barely managed to escape the advancing North Koreans. Awakened by the massive shelling, he struggled into shirt and trousers and raced for his jeep. Small arms fire chipped stone from the outside walls of his house. After a harrowing night-time drive through darkened streets filled with North Korean troops, Darrigo reached the ROK 1st Division headquarters at Munsan just minutes before it was overrun. He spread the alarm up the chain of command. The U.S. Ambassador, John J. Muccio, received Darrigo's sketchy report and cabled the State Department with a priority night dispatch: "According to Korean Army reports, which are partly confirmed by [a] KMAG field adviser report, North Korean Forces invaded ROK territory at several points this morning. It would appear from the nature of the attack and the manner in which it was launched that it constitutes an all-out offensive against the ROK."[1]

A United Press correspondent, Jack James, sniffed out the story and beat Muccio by wiring it to New York as an urgent news flash. "Fragmentary reports indicate North Koreans launched Sunday morning attacks generally along entire border. Headquarters ROK's 1st Division fell 9:00 a.m. Tanks supposed [to have been] brought into use at Chunchon 50 miles northeast of Seoul." James scooped his buddies; they were still sleeping off a late-night drinking binge.[2]

Muccio's encrypted cable arrived at the State Department's communication room at 2126, where it was decoded. Secretary of State Dean Acheson held the communique up for several hours trying to verify its contents before calling President Harry S. Truman at his vacation home in Independence, Missouri. Truman had just finished dinner and settled down in the living room to read when the security phone rang. It was Acheson: "Mr. President, I have serious news, the North Koreans are attacking across the 38th parallel."[3]

As the North Koreans approached the capital, harried embassy staffers threw boxes of classified papers and documents on a bonfire in the parking lot. They piled suitcases, boxes of clothing, and personal effects in the building's hallways. Muccio was eating lunch with Colonel Sterling Wright, chief of the KMAG, when two North Korean Yaks strafed the building. The two jumped into a vehicle and took off, starting a mass exodus of employees.

The ambassador, his staff, and the Marine Embassy Guard crossed the Han River Bridge, just hours before it was blown up by panic-stricken ROK engineers. Thousands of Korean troops were trapped on the outskirts of Seoul, along with all their heavy equipment and rolling stock. Hundreds were killed when the span tumbled into the river. The engineer commander was summarily executed for cowardice.

Trygve Lie, Secretary General of the United Nations, called the Security Council into emergency session and declared North Korean aggression a breach of the peace and demanded their immediate ceasefire and withdrawal. Two days later, after hearing nothing from the North Koreans, the Security Council passed another resolution, calling upon UN members to provide economic and military assistance to embattled South Korea. The United Nations was in the fight. Fortuitously, the Russian delegation was absent when the vote was taken or certainly they would have vetoed the resolutions. Documents from the Soviet archives suggest that Stalin supported the North Korean invasion because he didn't think the United States would get involved. U.S. Secretary of State Dean Acheson may have inadvertently given the Soviet leader that idea at a press conference in mid-January 1950 in which he described the American sphere of interest in the Pacific and did not explicitly mention Korea.

Acting quickly, President Harry S. Truman ordered American naval, air, and ground forces into action. The first contingents to arrive were hastily assembled occupation troops from Japan. They were understrength, soft from occupation duty, and short on heavy weapons and equipment. General Lemuel C. "Lem" Shepherd, commander Fleet Marine Force, Pacific, based in Hawaii, considered, "In retrospect the Army had a couple of 'makee-learnee' divisions in Japan. It was during the Occupation period. The men were living in the lap of luxury in Japan. They weren't worrying about any war. A lot of them had come in after World War II, and had no combat experience—and there were very few veterans there."[4]

The American formations were immediately thrown into battle against the North Korean advance. They were chewed up by the tougher, Soviet-trained and Soviet-equipped NKPA, who totally outfought the unprepared and ill-equipped Americans. They retreated in the face of the North Korean onslaught, trading space for time in an effort to regroup and establish a sustainable defensive perimeter. Even with the arrival of additional reinforcements, American forces were pushed farther and farther south, toward the vital seaport of Pusan. Shepherd felt there was a definite quality difference in the opposing forces. "They [U.S. forces] were not trained soldiers. All of a sudden they were thrown into battle against a strong enemy. These North Koreans were fighters and had successfully overrun South Korea. I can't blame or criticize the Army too much—they just were not prepared for combat against a determined enemy."[5]

CHAPTER 21

Send in the Marines

General Clifton B. Cates, Commandant of the Marine Corps, was closely following events in Korea. He pushed for the deployment of the Fleet Marine Force but was stymied by the inaction of the Joint Chiefs of Staff (JCS). General Cates could not even discuss the issue directly with them, as the Corps was not a regular member, only sitting in when invited. Exasperated, the commandant prodded Admiral Forrest P. Sherman, Chief of Naval Operations, into sending a "back channel" message to General Douglas MacArthur, Commander-in-Chief, Far East (CINCFE), and supreme commander of UN forces in Korea, asking if he wanted the use of a Marine brigade with supporting air. "Forrest, it looks like the Army's 24th Division is in a pretty bad spot over there. We can furnish a brigade by draining our two divisions. Why doesn't MacArthur ask for Marines?" Sherman asked. "How soon could you have them ready?" "We can have them ready as quickly as the Navy get the ships," Cates replied. "Leave it to me," Sherman assured him. "I'll send a 'blue flag' [a private message between senior navy commanders] to Joy [Vice Admiral C. Turner Joy] and tell him that he can inform MacArthur that the Marines can have brigade and an air group."[1]

General MacArthur, with his back to the wall in Korea, fired off a message to the JCS: "Request immediate dispatch of a Marine Regimental Combat Team and supporting Air Group for duty this command—MacArthur." In the meantime, General Cates sent the 1st Marine Division at Camp Pendleton, California, a "be prepared to deploy" warning order. He continued the pressure on the joint chiefs by showing up uninvited when they met to discuss and finally approve MacArthur's request. Cates' diary for 3 July noted: "Orders for employment of FMF approved."[2]

General Cates' warning order reached Camp Pendleton, the home of the 1st Marine Division, and was delivered to the assistant Division commander, Brigadier General Edward A. "Eddie" Craig, in the early morning hours of 3 July 1950. The commanding general, Major General Graves B. Erskine, was out of the country after being appointed as Chief of Military Group, Melby–Erskine Mission, a joint

State Department–Defense Department Mutual Defense Assistance Program survey mission to Southeast Asia.

Craig recalled that, "My wife and I had spent a very pleasant weekend at Pine Valley in the eastern San Diego County mountains and were returning to Camp Pendleton when we heard on our car radio the news that the North Koreans had invaded South Korea. I remarked to my wife, 'Well this is it again and it looks like another war for the Marines.'" Shortly afterward, he received a phone call from the assistant commandant, Major General Oliver P. Smith, ordering him to take command of the 1st Provisional Marine Brigade and have it ready to move out at the earliest possible date.[3]

Craig had his work cut out for him. The Division was seriously under-manned because of cuts imposed upon the Corps by Secretary of Defense Louis Johnson after World War II. Shepherd noted that, "Louis Johnson hadn't helped us along, and the Marine Corps was just about to go out of existence. We had only about 60,000 to 70,000 Marines at the time. To form the brigade took a great deal of effort just to get out the initial orders." Craig was able to field one understrength infantry regiment but he had to strip the Division to do it. Smith said that after forming up the brigade, "it left only about 3,500 men at Pendleton, who were all short timers—that's all that was left." The air component of the Brigade, Marine Air Group (MAG) 33, had to do the same thing.[4]

The Marine Corps Supply Center at Barstow, California, was ordered to equip the Brigade with rolling stock—tanks, trucks, jeeps, and amphibious vehicles. At the end of World War II, the Marine Corps established a stockpile of war reserves. Codenamed "Operation Roll-Up," everything that could be shipped back from the Pacific was repaired and squirreled away in this desert center, including "abandoned" Army equipment that could be rehabilitated. The center went into high gear. Reconditioned rolling stock jammed the highways between the two bases.

To make up some of this personnel shortfall, Marines from all over the United States were ordered to "get to Camp Pendleton NOW." By train, plane, and bus, dozens of former recruiters and guard company troops poured into the base. One company commander recalled, "These men were shipped from the posts and stations by air, most of them arriving with just a handbag. They didn't have dog tags and had no health records to tell us how many shots they needed. Their clothing consisted of khaki only, although a few had greens. They had no weapons and their 782 gear [web equipment] was incomplete. We had a problem of trying to organize these men into platoons and getting them squared away before our departure date."[5]

The Brigade had just seven days to get organized—but somehow they did it. On 15 July 1950, the 6,500-man 1st Provisional Marine Brigade sailed past the breakwater of San Diego harbor, less than 30 days after the North Korean invasion.

CHAPTER 22

Chasing the North Koreans

At the urging of Admiral Arthur W. Radford, Chairman of the Joint Chiefs of Staff, Shepherd flew to Japan on 10 July to see General MacArthur. Always the gracious host, MacArthur welcomed Shepherd as an old comrade-in-arms. "We had a lengthy conversation in his office," Shepherd said. "You know he always wanted to talk. My God, talk, talk, talk, forty minutes, telling me all his experiences. We talked about Korea, we talked about this and that, and as we got up to go, he very courteously—he was always very courteous—he got up and went to the door of his office." A large map of Korea hung next to the door. MacArthur put his hand on Shepherd's shoulder and pointed, with his ever-present pipe stem, to a spot on the map adjacent to Seoul on the west coast of the peninsula. "Lem, if I had that 1st Marine Division as I had at Cape Gloucester, I'd land here at Inchon and cut the North Korean lines of communication." Shepherd was not taken aback, he had been thinking about the commitment of Marines a great deal. "[If] we have only a Marine brigade in Korea, its identity will be lost among all those Army divisions. On the other hand, if we could get a Marine division ordered to Korea, it would be a unit of sufficient size to take care of itself independently. With a major general in command, he would not permit his division to be pushed around."[1]

Shepherd had made up his mind to push for the commitment of the 1st Marine Division if the opportunity presented itself—and here was the opening he needed. "General, why don't you ask for them? They're under my command, as part of FMFPAC, but I can't order them from the West Coast to the Far East without the Joint Chiefs of Staff approval." Shepherd had received a report from an aide that President Truman was going to call up the reserves. "It was on this promise that I based my decision, because I knew that we had expended everybody on the West Coast to get the brigade going, but with the reserves being called up, we would be able to mount out a full division."[2]

MacArthur, not batting an eye, said, "That's the kind of talk I like to hear," and immediately he asked Shepherd to write the message for him. "Sit down at my desk and write a dispatch to the Joint Chiefs of Staff, requesting that the 1st Marine Division be sent out to my theatre of command."[3]

Shepherd took one look at MacArthur's huge desk, four times the size of his own, and knowing that Mac Arthur would scrutinize every word, he was terribly disconcerted. After all, the Far East commander had five stars and Shepherd was a junior three-star. MacArthur had an aura, a presence that was almost larger than life. "It really shook me, so I said, 'Well, General, I will go out to the office of your chief of staff [Major General Edward M. Almond] to draft this message and bring it in to you for approval.'" Shepherd scrounged a message pad and jotted down his thoughts. It took three drafts before he got the delicately worded message in a form that he thought was suitable. "I finally came up with a draft that I believed suitable. It was a delicate dispatch to compose. Here I was, recommending that a Marine division be sent to Korea, and the Commandant [of the Marine Corps, General Cates] didn't know anything about what I was doing. It was a hell of a spot to be in, but the ball had been dropped in my hands and I felt I must run with it." MacArthur approved the request without change, but the Joint Chiefs turned it down—and three more—before finally approving the fifth message.[4]

The Commandant, Lieutenant General Clifton B. Cates, ordered that the 1st Marine Division be brought up to full wartime strength within three weeks, even though it required approximately the same number of Marines as existed in the entire Fleet Marine Force. Mobilized reserves would have to fill in the gaps.

All Marine activities were ruthlessly combed to expand the 1st Marine Division. By the end of the month, the first reservists were flooding into Camp Pendleton, California.

The windows of Headquarter Marine Corps blazed with light in the late summer evening. Early that afternoon, a grim-faced President Truman had authorized the call-up of the reserves. Now, Headquarters staffers were hard at it, preparing mobilization orders for the 33,000 Marines of the Organized Reserve.

9th Marine Corps Reserve Infantry Battalion

In Chicago a sleepy-eyed duty non-commissioned officer (DNCO) slowly responded to the persistent ringing of the entrance bell. He jerked the door open, ready to give "what for" to the wise guy who had just disturbed his sleep. Before he could say anything, the "intruder" thrust a telegram into his hand, apologized for the lateness of the hour, and shoved off. Mumbling obscenities, the by now wide-awake DNCO ripped open the envelope and glanced at its contents. The military verbiage took him a minute to decipher. He did a double-take. "This is it," he exclaimed, and ran down the passageway to the telephone. Chicago's 9th Marine Corps Reserve Infantry Battalion had just received mobilization orders—it was going to war.

Ray Davis, Inspector-Instructor (I & I), was proud of this battalion of reserves. They were a dedicated and hard-working group of citizen soldiers who trained one weekend a month and attended a two-week summer camp once a year. "The reserves had great spirit—an esprit, which drove them to be good Marines at night or weekends, after holding down their regular civilian jobs by day or all week long." Many of the men were World War II veterans, but most were youngsters just out of high school—a typical reserve unit. When the order for extended active duty arrived they had just returned from a highly successful training exercise at Camp Lejeune, where they had been classified as "nearly combat ready."[5]

Davis remarked that, "Camp Lejeune was another one of those breaks where I got involved with the right people. Litzenberg was in charge of reserve training, and noted how well the battalion performed." When he was assigned as the 7th Marines commander, he needed a battalion commander and asked Davis to take one of his battalions to Korea. "Without that I might have been left out of the war somewhere," Davis joked. "Litzenberg was another masterful tactician. He had a better feel for going and getting the enemy than most people I've been around."[6]

Within hours of receiving the notification, the reserve center was a frenzy of activity. Working parties hurried back and forth. Long lines snaked around the passageways—shots, equipment issue, wills and power of attorney, a host of pre-deployment activities—including "the standard problem people that wanted to stay home," Davis recalled. "We set up a hearing process for those who didn't want to go at all. We had several days of hearings to see what criteria they met. The most serious problem was the physical failure rate as the reserves reported to take their final, before-going-to-active-duty physical. All of these failures somehow had a relation to the Marines mental attitudes. The doctors were finding them Not Physically Qualified (NPQ). I looked at the many reports ... and I couldn't believe the findings."[7]

He found out the two doctors that screened them worked together at the Veterans Center. They found each other NPQ! Davis fired the two doctors, got the men re-examined, and they were found qualified

"I got in trouble with the high school football team," he chuckled. "I finally went along with the solution with the principal and the superintendent when they came to see me. I agreed to let them stay if they signed an agreement to go after the end of the season and they graduated. The deal was struck and the boys went on with their season." The end result was that, "We finally put 700 men on the train."[8]

A troop train wound its way from the East Coast across the continent, picking up Marines along the way. The 9th Battalion, in combat gear and carrying weapons, proudly marched down State Street past hundreds of well-wishers to the train station. Wives and sweethearts tearfully waved a last good-bye as the battalion climbed aboard the passenger cars for the three-day trip to Camp Pendleton. Ray Davis watched the train pull away, crestfallen that he wasn't going with them. "It was a hell'va good battalion," he said proudly.[9]

Ray found out later that the battalion had been split up. When the battalion got off the train at Camp Pendleton, they formed up, counted off in 75-man increments and marched off into the night. The battalion organization was completely destroyed.[10]

Within days, orders arrived assigning Davis as commanding officer, 1st Battalion, 7th Marine Regiment, then forming at Pendleton's Tent Camp Two, an old World War II encampment 21 miles from the main base.[11] Litzenberg commented on his selection of him as a battalion commander. "I had never met him before, but I knew of his reputation in World War II. He was also recommended as an outstanding officer. I put the formation of the whole battalion into his hands. I did take two or three staff officers, a few non-commissioned officers, and some privates and gave them to him to form the nucleus for the new battalion. Colonel Davis was, I think, unhampered in the formation of his battalion."[12]

When Davis arrived at Camp Pendleton on the morning of 21 August, he was greeted by Colonel Litzenberg. "Where the hell've you been?" the old man barked. Before Davis could answer, Litzenberg followed up with, "You've got five days to gather 800 men to fill your battalion!"[13]

Davis found there were very few troops, only a small handful of veteran officers and NCOs. His battalion existed only on paper and he had just seven days to get it ready to deploy. He called a meeting. "We have a week to form a battalion," he told them. "At no time in our careers will we be faced with greater responsibility—sixty per cent of our men will be reserves. Some of these men will be veterans from the last war, many will be youngsters who have been in reserve organizations. It is our job to get them ready for combat." With that admonition, he decided to go outside the established personnel system and "recruit" his battalion.[14]

The organization of the reserve reception center was just beyond belief. Thousands of men were streaming into Camp Pendleton from all over the United States; recruits just out of Boot Camp, old timers from posts and stations, and reserve units called back to the Colors. They flooded the base, forming huge working parties engaged in getting the 1st Marine Division ready to go to war. "I decided to take matters into my own hands," Davis said. "So, on the third day, I was still 300 men short. The executive officer and the operations officer got about a dozen trucks and rode around the base, everywhere they would find a bunch of troops lounging around, working parties, whatever, and the two officers would shout like Pied Pipers, 'Anybody want to go to Korea?' … and that's how I got the last 300 men."[15]

The "volunteers" climbed aboard the trucks and were taken to Tent Camp Two, where veteran sergeants collected name, rank, and serial number. Other NCOs were dispatched to locate their record books. "There was a huge pile of service record books stored under canvas," Davis explained. "My admin men went through them, matching them with the names of my volunteers. In this way we gained several hundred spirited, ready-to-go-to-war men in just eight hours of 'recruiting.'"[16]

The first two days were used just getting the men, their equipment, and their administrative records. The third and fourth days were spent in firing their weapons, small-unit tactics, hikes in the rough terrain of the Pendleton hills, and the fifth day they were on the buses heading for San Diego to board the USS *Okanogan* (APA-220), a Navy assault transport.

O. P. Smith said the Navy "grabbed ships from up and down the coast; merchant ships, anything they could find. All the amphibious shipping was in the Far East. There wasn't any amphibious shipping on the West Coast. We took all the [equipment] down to the docks in San Diego and loaded it on the ships as they came in."[17]

3rd Battalion, 11th Marines, was also aboard the ship. One of its battalion surgeons had an occasion to talk with Davis in the ship's wardroom. "He was very agreeable to converse and it was easy to communicate with him. He was a soft-spoken Georgian from Stockbridge. Our discussion centered on my lack of knowledge and training of what a battalion surgeon was supposed to do. I will never forget his reply, for it was to be a source of ongoing confidence and encouragement for me. After listening sympathetically he said with a smile, 'Bob, when the time comes, you will know what to do.' This turned out to be such a truth."

Davis used the 18-day transit for day and night training. "The second day at sea I convinced the skipper that if he'd throw some trash over the fantail, I could test my weapons—my machine guns, rockets and mortars had not been fired—so the skipper did and the next morning we opened fire and the whole ship formation went to emergency general quarters because the skipper forgot to tell the commodore what we were going to do and he thought we were under attack. In addition to firing our rifles at every target we could find from the fantail of the *Okanogan*, we fired machine guns, mortars, rocket launchers and threw hand grenades at every piece of trash, orange crates, whatever the ship's crew tossed overboard. Naturally these Navy folks were aghast at first to hear my operational desires, but they really entered into the innovative scheme, and we had over two weeks of good, solid training from Marines who were super-motivated. This was no game; they were going to war on the next land that they saw, Inchon, the port city to Seoul."[18]

CHAPTER 23

Land of the Morning Calm

The September 1950 7th Marines Historical Diary noted: "The entire 7th Marines landed at Inchon on 21 September and was immediately committed to the line overlooking the Han River on the north-west [left] flank of the 1st Marine Division. During the period 22–30 September, the regiment was engaged in combat against the enemy which culminated in the capture of Seoul."

MajGen Edward M. "Ned" Almond, commanding general X Corps, sent a message to MacArthur just before midnight on 25 September stating, "Three months to the day after the North Korean Army launched their surprise attack south of the 38th Parallel, the combat troops of X Corps recaptured the capital city of Seoul." Unfortunately, his message had little effect on the North Koreans. It took four more days of heavy combat—and 500 Marine casualties—before the city was finally liberated.

Following its capture, the regiment was ordered to cut off the enemy escape routes northwest of the city. "One morning I felt totally relaxed, because we had no new orders from Regiment. The phone rang. Colonel Litzenberg asked: 'What's the problem? You are supposed to be moving out.' 'But sir,' I responded, 'I don't have any orders to move today.' 'You have now! Get going!' he growled and hung up. I hurried to my operations tent in time to find my embarrassed S-3 [operations officer] scrambling to get things moving."[1]

By now, the North Koreans were streaming north with American forces in hot pursuit. The 7th Marines was assigned: "To advance rapidly and seize blocking positions in the vicinity of Uijongbu, an important road center about 12 miles north-northwest of Seoul," 1st Marine Division Op Order 14-50. Davis' battalion was to execute a tactical feint on a broad front as though the regiment was going to attack the hill masses on either side of the road. Meanwhile, Major Maurice E. Roach's 3rd Battalion would attack straight up the road through a defile.

At 0630 on 1 October, the 1st Battalion jumped off in the attack and quickly seized its initial objectives. Hospital Corpsman William Davis recalled, "We accomplished this mission fairly easily, although we were under artillery and mortar fire throughout the day. However, the 3rd Battalion got held up clearing the minefield and both battalions were ordered to continue the attack along the ridges—1/7 on the right and 3/7 on the left. They ran into heavily defended enemy positions and halted for the night."[2]

Early morning on the 2nd, the two battalions advanced in the face of heavy enemy artillery, mortar and small arms fire from "bunkers on the slope and at the top of the peak," Corpsman Davis recalled. The two battalions were only able to gain 300 yards. The following morning, the attack continued against light enemy resistance. VMF-312 supported them with sortie after sortie. The attacking Marines began to overrun North Korean heavy artillery and supply dumps.[3]

Davis was pleased with the conduct of his battalion. "We had a few skirmishes with small enemy groups and we were able to exercise our mortars, artillery and aircraft weapons on live fire targets," Davis explained. "Just a lot of maneuver and a little bit of fighting. One of my company commanders got slightly wounded, nothing serious, just enough to sharpen up the wits of the troopers."[4]

At mid-morning on the 3rd, Litzenberg sent Major Webb D. Sawyer's 2nd Battalion straight up the road, which broke the enemy resistance. About 1700, the battalion secured Uijongbu and outposted the hills north and northeast. Litzenberg said "the regiment waited in the town for two days, until a ROK corps passed through us on their way to the 38th Parallel."[5] In the three-day fight, the 7th Marines had smashed three battalions of the 31st Regiment of the 3rd NKPA Division. The Regiment suffered 13 killed in action and 111 wounded. Davis, the combat veteran, remarked that World War II was so totally bloody that Korea initially wasn't all that bad.

Three days later, the 7th Marines returned to Inchon Harbor where they boarded Japanese LSTs for a tactical landing at the port of Wonsan on the east coast. Located 80 miles north of the 38th Parallel, the port had the best naturally sheltered harbor in the Korean peninsula.

The amphibious operation was disdainfully nicknamed Operation *Yo-Yo* because the ships had to steam back and forth for several days while the Navy cleared the estimated 2,000 Russian-made mines from the sea approaches to the harbor. Second Lieutenant Owen assumed the demanding duties as company embarkation officer. "We were assigned an old LST that our Navy had used in World War II," he said, "but which was now leased to Japan for use as a cargo ship. There was a shortage of shipping and we were informed we would be afloat for only a few days."

Unfortunately, the ship ran low on food and water because of the mine-clearing delay. Owen lamented that it was, "a three-week ordeal of misery and sickness ... the stench below decks made the air unbreathable."[6] The men were crammed on transports for days on end, enduring monotony that lowered morale and physical fitness. To make matters worse, dysentery broke out, further eroding morale.[7]

While the Navy tried to clear the mines, South Korean troops captured Wonsan after a hard-fought battle. To add insult to injury, Bob Hope waited for the Marines on the beach, much to Davis' chagrin. "When we finally got ashore, landing in World War II-type assault waves in the event the enemy was still in the area, we were greeted by big signs inviting us to the Bob Hope show. He never let me forget that he was ashore when we landed."[8]

U.S. Army personnel attached to the South Korean troops added another verse to the Marine Corps Hymn.

> Those tough and fighting Gyrenes
> Wherever they may go,
> Are always bringing up the rear
> Behind Bob Hope and the USO

The entire Division bivouacked among the low-lying hills and rice paddies west of Wonsan. There were a few buildings for the command post, but most of the men lived in tents scattered over a distance of 10 to 12 miles. Rumors floated around the encampment that MacArthur was quoted as stating, "This war is definitely coming to an end shortly." There was talk of early rotation. Signs started to appear, "DRIVE CAREFULLY—THE MARINE YOU HIT, MIGHT BE YOUR RELIEF."

CHAPTER 24

Chinese Volunteers

Litzenberg was not convinced that the war would soon be over. He gathered his officer and staff NCOs and warned them that on the drive north they could expect to run into Chinese Communist soldiers. "If there is anyone here who expects an easy walk to the Yalu River, ease it from your mind now. We are faced with a winter campaign and we're going to have to fight. It's important to win all of our battles, but it's most important that we win our first one when we meet the Chinese."[1]

On 1 November, the Division received orders to send a regiment to relieve a South Korean unit in contact with enemy troops on the road leading to the Chosin Reservoir. The South Koreans were fighting hard but were forced to give up ground. There were rumors their attackers were Chinese "volunteers."

A new radio operator, Corporal Roy Pearl, was assigned to Davis when he got ashore. Roy Pearl of Duluth, Minnesota, a reservist, was a World War II veteran, who left a wife and two small children at home in Duluth. Pearl had seen action on Bougainville, Peleliu, Guam, and Okinawa. Joining the Reserves after the war, he attended weekend drills and summer camps, drawing meager pay to supplement the income he earned servicing cars. Like most of his peers he answered the unexpected summons without complaint, but it was hard. One of his concerns was that his daughters, three years and three months old respectively, had not been baptized. "I was greatly relieved," he recalls, "when our minister agreed to stop by and take care of it in our living room." His first impression of Davis inspired confidence. He was "an ordinary-looking man of average height who looked as though he would be comfortable in bib overalls. He was from Georgia and soft-spoken. No gruff, no bluff. Never talked down to you. Made you feel comfortable in his presence."[2]

South Korean troops moved north to Hamhung, a rail center, in keeping with MacArthur's dictum "drive north to the Yalu," the river bordering North Korea and China/Manchuria.

With the liberation of Seoul and the restoration of the South Korean government, the only mission that remained was the destruction of the North Korean Army. Battered remnants of that Army were desperately attempting to escape north across the 38th Parallel. MacArthur, basking in the glow of one of the most decisive operations in military history, was intent on crushing them. All he needed was approval to cross the boundary. On 27 September, the Joint Chiefs of Staff, in the name of the president, gave its consent, with the proviso that "At the time of such operations there has been no entry into North Korea by major Soviet or Chinese Communist Forces, no announcement of intended entry, nor a threat to counter our operations in North Korea." There was great concern at the highest levels of the U.S. government that either of the two countries might enter the war. MacArthur shared no such concerns.[3]

On October 1, MacArthur authorized the release of a broadcast calling for the surrender of the North Korean Army, who did not dignify it with a reply. However, two days later, the Chinese forwarded their intentions through a third-party intermediary. The Indian ambassador in Peking met China's foreign minister in a hastily arranged meeting at his home over tea. After the usual small talk, the Indian ambassador was told, "If the Americans cross the 38th Parallel, China would intervene." This message was immediately relayed to the State Department, but Secretary Acheson pooh-poohed it, because the Indian diplomat "was not a good reporter." Retired Admiral Kichisaburo Nomura, Japan's ambassador to the United States in 1941, said, "If you go north of the 38th Parallel, they'll come in. They'll have to do that now to save face, live up to their own words."[4]

MacArthur's complicated strategy, Operation Plan 9-50, in which he assured the Joint Chiefs of Staff there was "no indication of Soviet or Chinese intervention," assigned Walker's Eighth Army the task of seizing the North Korean capital, Pyongyang. Almond's X Corps was directed to make an amphibious landing at Wonsan on the east coast and drive due west, linking up with Walker, thereby trapping the North Koreans between them. The plan further stipulated that at some future date, both commands would attack north to a line approximately 50 to 100 miles south of the Manchurian border. O. P. Smith thought the plan was totally unrealistic because the central mountain chain was swarming with these North Koreans who were making their way north to reorganize and they had all their weapons with them.[5]

Clear and Convincing Evidence

Armed Forces Security Agency (AFSA), a combined Army, Navy, and Air Force code-breaking organization under the control of the Joint Chiefs of Staff, developed "Clear and Convincing Evidence that the Chinese were massing on the north of the Yalu River." AFSA also intercepted a message indicating that "General Lin Piao, the commander of Chinese army forces would intervene in Korea." The intelligence was passed to the Joint Chiefs and General MacArthur, who told President Truman that the chances of Chinese intervention were "very little." "Early on the bitter-cold morning of 26 November, with trumpets braying, thirty Chinese divisions surged across the border …."[6]

The senior leadership of the 1st Marine Division not only lacked confidence in the plan, but also with the Corps commander. Almond was seen as a vain, overly aggressive officer, who let his ambitions overrule his judgement. O. P. Smith saw him as, "egotistical. He was a MacArthur man, and anything he said, nothing could change it. MacArthur was God."[7]

Almond's aggressiveness would have serious consequences for X Corps in the drive north during the dead of a Korean winter. Smith was also very concerned "over the lack of realism in the plans of the Corps and the tendency of the Corps to ignore the enemy capabilities when a rapid advance was desired. I found in my dealings with the Army, particularly with the X Corps, that the mood was either one of extreme optimism or of extreme pessimism. There did not seem to be any middle ground."[8]

General Smith and Almond were completely opposite in almost every quality except one, extreme pride, which doomed both men to dislike each other. Temperamentally, Almond was brash and dictatorial; Smith was refined and polite. Almond was a proud Virginian, who relished his regal position under MacArthur, Smith was a proud Texas Marine who resented being under Almond's command.[9]

The ROKs had captured several prisoners who revealed they were elements of the 370th and 372nd Regiments of the 124th Chinese People's Liberation Army (PLA) Division, known simply as Chinese Communist Forces (CCF) by the United States. Along with the 125th and 126th, the other two divisions of the 42nd CCF Army, the 124th, had crossed the Yalu during the period 14–20 October. The 7th Marines intelligence section reported that the CCF Fourth Field Army was crossing the Yalu into North Korea with the mission of preventing the X Corps from crossing into either China or Manchuria.

General Smith flew to Hamhung on 1 November to visit the 7th Marines headquarters on the northern outskirts of Hamhung. "Word had trickled in about the reverses suffered by the 8th Army in the west," Smith said, "[and] Litzenberg was rightly concerned over the situation." Litzenberg added that, "I discussed with our division commander the change in the nature of the war as a result of Chinese Communists' intervention. We were no longer, in my opinion, chasing a beaten and defeated enemy."[10]

Smith told Litzenberg that the 8th Army was not advancing, which would leave his left flank open, except for the small division reconnaissance company. "At any rate, the 7th Marines had orders to lead the advance of the 1st Marine Division up the single mountain road," Litzenberg explained, "to capture Yudam-ni, at which time the 5th Marines would pass through the 7th and lead the advance out to the road to the westward. This would put the Division in a position of being an anvil against which it was hoped the 8th Army could drive back the Chinese forces and entrap them."[11]

Davis was not privy to his commander's concern. "At that time, my anticipation was that the war was about over and that this was a security mission. With this kind of mission we set up shop in a valley while I collected up two or three jeeps to make a reconnaissance. My battalion was initially assigned to secure the Changjin Power Plant above Chinhung-ni; keep anyone from blowing it up and keep the roads open."[12]

Smith was under pressure from X Corps to advance. "Under these circumstances, there was no alternative except to continue forward," so the 7th Marines received orders to move north to relieve the 26th ROK Regiment in the vicinity of Sudong, increasing the gap with the Army unit.[13] The hapless 26th ROK Regiment was a newly formed unit, having been activated just prior to the Allied September offensive. It was made up of "draftees" who had been scooped up and formed into tactical squads, platoons, companies, and battalions. It did not receive any formal military training until April 1951.[14]

Davis sent out reconnaissance patrols to explore the route northward. One of the patrols, led by Captain Myron E. Wilcox, Jr., First Lieutenants William G. Graeber and John B. Wilson with three jeeps and a fire team for protection, reached the command post of the 26th Regiment near Sudong. The South Koreans told Wilcox that they had taken 16 Chinese prisoners who had admitted, under questioning, that they belonged to the 124th Chinese Communist Force (CCF) Division and said they had crossed the Yalu in mid-October.[15]

Davis decided to check out the patrol reports and loaded three jeeps with four or five riflemen riding shotgun, the battalion intelligence officer, and a Korean Army lieutenant interpreter. "I cruised around out there all day long," Davis remarked. "We stopped in every village and in every one of them reported that Chinese forces had been in the area. We got up to a schoolhouse up in the hills where a South Korean battalion had its headquarters," Davis explained. "They had half a dozen Chinese there in their quilted blue suits."[16]

The Chinese uniforms were either mustard-brown or navy-blue winter uniforms made of heavy cotton cloth with ribbed cotton padding that provided extra protection in cold weather. They wore headgear consisting of cotton-padded caps with brown tops and pile lining on the ear and neck flaps with visors. Most wore canvas-padded, high-top cloth shoes with rubber soles. The clothing did little to protect the soldiers from the extreme North Korean winter and thousands of Chinese soldiers died from exposure.

Davis was also shown a number of captured weapons. They included a hodge-podge of firearms, including Japanese Army and Nationalist Chinese rifles that had been surrendered at the end of World War II or captured from the Kuomintang (Nationalist Chinese) military forces during the civil war. There was also a pile of captured American weapons and ammunition, as well as Soviet "burp" guns and even a Chinese-made copy of a Thompson submachine gun.

The Chinese prisoners told Davis, through the Korean Army interpreter, that they were simply "volunteers" who had come to help their friends, the North Koreans. The South Korean battalion commander told Davis that the area was "full of these people and that we're convinced that they're here in organized units."[17]

At the power plant, the ROKs showed Davis a wire cage full of Chinese, who claimed they were "volunteers." Davis recalled, "A team from MacArthur's Tokyo headquarters came to investigate and apparently accepted the 'volunteer' notion, that there were only a few there to work with the North Koreans. In fact, the entire Chinese force was called the 'Volunteer Army.' This fact was confirmed to our great detriment later on as we were besieged by the Chinese."[18]

Further interrogation of the prisoners had yielded that they were members of the 370th Regiment of the 124th CCF Division, which along with the 125th and 126th Divisions made up the 42nd CCF Army. Roughly speaking, a Chinese army was the equivalent of a U.S. corps. On arriving from the Yalu, the 124th had deployed in the center to defend the Chosin Reservoir, the 126th had moved east to the vicinity of the Fusen Reservoir, and the 125th to the western flank on the right of the 124th Division.[19]

By this time it was late in the day, and Davis was concerned enough about the Chinese threat to complete the reconnaissance before dark and head back to the perimeter. "I wasn't thinking in terms of a major Chinese invasion but that was what it was, a forerunner. In the next few days we picked up a whole bunch of Chinese and had them there when Willoughby [Charles A., MacArthur's Chief of Intelligence] came over from Tokyo to prove there were no Chinese over here. Somehow he convinced himself and his interpreters that there was nothing to this and wouldn't believe the Chinese were coming in. He dismissed their capture as an isolated incident. However, everywhere I went in my jeep, my interpreter said the people were talking about the Chinese. My long-range patrols were finding Chinese and yet we were ordered to race up to the border and block the Chinese which was a big tactical mistake which cost thousands and thousands of casualties."[20]

"It was obvious that we were up against large numbers of Chinese," Davis said. "My patrols were finding massive Chinese out in the countryside. And the Chinese tactics were against them because they would line up in the snow in straight lines and come up against our defensive positions, completely exposed, and for the Marines it was just like being on the rifle range. They could kill them easily. Their tactics, their lack of weapons, lack of preparedness for the weather made it possible for us to survive against ten to one odds."[21]

Davis recalled, "Our intelligence folks told us that the Chinese Communist Fourth Field Army was crossing the Yalu River into North Korea with the mission of preventing our right flank force, Tenth Corps, from crossing into either China or Manchuria. The Eighth U.S. Army was going up the west coast in what General MacArthur saw as a giant pincer movement, or double envelopment, to squeeze all North Korean forces together as we cleared out North Korea, in the same way we had done on the west coast of South Korea. Our orders were to go up to the border and stop. The Chinese were already in the country but MacArthur's staff wouldn't believe it."[22]

Major General Almond, X Corps commander, inspected and interrogated the Chinese captured at Sudong. He confided to his subordinates that they were "just a bunch of Chinese laundrymen." He just wouldn't believe that large numbers of Chinese were facing his Corps.[23]

A highly classified National Security Agency review reported, "No one who received Comint [communication intelligence] product, including MacArthur's own G-2 [intelligence chief] in Tokyo, should have been surprised by the PRC [Chinese] intervention in the Korean War." The review pointed a finger of blame for the disaster directly at MacArthur.[24]

Litzenberg ordered the 1st Battalion to march to Majon-Dong and effect a passage of lines with the ROK battalion. Davis moved to a position about four miles north of the South Korean positions. Lieutenant Dan C. Holland, 1/7's battalion forward air controller, recalled that he, "Requested aircraft for patrols to our immediate front and received four Corsairs. They reconnoitered the area northeast and northwest of Sudong, reporting a large group of enemy troops [reinforced battalion or reduced regiment] about five miles northwest of Sudong in a bivouac area. After checking with LtCol Davis, I received permission to attack these troops. The four Corsairs attacked the troops, reported them dispersed, and could see no sign of any enemy in the area when they retired from the target. This was the first air strike, I think, that was run in Korea against the Chinese."[25]

VMF-312 flew 12 close air support missions in the Sudong area, and VMF-513 assisted with several more. The skyline on either side of the regiment was blasted with 500-pound bombs, 20mm shells, and high-velocity rockets. That afternoon the regiment formed a tight perimeter for the night.

The next morning, 1/7 formed a route column and proceeded toward the ROK lines. It caught up with the South Korean soldiers in a wooded area approximately one mile south of Sudong on the morning of 2 November. Roy Pearl watched the passage of lines. "The ROKs came down the slopes grinning and waving at us and pointing north. 'Many Chinese,' they said. They were moving more smartly than any South Korean outfit I saw, before or since." By 1030 the passage of lines had been completed and the battalion proceeded northward. Company A, the lead element in the regimental column, received ineffectual long-range small arms and machine-gun fire.[26]

The battalion set up defensive positions late in the afternoon. Company A formed a line on the right of the MSR (main supply route) that stretched across Hill 532 and part way up a spur of Hill 727, then bent rearward sharply to refuse the east flank. The company's 3.5-inch rockets were deployed in a roadblock. The 60mm mortar section and the company CP set up in the low ground. Davis deployed Company C across the MSR, opposite Company A. Company B dug in behind Company A and the elements of Company B on the right of the road. Davis' CP, the battalion 81mm mortars and a platoon of Company C were located in the low ground behind Company A. The 2nd Battalion, 7th Marines, extended south behind the 1st Battalion.[27]

At 2300, the Chinese crept down the slope of Hill 727 and probed Company A. The darkness was shattered by blaring bugles, the crump of detonating hand grenades, and the rattle of rifles and submachine guns. Both the 1st and 2nd Battalions were under a full-scale attack by the 371st Regiment, 124th Division at 0100. Fighting was at close range with grenades, rifle and machine-gun fire.

Roy Pearl was standing the midnight radio watch when, "I was yanked out of my reverie by the god-awfulest sounds—bugles and shepherd's horns and whistles—then saw the glow of flares descending in a neat row across the river." All at once the companies on both flanks were attacked. He heard Davis shout, "Listen up, Marines! The enemy is hitting the companies on the other side of the river. We are expecting an attack on this side momentarily. Get your weapons and ammo squared away and stand by. Good shooting!" Litzenberg estimated that two battalions attacked the 1st Battalion.[28]

As the fighting increased in intensity, the Marines manning the roadblock heard the clanking sounds of a tracked vehicle. Thinking it was a friendly bulldozer, they let the machine pass through. The big vehicle rumbled into Company A's CP and stopped, one headlight glaring at the exposed mortar crews and headquarters personnel. Staff Sergeant Donald T. Jones, section chief of the mortars, yelled "tank!" It was a Russian T-34 from the 344th North Korean Tank Regiment, supporting the 124th CCF Division.

The tank opened fire with its machine gun, scattering the lightly armed Marines and then rumbled into Davis' CP. "He turned on his big light," Davis recalled. An NCO thought it was a Marine vehicle and shouted, "Turn that fuckin' light off." The tank opened fire with its machine gun. "Instantly every rocket launcher in the battalion went after him," Davis remembered. "They fired, but sandbags saved it." However, a 75mm shell hit the turret and set the sandbags on fire. The tank, trailing flames and sparks, clanked around a bend in the road and disappeared. The tank was found abandoned nearby the next day.[29]

Davis yelled to the men in the CP, "Dig in and prepare to repel boarders!" Just as he called out the warning, an illumination round outlined four enemy soldiers heading toward him. Someone shouted "Fire!" Three of the soldiers fell dead, and the fourth raised his hands in surrender. One of Davis' officers, who had served in China, interrogated the prisoner and confirmed that all four were Chinese. They were later identified as being members of the 124th CCF Division. This was the Division's first positive intelligence that the CCF was engaged.[30]

As the night went on, Chinese infantry attacked. "My battalion had a fight with a Chinese regiment 140 miles inside North Korea," Davis explained. "I had 600 dead Chinese and a hundred captured. I had positioned the weapons company along a river across from a railroad. The Chinese didn't know we were there. They came down the railroad, making a lot of noise. I told the weapons company to keep quiet until they got in range. Just before daylight, we opened fire. A Bugle started to blow and the bugler was cut down right in the middle of a note. It was the most eerie thing you can imagine. After that there was no question in my mind the Chinese were there and in force."[31]

A third company-sized force was intent on penetrating the perimeter. Dawn revealed them marching in columns of fours toward a railroad tunnel. Davis recalled it was a "real turkey shoot. They were near where we had set up our six heavy water-cooled machine guns. Not one of them made it. The final count was over six hundred dead!" Pearl stood next to Davis. "These people were only a hundred yards away ... it was unreal ... our machine guns opened up and others joined in, including me. I was just getting warmed up when I felt a hand on my shoulder. It was Davis. 'You've had your fun, Pearl; now get back to your radio.'"[32]

The Chinese slipped past Davis' right flank and wedged their way between Major Webb D. Sawyer's 2nd Battalion and Major Maurice E. Roach's 3rd Battalion, setting in motion an ugly brawl for possession of the high ground, which lasted all the next day. The Chinese overran the regiment's 4.2-inch Mortar Company, causing several casualties and the loss of one of its tubes.

Chinese Tactics

The Chinese attacks demonstrated that they were well-trained, disciplined firefighters, and particularly adept at night fighting. They were masters of the art of camouflage. Their patrols were remarkably successful in locating the positions of the UN forces. They planned their attacks to get in the rear of these forces, cut them off from their escape and supply roads, and then sent in frontal and flanking attacks to precipitate the battle. They also employed a tactic which they termed *Hachi Shiki*, a V-formation into which they allowed enemy forces to move; the sides of the V then closed around their enemy while another force moved below the mouth of the V to engage any forces attempting to relieve the trapped unit.[33]

The Chinese tried whenever possible to infiltrate through enemy positions in order to plant a roadblock on the supply line, in hopes of inducing the enemy to retreat to regain contact with the rear. If UN forces stayed in position, the roadblocks were still useful in cutting off escape routes and supply.

In infiltration and assaults against front-line positions, the Chinese moved largely at night to avoid air strikes and reduce aerial observation. In attacks they tried to isolate individual outposts, usually platoons, by striking at the fronts, while at the same time attempting to outflank them. The purpose was to defeat forces in detail by gaining local superiority. If they could not destroy enemy positions, they hoped to induce the opponent to withdraw. When this failed, they got as close as possible to the enemy so that, when daylight came, U.S. aircraft would be unable to bomb them for fear of hitting friendly troops.

Advancing Chinese units generally followed the easiest, most accessible terrain in making their approaches: valleys, draws, or streambeds. As soon as they met resistance, they deployed, peeling off selected small units to engage the opposition. However, if they met no resistance, the whole column often moved in the darkness right past defensive emplacements deep into the rear of enemy positions. There were many examples of this in Korea. In some cases, entire Chinese regiments marched in column formation into the UN rear.

Once fully committed, the Chinese seldom halted their attack, even when suffering heavy casualties. Other Chinese came forward to take the place of those killed or wounded. The buildup continued, often on several sides of the position, until they made a penetration—either by destroying the position or forcing the defenders to withdraw. After consolidating the new conquest, the Chinese then crept forward against the open flank of the next platoon position. This combination of stealth and boldness, usually executed in darkness against small units, could result in several penetrations of a battalion front and could be devastating.

Since the Chinese tried to cut the defending force into small fractions and attack these fractions with local superiority in numbers, they favored the ambush over all other tactical methods. Attacking Chinese forces ranged in size from a platoon to a company (50 to 200 men) and were built up continually as casualties occurred.

The best defense was for the UN force somehow to hold its position until daybreak. With visibility restored, aircraft could attack the Chinese and usually restore the situation. However, Chinese night attacks were so effective that the counsel often went unheeded and defending forces were overrun or destroyed.[34]

By afternoon of 3 November, the only Chinese in the regimental area were dead—or about to be. Litzenberg had his victory over the Chinese—but at a high cost. More than 200 Marine battle casualties were evacuated. O. P. Smith remarked, "Litzenberg went on up the road and had quite a fight. He had 43 killed and a couple hundred wounded, but they absolutely decimated the 124th CCF Division.[35] Then we took it slow. With winter approaching, I was hoping the division wouldn't have to get up on that high plateau and, on that one road, advance beyond Koto-ri."[36]

On the 4th, after a relatively quiet night, the 7th Marines captured Sudong. The next day the regiment continued advancing against increasing resistance and on the 6th, it sustained a heavy counterattack north of the city by infantry supported by artillery and mortar fire. The regiment countered with artillery and air support. Colonel Al Bowser, Division G-3 (operations officer) reported, "A battery of 4 enemy artillery pieces continued firing under air attack until three of four pieces were destroyed." He was later able to inspect the guns and determined that they were 76mm horse-drawn weapons. "The majority of the gun crews had been killed in the gun positions by air while firing."[37]

Chinhung-ni

For the first 43 miles north from Hungnam, the 1st Marine Division's MSR was a two-lane highway passing through relatively flat terrain. At Chinhung-ni the road narrowed to one lane as it went up Funchilin Pass, climbing 2,500 feet in eight miles of zigzagging single-lane road clinging to the sides of the mountain; "a cliff on one side and a chasm on the other," as the official history described it.

"The battalion led the regiment's approach march north to Chinhung-ni," Davis explained. "Just before we went up on the plateau, we approached a little town at the foot of the pass, with a railroad station. There were a lot of tank tracks around. I was concerned and admonished the AOs [Aerial Observers] to get busy and find out where those tanks were, because we were pretty much exposed on the road. It was one of those Korean roads that was built right up along a river bank and into another sharp rise, so you were trapped on that road with jeeps, communication vehicles, and so forth."[38]

The AOs could not find the tanks. "Since they couldn't find them, I sent elements of the Reconnaissance Company [First Lieutenant Ralph B. Crossman] with two or three jeeps up ahead. Suddenly they radioed they were in contact with tanks! Initially they reported one, then quickly, too quickly, four more, hidden in the brush off the road. I personally felt a little 'undressed' facing one enemy tank, never mind four, with my .45 caliber pistol."[39]

Second Lieutenant Donald W. Sharon's recon platoon had unknowingly passed a Soviet medium T-34 tank hidden on the right side of the road. As the platoon moved forward, it spotted a number of Chinese and took them under fire. During the engagement, it spotted a second immobile tank hidden under a pile of brush. Thinking the tank was abandoned, Sharon, Staff Sergeant Richard B. Twohey and Corporal Joseph E. McDermott climbed up on it. Suddenly the periscope began to revolve. Quickly reacting, McDermott smashed the glass, while Twohey dropped a hand grenade inside and the three Marines jumped off just as the grenade exploded.

The tank engine roared and the vehicle lurched toward the three men. Twohey jumped on it again and dropped another grenade down the periscope.[40] After the dull thump of the second explosion, the T-34 stopped dead and began smoking. The tank was quickly given the *coup de grace* by 3.5-inch rocket and 75mm recoilless rifle crews. Simultaneously, a third tank erupted from a thatched hut where it had been hiding. A fast-acting forward air controller, First Lieutenant Dan C. Holland, radioed a section of Corsairs orbiting overhead. One of the gull-winged aircraft swooped down and unleashed a pair of five-inch rockets, which scored a direct hit. The T-34 blew up. Finally, a fourth tank was discovered and taken under fire, forcing the crew to bail out and surrender.

Early in the war, there were stories galore about Army troops running away whenever enemy tanks appeared, but not among the Marines. Davis almost got trampled by excited Marines. "Not only did the reconnaissance Marines call in air, but rocket-launcher Marines from my battalion and from the battalions behind me came roaring up, shouting, 'Where are the tanks!'"[41]

Lieutenant Holland explained, "Before we started our movement north, I requested air coverage for our column. I received four Corsairs, fully armed—500-pound bombs, one napalm, eight 5-inch rockets and a full load of 20mm cannon ammunition—awaiting my call. When we spotted the tanks, I immediately called them in on the target, 50 yards from our troops."[42]

During all this excitement, Davis raced forward with his driver, "alarmed that the tanks might shoot up my Charlie Company which was in an exposed position on the railroad just across the small river. I had 'armed' my jeep with two land mines. At a very narrow spot in the road over a culvert I posted my Marine runner with a land mine and gave him instructions to arm it and place it where the tank's track would hit—if one came down the road." Davis went forward to look at the battle site and then returned to advise his runner of the best escape route. The youngster looked a little unnerved and responded in a quivering voice, "My God, colonel, I thought you wanted me to hold the mine under the track!" Davis was taken aback. "The poor kid thought he was supposed to perform some sort of Kamikaze mission and get blown up with the tank." So many wanted credit for knocking out the tanks that Davis had to arbitrate before blood was spilled—between Marines. "I assigned and reported the kills: one to air, one to recon, one each to the two rocket teams. I also messaged regiment that I did not like to go hand-to-hand with tanks and asked, 'Where are our tanks?'" He was told they had been blocked by weak bridges.[43]

After this incident the Chinese vanished. "This was typical of the Chinese. Once they got hurt, they moved back," Davis explained. By the 8th, the 7th Marines were in the vicinity of Pohujang, a 3,000-yard advance representing an increase in altitude of approximately 1,000 feet. Marine units were approaching the divide and on the 10th, the regiment seized Koto-ri on top of the escarpment. Throughout the advance to Koto-ri, the regiment was continuously supported by close air support, including night intruder aircraft, and heavy artillery concentrations.[44]

CHAPTER 25

Attack of General Winter

On 10 November, the Marine Corps' birthday, Davis took a much-needed bath in a stream at the base of the Chosin Reservoir plateau, although he did say, "It was a trifle cold for a guy from Atlanta." Two nights later the temperature stood at 16 degrees below zero. "On our second or third day up on the plateau at Koto-ri, the Siberian winds struck, lowering the temperatures," Davis explained. "Vehicles died, everything froze, troops were frostbitten. It took two days to recover [with added clothing, heaters, warming tents, anti-freeze] before we were prepared to move north again." Lieutenant Holland said, "We had 30 to 35 knot winds blowing in our faces and sub-zero temperatures."[1]

The arctic weather struck so suddenly that it sent men into shock, and they had to be led, zombielike, to shelter. "It was bad," Davis commented. "My staff and I moved around among the troops, looking for characteristic candle-white splotches that signaled frostbite; and when we spotted it coming on, we would hustle the man to the nearest fire."[2]

Corporal Roy Pearl, Davis' radio operator, recalled, "I grew up in Minnesota, so I was used to temperatures like that, but the thing that shocked me was the suddenness of it. I saw several guys, some of them from the south, in tears. We dragged over some boards from a bombed-out house and, with the help of a splash of gasoline, got a fire going. Our C rations turned out frozen solid. It wasn't easy to heat them up, even over a roaring fire like that, because of the wind."[3]

The doctors reported numerous cases where men were admitted to the sickbay suffering from what appeared to be shock, which they diagnosed as simply the sudden shock of the terrific cold when they were not ready for it. The men recovered quickly after a shot of medicinal brandy and a chance to get warm by a fire.

Equipment died, particularly the battery-operated radios. Vehicles wouldn't start. Engines wouldn't turn over. Everything was dead. The drivers soon learned to run them all night long. A little too much oil or grease on a weapon caused malfunctions; carbines, machine guns and BARs (Browning Automatic Rifles) were particularly susceptible. Artillery recoil mechanisms froze, and the cannoneers had to push the tubes back in battery by hand.

However, the men quickly adapted; they found that hair tonic, which had alcohol in it, proved to be a fairly effective lubricant. Gasoline, purloined from an unattended vehicle, could be poured over dirt or gravel, producing a skimpy but adequate flame. Unused mortar propellant charges would produce a quick starter flame. A canteen with a couple of small bottles of sickbay alcohol would keep it from freezing. Corpsmen carried morphine capsules in their mouths to keep them from freezing.

The Division was hit hard by frostbite. Cold-weather clothing arrived just in time: heavy, knee-length, pile-lined, hooded parkas; wool caps; winter-weight, cold-weather trousers; flannel shirts; long johns; and heavy wool socks. To protect their hands, they had wool gloves and leather and canvas mittens with an ingenious "trigger" finger sewed into them. The new clothing was welcome, but it was not designed for humping the hills. After a few minutes the men were sweating and overheated, forcing them to strip off a layer or two.[4] The newly issued shoepacks caused feet to sweat, but wouldn't allow air to circulate. When the men stopped moving, the sweat-soaked felt inserts of the shoepacks would freeze, causing frostbite. They were also heavy and, despite their cleated soles, clumsy for climbing and slippery on ice. The parka hoods kept ears from freezing, but cut down on peripheral vision and made it difficult to hear.

CHAPTER 26

Out on a Limb

On 15 November, Almond ordered the 1st Marine Division to attack north to Yudam-ni, then west to assist the Eighth Army in its drive to the Yalu. He envisioned that the Army's 7th Infantry Division would cover the Division's right flank. Almond was slow to recognize the scale of the Chinese offensive, urging Army and Marine units forward despite the huge Chinese forces arrayed against them. Displaying his usual boldness, he underestimated the strength and skill of the Chinese forces, at one point telling his subordinate officers, "The enemy who is delaying you for the moment is nothing more than remnants of Chinese divisions fleeing north. We're still attacking and we're going all the way to the Yalu. Don't let a bunch of Chinese laundrymen stop you." As stated by a close associate: "When it paid to be aggressive, Ned was aggressive. When it paid to be cautious, Ned was aggressive."[1]

On that day, the 1st Marine Division was spread out from hell to breakfast. Litzenberg's 7th Marines had just reached the medium-sized town of Hagaru-ri, an insignificant village at the base of the Chosin Resevoir;[2] Murray's 5th Marines were spread along the MSR from Koto-ri to Majon-dong, where Puller's 1st Marines were encamped. It was 20 miles as the crow flies. Yudam-ni was another 14 miles north of Hagaru-ri, along a mountain road which wound its way up to the 4,000-foot Toktong Pass.

"The division and regiment were concerned over the vulnerability of the MSR to both the enemy and the weather," Smith noted. "What I was trying to do was to slow down the advance and stall until I could pull up the 1st Marines behind us and get our outfit together. The advance was kept at a slow pace in order to build up supplies and give the division an opportunity to move additional troops behind RCT-7 [7th Marines]. I told Litzenberg not to go too fast. He didn't want to go over the pass and down to Yudam-ni because we had this tremendous open flank. But the pressure was being put on me to get going. Finally, I had to tell Litzenberg to go on over and occupy Yudam-ni."[3]

General Smith ordered the Division engineer battalion to construct an airfield that could handle C-54 and C-119 aircraft at Hagaru-ri. The airstrip was completed

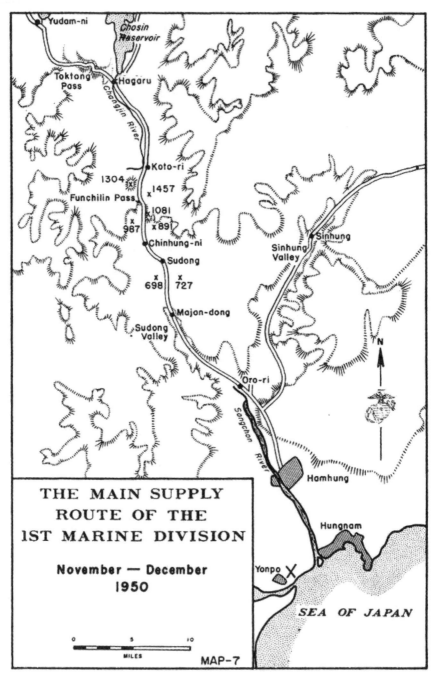

The 1st Marine Division's advance and withdrawal along a narrow mountain road in the dead of a North Korean winter was a tribute to the courage and discipline of the individual Marine. (U.S. Marine Corps, *U.S. Marine Operations in Korea: 1950–1953*)

in 11 days but at the time it was put into operation, it was only 40% complete, according to the estimates of the Division engineer. The space allowed only two planes to land that day, but the evacuation was begun, with the clearing of 60 wounded. The strip was truly a life saver.

Hagaru-ri

Davis' battalion led the 5th and 7th Marines toward Hagaru-ri along a narrow, winding road that left the men exposed to attack. "There was nowhere to go," Davis pointed out. "You were up against a bank, solid wall on one side and a sheer precipice on the other side … There was no such thing as a flank. What you would do would be to have a unit over on the far side of the valley, on the ridge, and somebody up on the ridges on this side. You just kind of screened your way along." Litzenberg said, "The day we marched to Hagaru-ri was an extremely cold and windy day and we had to walk into the face of the wind. It was a very, very uncomfortable day …."[4]

When the 7th Marines reached Hagaru-ri, at the southern tip of the Chosin Reservoir, Litzenberg established a defense perimeter around the town, with Davis' battalion holding the northwest sector and dispatching reinforced company-sized patrols three to five miles out, well within artillery support range. "We spent most of our time patrolling, trying to make contact," Davis said. "We covered dangerous areas with artillery fire mixed in with a lot of air support. We were fortunate to have four Marine aircraft on station from dawn to dusk. Several times the patrols made contact with the enemy. Normally the Chinese would open fire at long range and withdraw before the patrols could close on them. However, twice they stayed to fight which turned into an all-day action before both sides withdraw at dusk."[5]

Davis received orders to march toward Yudam-ni on the 24th (they had their Thanksgiving Day meal one day later). "I sent B Company to the pass area [Toktong Pass], about 9,000 yards 'airline' from Hagaru-ri, which in that country meant about eight miles by road over heavy grades." Company B moved out at 0900 to occupy a screening position. Approximately 500 yards from the objective the company came under enemy small arms and machine-gun fire from an estimated 150–200 enemy soldiers. Air strikes and artillery missions were called on the enemy position, driving them off. Company B occupied the high ground for the night.[6]

The battalion was ordered to establish defensive positions at Sinhung-ni and conduct aggressive patrolling to the north and west, paying particular attention to approaches to Yudam-ni from the west. "Patrols operating in advance and to the flanks of the battalion did not make contacts early in the advance, but later in the morning, one flank patrol received small arms fire from an estimated enemy platoon. Air and artillery fire drove the enemy back."[7]

Turkey Hill

Thanksgiving Day caught 1/7 on the road south of Yudam-ni. "My troops felt a little down on that last Thursday in November," Davis recalled. "We moved through Toktong Pass, which would later be very important in our combat lives, without incident, and seized the high ground south of the town of Yudam-ni." Davis talked Litzenberg into letting the battalion have a day off for the Thanksgiving meal. "I knew the men needed a lift." A very gracious Litzenberg told Davis he could hold in place for a whole 24 hours—and "by the way, I'll send up the fixings for T-day."[8]

"When the turkeys caught up to us, there were stacks of them," Davis recalled, "but unfortunately they were frozen hard as could be." The troops were overjoyed but Davis just scratched his head. "I just could not see how the cooks could pull it off, when it was so cold by now."[9]

Winds coming from Siberia had lowered the temperature to minus 18-degrees Fahrenheit. However, the troops needed the morale boost—and where there is a will, there is a way. Davis had a pow-wow with his mess crew. "We designed an innovative solution: two tents were erected one over the other for a double thickness; two stoves were fixed up inside and the frozen turkey were stacked around the stoves in the sealed tents." After several hours, they were ready and the troops were rotated, platoon by platoon, through the chow line, which was set up in a deep gulley, just south of "Turkey Hill" (Hill 1419), which earned the moniker from all the turkey bones scattered around.[10]

There was enough turkey that even some of the nearby units were able to enjoy the feast. Davis learned that a platoon on an outpost had been overlooked. "I felt totally ashamed, but we were able to find some turkey and a lot of shrimp to boil for them." Despite the circumstances, Davis looked back at the meal with something akin to fondness. "This was to be our last hot meal for the next ten days, though we didn't know it at the time."[11]

Crisis at Yudam-ni

The 1st Marine Division Operation Order 23-50 ordered Litzenberg's 7th Marines to seize and occupy Yudam-ni. "I was told to occupy a blocking position at Yudam-ni with the 7th Marines after Thanksgiving, and to have the 5th Marines go up the east side of the Chosin Reservoir until it hit the Yalu," O. P. Smith said. "I told Litzenberg not to go too fast. He didn't want to go over the Toktong Pass and into Yudam-ni because of that tremendous open flank in the west. But the pressure was put on me to get going. I finally had to tell Litzenberg to occupy Yudam-ni. General MacArthur devised a plan that rushed some troops from the 31st and 32nd Infantry Regiments [7th Division] east of the reservoir to relieve the 5th Marines."[12]

Smith wrote to the commandant that he was appalled at the plan to reach the Yalu without flank safeguards in the face of Chinese resistance. "We would simply get further out on a limb ... I believe a winter campaign in the mountains of North Korea is too much to ask of the American soldier or Marine, and I doubt the feasibility of supplying troops in this area during the winter or providing for the evacuation of sick and wounded."[13]

Davis' battalion took the lead, marching along the desolate road, past a dozen booby-trapped, unmanned roadblocks. Most of them were hastily constructed, about 3-feet high, formed from rocks, and brush. Resistance was light, only the occasional squad of enemy soldiers, who were easily brushed aside. The 1st Battalion reached its objective on the 25th and took up positions about two miles south on the high ground overlooking the forlorn hamlet of Yudam-ni.

The Chinese offered a token resistance—small arms, machine guns and a few mortar rounds. It was reported to be from a battalion of the CCF's 89th Division. After an air strike on the crest of the hill, resistance crumbled and the enemy soldiers melted away. However, civilian refugees insisted that a new CCF army was in the area. In fact, it was three fresh Chinese armies—the elite 20th, 26th and 27th,—some of the best troops China fielded during the Korean War. A Chinese division averaged 10,000 men, but there were rarely enough weapons to equip everyone. Normally one third of the men were unarmed and they waited to pick up captured weapons or from their own casualties during an attack.

The Division learned from two prisoners that the 89th Division, part of the 20th CCF Army, had crossed the Yalu River on 13 November, and had marched day and night to reach the Chosin Reservoir. Further, their mission was to attack the MSR after the two friendly regiments had passed.

Major Thomas Tighe, Davis' operations officer, thought one of the huts looked occupied. He had an interpreter order everyone out under threat that the hut was going to be burned down. Three Chinese soldiers timidly emerged with their hands over their heads. Under interrogation, the three freely admitted to being riflemen in the 60th Chinese Division. They also volunteered that two other divisions were in the area. The information was passed up the line. Lieutenant Colonel Frederick Dowsett, 7th Marines executive officer, doubted that ordinary private soldiers could be privy to such high-level information. He didn't put much faith in what they said. Despite Dowsett's seeming lack of concern, the Division was worried about the Chinese cutting its relatively long and exposed MSR.

Early on the 26th, O. P. Smith dropped in to talk with Litzenberg—and drop he did, literally. His helicopter tried to hover in the thin mountain air; instead it dropped like a stone for the last 15 feet. Davis saw the "crash" and ran over. Smith emerged, nodded, and asked courteously where the regimental CP was. "Right over there, general." Davis pointed and asked, "Are you all right?" "Fine," Smith nonchalantly replied, and strode off.[14]

Smith and Litzenberg discussed the current situation, which both officers thought was deteriorating. During the meeting, Smith told Litzenberg "to use as much of his regiment as he could to try to clear the road back to Hagaru-ri."[15]

Late in the afternoon, the vanguard of the 7th Marines reached Yudam-ni, which it found deserted except for a few civilians and enemy dead. Two companies of 2/7, D and E, also arrived and were immediately attached to 1/7, giving Davis five companies. The arrival of two battalions the next day brought Marine strength to five infantry and three artillery battalions—a little more than 8,000 men and 48 artillery pieces.

A North Korean civilian disclosed that he had been forced to act as a guide for "endless numbers of enemy troops," supported by horse-drawn artillery. Another report indicated that in the past two or three days, there had been at least ten enemy patrols seeking information about the MSR. Several prisoners stated that the missions of their units were to attack the MSR after two Marine units had passed their east flank. The attack was to take place at night, to avoid detection by air elements. Concealed in the mountains around the Marine positions were 80,000 to 90,000 Chinese infantrymen. First Lieutenant Joseph R. Owen commented, "Yudam-ni, that's where the shit hit the fan."[16]

Before dawn on the 27th, Davis sent a patrol from Company B to search the hills to the south and southwest of Yudam-ni. The other two companies were held in reserve. The men of Company B were glad to be moving, after suffering through an impossibly cold night. Around midnight temperatures bottomed out at -25 degrees. Marines on the perimeter rotated through warming tents, which gave them an opportunity to thaw out and get something hot to drink, but it was still damn cold. One officer commented, "It was a clear, starlit night, like a Christmas-card scene with the mountains and the evergreens and the snow. But the wind was a killer."

By early afternoon, the weary Company B patrol was climbing one of the many ridges in the area. The point spotted enemy soldiers on the ridgeline ahead. As they continued to climb, other groups appeared. Suddenly, heavy firing broke out from all directions, and Marines began to fall. Air support was called in. "Our Forward Air Control officers had been pilots with the squadrons that were flying support," Davis recalled. "One time when the situation was tense, I overheard a casual conversation between my FAC and a flight leader. 'See you tomorrow morning, buddy.' Danny Holland, my Forward Air controller yelled, 'Damn you! You stick around up there till I let you go, Pardner (everyone was Pardner to Danny), or I'll tell your wife what a no-good bastard you really are!' Needless to say, those four aircraft remained on station until Danny expended their loads and then told them to go home to rearm and return."[17]

Davis learned of the ambush over the radio net. "Captain Wilcox, commander of Baker Company ... was shot in the mouth while talking to me on the radio! I ordered the patrol to break contact." Litzenberg gave him permission to lead Captain

John F. Morris' Company C to the rescue. The patrol was able to break contact under cover of darkness and reach the road just as the relief force arrived.[18]

Davis "fired mortar illumination rounds to mark the way ... and used truck lights to guide them into our position." The wounded were loaded into empty trucks and sent to Hagaru-ri for treatment. "The men were silent, spent from the cold and brutal day. Captain Wilcox had been a good skipper," Lt Owen said. It was the last convoy to get through before the Chinese cut the road. Litzenberg ordered Davis to leave Company C on Turkey Hill, about 4,000 yards south of Yudam-ni to protect the MSR.[19]

Meanwhile, Companies D and E in the hills above Yudam-ni were fighting for their lives. Captain Walter Phillips' Company E reported that it was barely holding on. "We've taken too many casualties. We're holding, but we can sure use some help." Davis recalled, "They came under heavy attack by waves of Chinese. Their situation turned desperate soon after dark. Communications were difficult; I was not fully aware of their situation or precise deployment." Roy Pearl remembered, "It looked like the enemy was breaking through the two hills to the north, and the battalion command post was in danger. Colonel Davis ordered [everyone] into a makeshift defense line around the headquarters tents."[20]

Davis stayed in the tent, ignoring the danger. Pearl stayed with him. "He [Davis] was very busy assessing the overall situation as reports came in by radio, phone, and runner. The only time he raised his voice in all the weeks I served with him was when Captain Hull reported by radio that Dog Company was no longer on the hill. The colonel's voice got loud: he told Captain [Milton A.] Hull to get his people together and retake that hill and stay there!"[21]

Davis recalled, "I don't hesitate to say I was tormented for hours by the situation: Easy Company barely holding onto [Hill] 1282, Dog Company driven off 1240, and, later on, the mess with Fox and Charlie Companies got into. Only one of my companies—Baker—was in anything other than an emergency situation." Captain Hull gathered the remnants of his company. "Okay, let's go get the bastards." At dawn reinforcements arrived to find 16 survivors on top of the hill. One of them asked a wounded rifleman where the company was. "This here's it," he croakily replied. "This here's Dog Company, 7th Marines."[22]

Roy Pearl monitored a radio in the backseat of a jeep with Davis at the wheel. "I kept picking up this faint transmission ... I thought I could hear gunfire in the background and someone shouting." He asked Davis to stop the jeep and turn off the motor. "I finally determined that the signal was from the Company C radio operator. He said Company C was surrounded and needed help." Davis learned that, "With darkness came many, many Chinese Communist soldiers. Apparently our troops climbing from the main supply route up onto Turkey Hill in the darkness met Chinese coming down the hill." Pearl handed Davis the handset. "I could hear the relief in the man's voice when he realized he was talking to his battalion

commander," Davis recalled. "I don't recall exactly how the conversation went …
but I got across the basic message: Hang on! We're on the way."[23]

"It didn't take us long to get saddled up. I told the two company commanders,
[First Lieutenant Eugenous] Hovatter and [First Lieutenant Joe] Kurcaba, that we
were going to strike off down the road very fast and see how far we could get before
moving into the hills. About two miles later I sent Able Company up the slope,
keeping Baker down below. Lieutenant Hovatter soon radioed that he had found a
path by which Able Company could outflank the enemy." Tom Tighe worried about
the way Davis exposed himself. "From the ditch beside the road I suggested that
the colonel take cover. Davis smiled and explained that he could better coordinate
the tactical moves from the road, where he could see the situation as it unfolded. It
may have been foolhardy of him, but the men of 1/7 were glad to have the battalion
commander up front like that, sharing the danger and risk." The coordinated attack
worked, and the enemy was caught in a crossfire. Pearl saw "the Chinese break up
into small bands, running every which way."[24]

Small arms fire peppered the road around Davis. "A jeep driver ran up to me and
said, 'Colonel, won't you at least get down behind the jeep?' It was bothering him so
much that I decided to do as he requested, and I continued my radio conversation
crouched next to one of the rear wheels." Captain Holland coordinated air strikes.
"From early in the morning until dark I ran repeated air strikes. The last strike was
run after the sun had gone down and the pilots could hardly see the terrain. It was
so dark that I was even afraid for the pilots."[25]

Company C was finally extracted and the force pulled back to Yudam-ni. Davis
was dejected. "I've always thought a better job could have been done supporting
those Marines out there."[26]

While Davis struggled to hold the vital hill positions, the Chinese hurled its
infantry against the Marine positions on the high ground, threatening to engulf
the entire perimeter. "One of my companies on top of a hill saw three waves of
Chinese coming through the snow at them. The first wave had rifles, the second
wave had hand grenades and the third wave didn't have anything. They would pick
up weapons from the first two waves."[27]

The battlefield echoed with the sounds of whistles, bugles, and weird oriental
chants as the enemy advanced. The Marines had their backs to the wall; the Chinese
were determined to chop them up. A political commissar wrote, "Kill these Marines
as you would snakes in your homes!" The two regiments held, but the furious
two-day defense cost them more than 1,200 casualties. Davis said, "The artillery
worked over the ridges around us, and I think this had a great deal to do with
keeping the CCF down."[28]

Smith sent report after report to the Corps commander about the massive Chinese
force they were up against. "Every four hours we sent in a report of what was going
on, but apparently they [Corps] were stunned; they just couldn't make up their

minds that the Chinese had attacked in force, you see. They just had to re-orient their thinking. It took them two days before we actually were told to withdraw to Hagaru-ri and advance to the coast."[29]

On 30 November, X Corps finally issued Operation Order No. 8, directing the 1st Marine Division to withdraw to Hagaru-ri. The Division knew that withdrawing the 5th and 7th Marines would be formidable task. "The only feasible thing to do was to pool their resources," O. P. Smith stated. "The two regimental commanders drew up a joint plan … which was flown to me by helicopter and which I approved." The 7th Marines were to lead out from Yudam-ni to Hagaru-ri, while the 5th Marines covered the rear.[30] Normally, Brigadier General Edward A. Craig, the assistant Division commander, would have coordinated the withdrawal of the two regiments but he was on emergency leave due to the death of his father.

Colonel Al Bowser, Division operations officer, told his assistant to start planning. "My God," he exclaimed. "It never occurred to me that the Marine Corps would be involved in a retro-grade movement."[31] As the plan evolved, someone brought up the word "retreat". Smith responded, "Well, really, in the tactical situation in which we find ourselves, having to fight forward … this is really not a retreat, because in every case we must attack." At a news conference the next day, a reporter asked, "What do you think of this, because the Marine Corps is retreating?" Smith bristled and replied, "Retreat, hell, we are simply attacking in another direction."[32]

On the 30th, Almond flew in to talk with Smith. "I received an order to displace a regiment to return to Hagaru-ri and rescue the Army outfits east of the Reservoir. My God, at that time we were ourselves being attacked by three or more enemy divisions." Almond also authorized the destruction of the Division's equipment and supplies. Smith replied, "I would have to fight my way back and could not afford to discard equipment … I intended to bring out the bulk of my equipment." The vehicle train—trucks, jeeps, and artillery prime movers—moved within this defensive bubble, with the wounded, extra ammunition, and supplies. The road back led through a mountain pass that was being held open by one valiant Marine company.[33]

CHAPTER 27

Toktong Ridge Runners

As the regiment fought its way north, Captain William E. Barber's Company F, 2nd Battalion, 7th Marines was dropped off in the center of the Toktong pass to guard the MSR. He selected a hill near the village of Shinhung-ni as the most defensible place for the company. Reinforced with heavy machine guns and an 81mm mortar section, the company numbered 220 officers and men. At 0430 on the 27th, the 3rd Platoon was hit by an estimated company of Chinese infantrymen who overran the position, killing or wounding 24 of the 35 Marines; three others were missing. The fighting quickly spread until the entire perimeter was under attack. At daybreak the Chinese broke off the attack, leaving more than 450 dead on the battlefield. Hundreds of grotesque shapes covered the ground, many of them within feet of the Marine positions. The battered Company F survivors crawled through the cordite-stained snow into the killing zone to retrieve frozen Chinese bodies, stacking them in gruesome layers like sandbags around their foxholes.

Isolated and surrounded by overwhelming force, Company F began a heroic five-day ordeal by fire. Their plight was not forgotten; four attempts were made to reach them by road, but each failed under withering Chinese fire from the ridges. The company was in desperate shape, with little, if any, food, and heavy casualties. One more attempt had to be made.

The Plan

On the evening of the 29th, Colonel Litzenberg called Davis and told him to meet him at his command post, a small tent located at the southern edge of the village. "Litz sent for me," Davis recalled, "and told me about the desperate situation. 'Ray, we're in serious trouble, we've got to get the pass open and that company rescued. On 1 December we will probably execute a plan to advance from the valley south of Yudam-ni to Hagaru-ri, where we expect to join the 1st Marine Regiment.'"[1]

Further, he explained that Davis should start planning to take his battalion and move from the valley south of Yudam-ni, across the trackless mountains, to secure the 5,000-foot pass between Yudam-ni and Hagaru-ri. The pass was a key terrain

Davis' 1933 high school graduation photograph.

Second Lieutenant Davis, The Basic School, Philadelphia, 1938.

Davis as a member of the Reserve Officers Training Corps, Georgia School of Technology, in 1937.

Davis' Special Weapons battery was assigned to protect Henderson Field, Guadalcanal, as seen from a USS *Saratoga* aircraft in August 1942. (National Archives 80-G-16312)

Davis was heading ashore when these Japanese Navy Type 1 land-based attack planes (later nicknamed "Betty") began an attack on the amphibious ships off Guadalcanal, D-day, 7 August 1942. (National Archives 80-G-17066)

A water-cooled .50-caliber antiaircraft machine gun in position near the runway on Guadalcanal. Davis' Battery A was equipped with these heavy machine guns. (USMC photo 50850)

Davis' battery was equipped with the Swedish-designed 40mm antiaircraft guns positioned near Henderson Field, Guadalcanal. (USMC photo 51761)

A view of "The Pagoda" that served as flight operations headquarters for the U.S. Marine Corps and U.S. Navy fliers at Henderson Field, Guadalcanal, from August to October 1942. During July 1942, this building was built by the Japanese on a small rise to the north of the runway. The flagpole, visible on the left side of the roof, was used to indicate incoming air raids. In early October, its radio equipment was moved into the newly dug radio tunnel. After the Japanese battleship bombardment on 13–14 October 1942, General Geiger concluded that the roof was reflecting the flares and it was being used as a registration point, so ordered it to be bulldozed over the side of the hill. (USMC photo 50921)

Cape Gloucester invasion, December 1943. Marines boarding USS *LCI-340* on the day before Christmas, 1943. The day after Christmas, they landed at Cape Gloucester on New Britain Island. Photographed at Oro Bay, New Guinea. Note the M-1 Garand rifles carried by most men, and telescope-equipped M1903 "Springfield" rifle at left. (National Archives USMC 72064)

Marines and Coast Guardsmen landing on Cape Gloucester, circa 26 December 1943. An LVT (1) leads the way as some men carry stretchers and others push a jeep toward the beach. (National Archives 26-G-3046)

Retreating at first into the jungle of Cape Gloucester, Japanese soldiers finally gathered strength and counterattacked their Marine pursuers. These machine gunners pushed them back. (National Archives 127-N-71981)

A relaxed Major Davis on Cape Gloucester. (USMC photo)

Battle of Cape Gloucester, New Britain, December 1943–January 1944. *LST-18* and *LST-463* standing by to embark troops. Photographed by USS *Nashville* (CL-43), 24–26 December, 1943. (National Archives 80-G-57464)

Climbing down cargo nets from the assault transports into landing craft on D-day, 15 September 1944. (USMC photo)

As supporting naval and air units pave the way with high explosives, Marine-laden assault craft from the first wave move in for the attack on Peleliu. The Leathernecks hacked out a mile-and-a-half-long beachhead after bitter fighting. (USMC photo 94875 by Sgt. William A. McBride)

Assault elements moving off the beach under fire and pinned down. While running across the beach, Davis was wounded in the leg. (USMC photo 95256 by PFC John Smith)

Marines of the 1st Division pinned down by heavy enemy mortar fire remain near their equipment as they hit "Orange Beach 3" on Peleliu Island, in the Palau group of the Caroline Islands. Amtracs, hit while carrying the green-clad Leathernecks ashore, burn in the background. (USMC photo 94937 by Pvt. Robert Bailey)

A photograph of Ray and Knox Davis at their wedding. (Davis family photo)

APA-53 underway in San Francisco Bay, California, circa late 1945. The decks are crowded with homecoming servicemen. (Courtesy of Donald M. McPherson, 1973, U.S. Naval History and Heritage Command Photograph)

The Davis family after World War II.

The Davis family at home in the 1950s: Willa Kay, Gilbert, Raymond, Knox and Miles. (Davis family photograph)

Lieutenant Colonel Davis with his Medal of Honor. (USMC photo taken in 1959)

South of Koto-ri, 10 December 1950. A blown bridge at the site of a concrete power plant. Marine engineers had to install a temporary bridge to enable the 1st Division to escape the Chinese trap. (USMC photo by Sgt. W. R. Keating)

Lieutenant Colonel Davis in Korea. (USMC photo)

Marines of the 1st Marine Division prepare to move out along a snow-covered road during the Chosin Reservoir campaign. (USMC photo)

Hagaru-ri, 18 November 1950, Colonel Homer Litzenberg presenting awards for valor to Marines of the 7th Regiment. From left: LtCol Ray Davis, Corporal Earle R. Deifert, Staff Sergeant Earle E. Payne, Colonel Homer Litzenberg. (USMC photo, Corporal L. B. Snyder)

Koto-ri, 9 December 1950. Marines of the 1st Marine Division "advancing in the opposite direction," through the snow-covered hills of North Korea. (USMC photo by Sgt. F. C. Kerr)

President Harry S. Truman awarding the Medal of Honor at a White House ceremony to Lieutenant Colonel Raymond G. Davis for heroism "above and beyond the call of duty" for actions during the Chosin Reservoir Campaign. (USMC photo)

Major General Davis in Vietnam. (USMC photo)

Change of command, 3rd Marine Division in 1968. Davis on the left and Major General Rathvon Tompkins on the right.

Lieutenant General William B. Rossen, Commanding General, PVC, making remarks at the change of command ceremony whereby Major General Raymond G. Davis (on the left) assumed command of the 3rd Marine Division from Major General Rathvon M. Tompkins (on the right). (USMC photo)

Major General Davis, Commanding General 3rd Marine Division, visiting one of his battalion commanders in the field. (USMC photo)

Major General Davis with Major General Simpson (center) on a visit to Brigadier General F. E. Garretson at Task Force Hotel, near Khe Sanh, Vietnam. (USMC photo)

Medal of Honor recipients, Major General Raymond G. Davis and Lieutenant Colonel Archie Van Winkle during a field visit near Khe Sanh, Vietnam. (USMC photo)

Major General Raymond G. Davis and Colonel Robert H. Barrow, Commanding Officer 9th Marines, promoting Davis' son, Miles, to first lieutenant. (USMC photo)

Captain Thomas F. Hinkle (Wilmington, Delaware) (upper left) points out a spiked gun barrel to fellow Leathernecks from the 9th Marine Regiment. The Russian-made 122mm howitzers were destroyed by the enemy, as the Marines advanced on them. Leathernecks captured several of the big guns as the enemy retreated during Operation *Dewey Canyon*. (USMC photo A193689 by SSgt Bob Jordan)

Major General Davis pulls the lanyard firing the 175mm gun at North Vietnamese positions. (USMC photo)

Davis presenting the Purple Heart to his son, Miles, for wounds received while serving as a platoon commander in the 9th Marines. (USMC photo)

The Davis family with the Commandant of the Marine Corps, General Leonard F. Chapman. (USMC photo)

General Davis being promoted at Headquarters Marine Corps by General Leonard Chapman, Commandant, and Knox. (USMC photo)

Retirement ceremony at the Marine Barracks, 8th and I St. Washington, D.C., March 30, 1972. General Davis, a Medal of Honor recipient and veteran of nearly 34 years of Marine Corps service. (USMC photo A702500).

Davis with Vice President Cheney at the White House.

General Davis and Knox after retirement.
(Davis family photo)

Knox christening the USS *Chosin*, while the family look on, 14 October 1989.

General Davis wearing the Medal of Honor at a Georgia veteran function after retirement. (Davis family photo)

Davis with his daughter, Willa, at her wedding.

General Davis and his wife Knox at the ceremony commemorating the 50th anniversary of the Korean War in 2000. (U.S. Navy photo by PH1 Tina M. Ackerman)

Lieutenant General James Mattis, Commanding General, Marine Corps Combat Development Command, and Knox cut the ribbon during the General Raymond G. Davis Center dedication ceremony, 10 September 2005. (USMC photo by Cpl. Sara A. Carter)

feature and if the two regiments were to get to Hagaru-ri, the Marines had got to control the pass in order to get the vehicles and wounded out over the road.

Litzenberg explained, "Our situation at Yudam-ni was not a pleasant one. We were in a valley with five Chinese divisions around us. There were 8,000 of us and perhaps 50,000 Chinese—a conservative estimate—with another Chinese division somewhere in the offing. We knew the Chinese had the only road available to us well blocked ... we had to take the Chinese by surprise and throw them off balance. The pass was the key to the situation. Without that in our possession, we didn't feel we could fight our way up the road. This was one of the most difficult operations, I guess, Marines have ever been called upon to perform."[2]

Litzenberg gave Davis a secondary objective, the relief of Company F. Davis said that Litzenberg was very concerned about Company F, which had been under attack for 48 hours about a mile west of the pass. "Nothing works," Litz said, referring to four prior efforts to get them out using the road. Each time the Chinese were able to stop the relief force. "You have got to get to them," Litzenberg emphasized. "Come back here in twenty minutes with a plan!"[3]

Major M. E. Roach commanded a provisional battalion occupying a position immediately adjacent to 1/7's command post. He said he had, "a close personal relationship between LtCol Davis and myself during the planning phase of the breakout. Jointly LtCol Davis and I studied aerial photographs and maps and discussed our plans ... from my study of the impending operation I knew that it would require super-human effort to push it to a successful conclusion."[4]

"I had been over the road. It was just a little narrow 12-foot road chiseled out of a 300-foot cliff of rock and I knew that a road approach was hopeless," Davis explained. "Instead, I planned a bold, night cross-country march over the ridges to the high ground overlooking Fox Company's position. In effect, my troops were going to move 7,000 yards, as the crow flies, before we could get the job done. In actual distance I would say we would have to walk twice as far if we counted the steps in moving around the ridges, not including the extra strain on account of the grades."[5]

"The Chinese didn't have artillery or air so we were able to hold them off and fight our way out. We had two regiments on one side of the mountain and the rest of the division on the other side and we had to get them back together. I had 800 Marines out in that condition and didn't have a single complaint or one beef, because they were going to rescue fellow Marines ... one for all, all for one, really stuck with me."[6]

Stripping for Action

Davis, together with his executive officer, Major Raymond V. Fridrich, and the operations officer, Major Thomas B. Tighe, worked up a plan. "My first problem was to get the battalion furnished so that it could sustain itself for two or three days in the hills. We streamlined the battalion," Davis explained, "leaving all vehicles, all wounded, and disabled, six of my heavy (81mm) mortars, and heavy machine guns, all supplies and equipment not carried by the troops. Riflemen carried a full belt and two bandoleers of ammunition. We were loaded down with grenades, but I do not remember how many each man carried. Gun crews were doubled up; ammunition was strapped to litters; men carried a spare mortar round in their big parka pockets; some carried extra belts of machine-gun bullets. We carried one hand-crank ANGRC-9 radio, because our battery-powered sets were dead, with rare exceptions." The artillery liaison party carried a pack set SCR-610 for calling in artillery support. The forward air controller carried extra portable radios while the battalion air liaison officer remained behind on the road with a jeep-mounted radio to guide strike aircraft to the FAC. Planning complete, "I went back to Litzenberg and briefed him on my plan. I told him that I'm going to streamline my force and fight our way to the north and go around through the mountains and get the job done."[7]

Lieutenant Colonel Fox Parry, commanding officer, 3rd Battalion, 11th Marines, happened to be in Litzenberg's small CP tent when Davis presented his plan. "The regimental commander was sitting on his cot, the battalion commander on the ground, holding a map. My principal recollection of this meeting is of Ray's cool determination and his matter-of-factness. Ray was as self-possessed as if he were about to set out on an evening stroll. Neither man raised his voice nor did a hint of passion insinuate itself into the tiny command tent. They were two men going about their business."[8]

Parry said that, "Litzenberg was taking a terrific gamble. He was sending Davis off into the frigid gloom away from the main body ... the chances of a mishap were everywhere. Davis' map was primitive. Maintaining companies in close contact and headed toward the objective through snow, ice, darkness, and treacherous mountain slopes would require a heroic effort. If he got in trouble, he was on his own. With an everyday farewell and a shyly confident smile, Ray got up and headed quietly down the hill ...." Davis recalled that Litzenberg, with characteristic bluntness, growled, "Plan approved, get going!"[9]

Davis called his company commanders together for a briefing. He took a stick and drew up the plan of attack in the snow. "Surprise will be our essential weapon," he said. "Marines don't ordinarily attack at night so the Chinese won't be expecting us. We'll move out in single file, along an azimuth of 120 degrees. Every three minutes a star shell will burst along the azimuth to guide us."[10]

Davis directed the officers to carefully screen their men, ensuring that only the able-bodied were taken. All walking wounded and disabled—mostly those men who had frostbitten hands and feet—were left with the vehicles on the road. He was concerned about the physical condition of his men because the extreme temperatures, coupled with dietary deficiencies, were taking their toll, as evidenced by a growing sick list.

Water was also a problem because canteens were frozen and it was impossible to melt enough snow to satisfy their thirst. "The experts who said snow would do to drink never tried it for three days with dry crackers and chocolate bars," Davis remarked derisively. "The thirst was nearly unbearable."[11]

"We constantly ate the stuff to get our thirst under control," Davis explained. "It didn't help much. Even when we added a little sickbay alcohol to our canteens, the water in them remained frozen. One of my runners was determined to get water somehow. In his efforts he would gather twigs and anything else lying around and try to start a fire. Every time we stopped, he'd build one of these little fires. Then he'd pack his canteen cup with snow. When it melted he'd add more snow. The little fire would go out and he'd have to get it going again. He'd work, work, work until I finally said to him, 'You can't melt enough snow to make the effort worthwhile.' He, too, eventually reached that conclusion and just gave up."[12]

Each man was given four rations, but most took only small cans of fruit, reinforced candy bars and dry crackers because the rest of the meal was frozen and inedible. Attempts were made to thaw them, but the effort succeeded only in creating a half-frozen mush which caused dysentery. The "runs" added insult to injury because the multiple layers of clothing and gloved hands made it nearly impossible to answer the call of nature in time. With this low-calorie intake, the men started losing weight—15 to 20 pounds, and this from riflemen who were already lean. It had been three days since their last good meal, Thanksgiving turkey, and it would be several more before they would have hot food again.

Every man took along a sleeping bag for warmth and for an unstated but more ominous reason—the bag would be needed if they got cut off in the mountains. Treating the wounded was so difficult that corpsmen, after initially patching them up, would stuff the casualty in a sleeping bag, to be hauled along on a stretcher by the reserve company. For many, the bag was a lifesaver. Counting ammunition, sleeping bag, equipment and weapon, each man carried approximately 120 pounds.

With the battalion ready to go, Davis got in touch with Litzenberg and found him in an impatient mood. He pointed out that if the men sat around much longer they'd freeze to death—thermometers registered 16 degrees below zero. "I called the company commanders and told them, 'We're going now—we're just going.'" Roy Pearl hefted his radio: "We had perfect confidence in Colonel Davis," he said.[13]

Ridge Running

Davis planned to break away from the road about four miles south of Yudam-ni. His first objective was Turkey Hill, the heavily defended snow-covered peak, 1,000 yards east of the MSR.

The battalion was already in a good position to commence the march. "1st Battalion, for the most part," Davis explained, "was already extending across the flat in the southwest valley, and into the hill mass on the left flank." As the 5th Marines returned from Yudam-ni they were tasked to relieve Davis' battalion, one company at a time.[14]

Litzenberg ordered Company H, 3/7, to seize the crest, after which 1/7 would pass through it and continue the attack south, paralleling the MSR, to Hill 1520 and then strike east to Hill 1653. The last objective would place them in a position about a mile and a half north of Barber's position and behind the Chinese defenses.

"At 0900 on 1 December, Company H jumped off in the attack but approximately two miles southeast of the line of departure it ran into stiff resistance from a company of Chinese entrenched on the high ground overlooking the MSR. The enemy's position was well concealed from observation by a thick grove of trees, camouflaged, and well dug-in positions, in deep snow drifts."[15]

Murderous Chinese fire ripped through the Marine ranks from concealed positions along a series of fingers that ran from the hilltop. The assault was slowed by steep slopes and snow which forced the attackers to crawl on their hands and knees, hauling themselves up by grabbing tree stumps, shrubs—anything they could find. Casualties were heavy, and when its commander, First Lieutenant Howard H. Harris, fell wounded, the assault ground to a halt.

"We put our mortars to work on the ridge line where the enemy fire was coming from," Davis explained. "The underbrush was very thick and we couldn't see them very clearly. So, we plastered the hill with mortar and artillery fire." Davis ordered Company A to continue the attack along the line of the ridge, Company B on the slope to their left, with Company C in reserve.[16]

Eugenous M. Hovatter's Company A encountered stiff resistance from "a numerically superior enemy force entrenched in reinforced positions on Hill 1419, which is the commanding ground in the area. At this point in the attack (at about 1600), my company was assaulting along the ridge line leading to Hill 1419. My assault platoons were engaged in fierce hand-to-hand fighting with forward elements of the enemy force, and were becoming seriously depleted by casualties. The progress of the 1st Battalion at this point had almost come to a standstill, with the crest of the hill still approximately 500 yards away."[17]

Davis, at Hovatter's company CP, "coolly braved intense enemy automatic weapons fire, and went forward among the assault troops intermingled with enemy elements, to get a first-hand look at the situation." The crest of Hill 1419 was finally reached. "Lieutenant Colonel Davis reached the [crest] while fierce fighting was still in progress. Without any consideration for his life, he moved about on the position, and in front of the leading assault squads while making a reconnaissance to continue the attack. Mopping up operations were still in progress when Colonel Davis returned to my CP area, where he remained calmly while enemy were engaged within a few feet from him."[18]

Davis called in an airstrike to soften up the objective. "Two planes made about three passes each at the hillcrest using rockets and machine guns." Company A's lead platoon, commanded by Second Lieutenant Leslie Williams, moved forward into the heavy fire, shot its way into the Chinese position and took them on in hand-to-hand fighting.[19]

Williams received the Navy Cross for this action. Williams' platoon's gallant fight succeeded in taking the position and restoring the momentum to the attack, but it took until 1930 to secure the hill. The fighting had been so severe that Litzenberg attached Company H to 1/7 to make up for its losses. One officer noted that when he passed through the assault platoon there were only four or five men left.

Davis had his jump-off point, but had to act quickly because his men were drenched with sweat from their exertions and would freeze if he didn't get them moving. "As we reorganized in the dark," he said, "the cold wind struck. Artillery in the valley was reporting 24 degrees below zero; in the wind on our mountain top it could have been 75 degrees below zero, with the wind chill!" While the last of the day's casualties were being evacuated to the road, he ordered Company B to send a patrol to the southeast to check on enemy activity. The remainder of the battalion formed a hasty perimeter and reorganized.[20]

By 2100 they were ready to move out. First Lieutenant Kurcaba's Company B took the lead, followed by Davis and his command group; Company A, under First Lieutenant Hovatter; Captain Morris' Company C, and battalion headquarters group. Company H, under 2nd Lieutenant Minard P. Newton, brought up the rear. Darkness and terrain dictated that the battalion move in a column formation—one Marine behind another—without security elements out front or on the flanks. The battalion had been reduced to less than 500 men—companies A and B were at half strength, Company C had 50 men left and Company H had about the same.

Davis tried not to think about the consequences. "I was trying not to worry about the weakness of the battalion's radios or about how we were going to deal with casualties on the steep icy slopes in the dark." He finally turned to Lieutenant Chew-Een Lee, a Company B platoon commander, and ordered, "Move out smartly." Lee's platoon moved out, followed by a single file of men that soon formed a column half-a-mile long.[21]

Darkness and blowing snow hid Hill 1520, their second objective, 1,500-yards away over the forbidding terrain. The lead platoon had to wade through knee-deep snow along a narrow mountain trail, slowing the column movement and forcing the rotation of the exhausted men. The newly formed path froze and became ice-glazed. The treacherous footing caused serious falls among the heavily loaded men and made it especially difficult to climb the snow-covered slopes.

The men were sweating heavily. The many layers of clothing trapped the moisture and kept it from evaporating, increasing the risk of frostbite if they didn't keep moving. Men stumbled into each other or fell in the snow, creating gaps which had to be closed. The column stopped and started, while unit leaders struggled to keep the men moving.

Lieutenant Lee, at the head of the column, needed a direction to guide on. "At one point," Davis described, "I got myself all hunched down in an abandoned Chinese hole with my map and compass, and flashlight. Naturally, we didn't want the enemy to know we were there, so before I turned on the flashlight, I made sure I was tucked in under a poncho. I then got oriented to the azimuth in relation to the next hill mass, turned off the light, and climbed out. The three company commanders were standing there shivering, waiting for orders—and suddenly I couldn't recall what I had done down in the hole! The temperature was so severe that I found it difficult to think." He had to repeat the process, this time with another officer. "Everybody had to repeat back to you two or three times to be sure of what was supposed to happen. We were absolutely numb with the cold. It was hard to believe." Company B's men were so numb that the company commander had them jog in place to get their blood flowing.[22]

Despite the low-hanging clouds and swirling snow, Davis could see a few stars, one of which seemed to be in the general direction of their objective. He had Lee guide "toward the star" and, as an added precaution, arranged for the artillery to fire star shells and white phosphorus rounds to mark the direction of march. However, as the point descended into a valley, it lost all sense of direction. Lee whispered, "Haven't seen a starburst in ten minutes. Tell them back there that we can't go any faster unless we want to walk in circles—or over a cliff!" The column started drifting south, toward the road and the Chinese positions, which had been targeted for artillery bombardment.[23]

Davis sensed the deviation but could not raise Lee because the radios were frozen and useless. "I passed the word to stop the column to get everyone back in line. No response." He sent his runner forward and still nothing happened. In desperation, Davis and Pearl left the trail and beat a parallel track toward the head of the column. As he pressed forward, he found out why the men had not reacted to his orders—with parka hoods tied tightly around their ice-covered faces, they simply could not hear. "I made quite a racket thrashing through the snow," Davis recalled. "That drew complaints. 'Quiet! Knock off the noise!' I could hear Corporal Pearl behind me explaining that it was the battalion commander who was making all the commotion."[24]

At one point, Davis collided with one of the men, who was horrified that he had knocked his battalion commander to the ground. Davis finally reached the head of the column, out of breath and exhausted by the effort. Bill Davis (no relation) remembered, "We couldn't believe it. Here was Colonel Davis going up and down the column. I was in good shape, and I was dying. He was phenomenal."[25]

About 0230, at a point approximately 3,000 yards north from where Company F was trapped, Captain Hovatter observed Davis. "At the time, Colonel Davis was with Company C, which was assaulting an enemy strong point." Major Tighe recalled, "The battalion surprised and attacked a group of enemy troops estimated to be of company strength. They had the advantage of high ground, and on becoming aware of the 1st Battalion's presence, rolled grenades down the hill and directed automatic weapons fire on our troops. At this point the battalion had been attacking in sub-zero temperatures over extremely mountainous terrain covered by a minimum of eight inches of snow in excess of nineteen consecutive hours."[26]

Davis, immediately realizing the seriousness of this situation, rallied the men in one final concentrated effort and personally led the assault. Major Tighe stated, "It was miraculous that Lieutenant Colonel Davis was not killed or seriously wounded as he was a continuous target for enemy grenades, small arms and automatic weapons fire. On one occasion during the final assault he was knocked from his feet and momentarily stunned by a missile which failed to penetrate his helmet. However, he continued the attack and gained the objective without serious injury although he had two bullet holes through the sides of his parka."[27]

Companies B and C deployed in two columns and began their assault, supported by the battalion's two 81mm mortars and four heavy machine guns. Exhausted Marines somehow found the strength to push forward. A cacophony of sound erupted, shattering the stillness with the roar of rifle and machine-gun fire, shouted commands, oaths, and tension-releasing bellows of the attackers. Exploding grenades and mortar rounds flashed in the darkness. Marines closed with the Chinese, who, surprised and overwhelmed by the violence of the assault, died in their foxholes, except for a few who escaped or were taken prisoner.

An NCO called Davis over to look in one of the foxholes. Reaching down, he dragged a Chinese soldier out of the hole, totally frozen, except for his eyes, which showed a flicker of movement. A half-dozen more were found frozen to death, their thin, padded winter uniforms and tennis shoes with no socks unable to keep them alive in the terrible cold.

As the combat-induced adrenaline rush wore off, the Leathernecks started dropping like tenpins, completely spent after five exhausting hours on the move. Davis called a halt for a few hours of sleep, but there was no way to get warm. Private First Class Theodore B. Hudson recalled, "When we stopped for our break, I got chilled pretty bad and started shaking all over. There was no way to get out of the wind." Before climbing into their sleeping bags, the men were warned to change socks lest they get frostbitten feet. Corporal Walter H. O'Keefe remembered, "We took off our boots, changed socks, put the wet ones underneath our shirts and put our dry socks on. It was nice to be able to wiggle our toes, to get the circulation going again."[28]

"Immediately upon capturing this position, a perimeter defense was established and due to the extreme exhaustion of all personnel and the necessity for treating additional casualties, it was decided to defend the position until daylight."[29]

Davis had two-man teams of officers and NCOs move along the perimeter, trying to keep one man in four awake, which was difficult despite the occasional small arms fire. "I found one platoon that had sat down and it struck me then they were all in a state of a coma. I asked them what outfit they were from and they could not even answer. There was nothing to do but shake them physically and get them started doing something. [Chinese] bullets were striking in the snow right among us and I noticed some of our men were so badly shocked that they would not move to get out of the way. It took a good 19 minutes of manhandling to get the mortar section of C Company aroused sufficiently that it would set up." Owen said, "… the men had long passed the point of exhaustion. They were functioning now on instinct."[30]

"I tried to get Fox Company on the radio, but failed," Davis said. "I was not sure of my orientation. So, for these reasons, and because of the exhaustion of the men, I asked regiment for permission to set up a perimeter until daylight." Some of the men were able to get into crevices and behind rocks which gave them superficial protection from the wind.[31]

Davis settled down next to a small rock formation for a short nap. "As I was getting settled, I saw one Marine sitting on a rock 20 feet away. I sat up to tell him to get down, and just then a bullet tore through my hood and skinned my forehead." Major Tighe watched as "Colonel Davis turned over on his side and, in that nerveless way of his, fell asleep immediately." Later a chunk of shrapnel bounced off Davis' helmet. Others were not so fortunate, joining the wounded after being treated and stuffed into sleeping bags at the rear of the column.[32]

At 0300, with less than three hours of rest, the battalion moved out toward its final objective, Hill 1653, about 1,500-yards north of Barber's position. The respite seemed to revive the men, although for the 27-year-old O'Keefe, called "Pop" by the younger Marines, it was an ordeal. "So when word came to move out, regardless of how I felt, in the old Marine Corps tradition, I got up on my feet and put one foot forward and started moving, and the kids were right behind me."[33]

The advance proceeded without contact until it approached the hill. The Chinese opened up with long-range small arms fire from all four directions. A group also threatened to overrun the last company and the wounded, but it was beaten off, and the 22 stretcher casualties were brought forward for better protection. "We had sustained a dozen casualties, including three dead, in the firefight," Davis recalled. "We buried the latter in the snow and brought the wounded along on stretchers and canvas fold-up litters. We had no choice but to leave the dead behind."[34]

Company C jumped off in the attack, seizing a spur, which covered Company A's drive on Hill 1653. Corsairs from VMF-312 (the "Checkerboards") covered the attack on the final objective, forcing the Chinese to withdraw when the column approached from their rear. "During this action, Lieutenant Colonel Davis again positioned himself with the forward most elements of his command, which by this time were receiving heavy mortar, machine-gun and small arms fire. After considerable hard fighting, some of which was hand-to-hand combat, the battalion was able to penetrate the enemy's positions surrounding F Company."[35]

As Davis reached the spur, he saw Company F's perimeter. "There it was, plain as day, about 800 yards off." Pearl called out to him greatly excited, "Colonel, I've got Fox 6 [Barber] on the radio!" After trying to reach Company F for two days, they finally got through. This first contact was an emotional experience for both officers.

"Bill Barber brought tears to my eyes when he volunteered to send a patrol out to lead us into his position. Here was this beat-up company—118 casualties—26 killed in action, three missing, and 89 wounded—almost half of his original complement of 240. Six of seven officers wounded, including Barber, who had been carried around on a stretcher because of a leg wound, and still maintained its esprit de corps." Barber's artillery officer and air officer set up fires around their perimeter except for one entry point.[36]

As a matter of record, Colonel Davis was the first man to enter the surrounded company's perimeter at 1125 on the morning of 2 December 1950. Company B completed the link-up. One of the company's officers remarked, "The snowfield that led up to the embattled company's position was covered with hundreds of Chinese dead. Many of them seemed asleep under blankets of snow, but their bodies were frozen in spasms of pain. There were jumbles of corpses in padded mustard green uniforms." A Company F Marine recalled, "We saw a column of Marines straggling in toward us, but when they got here we realized that they were in just as bad shape as we were." "People," another of Barber's Marines shouted, "You look like shit!" A rescuer saw "Dead Chinese ... piled up like sandbags to from barricades and gun pits. Dead Marines were neatly piled to one side of the aid tent, wounded on the other side." Pearl said, "I stood around with a grin frozen on my face, until I saw a sight that wiped it off real quick: the stack of dead Marines between the aid tents."[37]

Davis recalled, "When I saw Barber, he was hobbling about and could just barely walk. I think we just shook hands and looked at one another for a few minutes until we got unchoked, and then I told him he had done a wonderful job." Company F had suffered almost 50 percent casualties. The company had held off a Chinese regiment for five days.[38]

Lt Harrol Kiser remembered, "When I got there I could see how the men who could still move had taken the bodies of the dead Chinese and stacked them around their positions to use as sandbags." Davis passed his men through Company F and seized the high ground overlooking the road.

The trek was too much for two of Davis' Marines, who died from the physical and mental strain in the freezing cold. O. P. Smith recalled, "When he [Davis] made that trip across country to relieve Toktong Pass, two of his men just couldn't take it. They were out of their heads and [he] had to put them in improvised straightjackets. The two died after reaching Fox Company's position."[39]

Captain Hovatter noted in a statement that, "Throughout the morning of 2 December, when the 1st Battalion was approaching the F Company position, and encountering mounting resistance, I observed Colonel Davis constantly moving among and forward of his leading assault element. During the relief of F Company, my company was fighting a holding action on the left flank. Upon reaching the F Company area at about 1530, Colonel Davis was still working tirelessly and fearlessly under continuous fire, setting up a hasty defense of the area and clearing additional portions of the MSR at a time when a major portion of his troops were too battle weary and exhausted to continue the fight."[40]

Litzenberg was heartened when Davis radioed that he had reached Company F. "When I received word that the 1st Battalion had possession of the pass, I no longer had any doubts about our ability to come out of Yudam-ni with our guns, our wounded, and our vehicles, because I knew possession of that key terrain meant that we could open the road … the tactical maneuver of Davis' battalion unlocked the gate and let us out of Yudam-ni."[41]

"My main concern soon became the security of the main force from Yudam-ni," Davis explained. "I wanted to ensure that no pockets of enemy would fire on them as they came near Toktong Pass." Company A halted on the north side of Hill 1653 to provide manpower to evacuate casualties. Twenty-two wounded had to be carried by litter to safety. Tragically the regimental surgeon, Navy Lieutenant Peter E. Arioli, was killed by a Chinese sniper's bullet while supervising the task.[42]

Company B remained on the hill to eat some of the airdropped rations and then went on to a position that overlooked the MSR. Company A followed and the two companies set in for the night. Companies C and H were kept in the perimeter to rest. Weapons and H&S Company were used as part of the Company F's perimeter defense.

Tighe recalled, "During the remainder of the day, the battalion consolidated its new positions and was resupplied by air. Repeated night attacks were repulsed during this period with considerable loss to the enemy."[43]

Advance Guard

On the morning of 3 December, the battalion continued the attack and seized and held the high mountain pass between Yudam-ni and Hagaru-ri against repeated enemy attacks, until the main body reached this point in their advance.[44]

Davis continued with the mission to clear the passes. "I formed two task forces. My operations officer, Major Tom Tighe, took one force to clear the southern passes and I took the other to clear the northern passes. At the same time, I moved my people toward Hagaru-ri to get a head start. I also had the troops build fires around the area to draw the Chinese out."[45]

The next morning, Davis led the remnants of the battalion and the survivors of Company F off the hill and joined the head of the column on the road. In accordance with Litzenberg's plan, 1/7 then became the advance guard of the main body. Behind the battalion stretched the regimental trains of the 5th and 7th Marines: hundreds of trucks, jeeps, artillery prime movers—an assortment of battered and shot-up vehicles loaded down with wounded and dead Marines, estimated to be 1,100. Hundreds of other lightly wounded and frostbitten survivors—800 or so—shuffled alongside them, while the remnants of infantry battalions attacked along the ridges, keeping the Chinese at bay.

Davis left Company C as a flank guard to protect the column and fall in behind the last unit as it passed by. Unfortunately, a long break in the column misled them into believing it was the last unit and the company left their position. A Chinese unit slipped in the break and attacked the rear of the column. Nine 155mm howitzers with tractor prime movers were abandoned and later destroyed to keep them from falling into the hands of the enemy. "Colonel Litzenberg was most unhappy," Davis recalled.[46]

The point of the advance guard—Davis, LtCol Frederick R. Dowsett, executive officer, 7th Marines, a scout from the intelligence section 1/7 and two riflemen—reached the Hagaru-ri perimeter shortly after dark. "Dowsett had received a radio message telling him to be sure and halt, identify himself, and give the password before trying to enter the perimeter," Litzenberg explained. An outpost was guarding the road. Dowsett shouted, "We're coming in. I don't know the password, but don't get in our way."[47]

Fortunately, LtCol Beall, CO 1st Motor Transport Battalion, was at the outpost and recognized Dowsett's voice. He ran forward and threw his arms around his old friend, in an emotional bear hug. Davis took position at the head of his battalion as he led them into the Hagaru-ri perimeter. He talked to his men: "Let's go in like Marines; shape up and stand tall." Owen said, "The walking wounded and some who were unharmed but who staggered from exhaustion, formed up into three files, shouldered their weapons, and marched in ragged step. Slowly the tread of their thick, rubber-soled shoepacks on the icy road became a steady, sure cadence, and the haggard and hurt Marines put their heads high." A doctor who witnessed the column's arrival exclaimed: "Look at those bastards! Those magnificent bastards!"[48]

All units of the 5th and 7th Marines closed on the Hagaru-ri perimeter by 1600, 4 December. Bowser thought that the "CCF appears to have missed its greatest opportunity ... there were strong forces in the general area, but seemingly they could not be grouped to take advantage of the situation."

Litzenberg praised the performance of the regiment. "They performed tasks that I still can't believe. The only rest we got we snatched when the column was held up by a road block. When the road block was overcome, the column moved forward. The distance from Yudam-ni to Hagaru-ri was roughly 16 miles, which took the column 59 hours to negotiate or a quarter of a mile per hour average."

"At Hagaru-ri, Colonel Davis called all the officers in the battalion together and explained to us the difficult situation we were in," Lieutenant Owens recalled. "Colonel Davis said, 'If any of my officers don't think they can make it all the way, the planes are leaving right over there. You can just sign up and fly out.' None of the officers flew out."[49]

CHAPTER 28

"Retreat Hell"

The regiment's rifle companies were so depleted that Colonel Litzenberg requested the assignment of officers and men from other elements of the Division in order to strengthen them. "The 11th Marines furnished 300 officers and men," Litzenberg noted. "These were distributed as to equalize the strength of infantry companies at 90 to 100 men." Distributing many of the cannoneers did not affect the effectiveness of the artillery battalions. Bowser pointed out that, "Artillery units at Hagaru-ri and Koto-ri were expending ammunition through the muzzle which they could not carry south. There was no shortage of targets and the shoots were put on targets and likely areas where the CCF might be hiding, the effort being to generally soften up the enemy forces along the MSR from Hagaru-ri to Koto-ri."[1]

The Division organized two trains of motor vehicles, one with the 5th Marines and one with the 7th Marines. The regiments further subdivided the trains into serials. General Smith ordered that no vehicle should be left behind that could roll, and that no material would be left behind that could be carried. The Division also specified that 2 days' "C" rations would be distributed between individuals and organic transportation; that each individual carry up to one unit of fire per weapon; and that weapons on vehicles would have a minimum of one unit of fire.[2]

On 4 December, C-47s delivered 48 tons of supplies and another 40 C-47 aircraft from Ashiya Air Base in Japan parachuted 200 tons of supplies into the Hagaru-ri perimeter. In addition, a record-setting total of 232 bombing sorties rocketed, bombed, and strafed the area in support of the X Corps, including 136 by the 1st Marine Air Wing.

General Almond flew into Hagaru-ri perimeter and bestowed Distinguished Service Crosses on General Smith, Colonel Litzenberg, Lieutenant Colonels Murray (5th Marines) and Olin L. Beall (1st Motor Transport Battalion). Smith tolerated the ceremony but thought that Almond dispensing decorations was

Hagaru-ri Airstrip

General Smith's letter to the Commandant of the Marine Corps noted: "We had at an early date realized the importance of Hagaru-ri as a base. On November 16th Field Harris [MajGen Field Harris, Commanding General, 1st Marine Aircraft Wing] and I had tentatively approved a site for a C-47 strip at Hagaru-ri. Work had begun by our 1st Engineer Battalion on November 19th and the strip was first used by C-47s on December 1st, although at the time it was only 40% completed. This strip was essential for the evacuation of wounded and air supply in case our road went out either due to weather or enemy action. Hagaru-ri had to be held to protect this strip and the supplies, which we were accumulating there."

"On the advice of the aviators it was decided to bring in a C-47 for a trial run on the afternoon of 1 December. The plane landed successfully at about 1500 and took off 24 wounded. It took about a half an hour to load a plane with litter patients. Ambulatory patients go very much faster. At first we could accommodate only two planes on the ground simultaneously. Eventually, as the field was improved we were able to accommodate six planes on the ground without blocking the runway. Hours of daylight were from about 0700 to 1745 and use of the strip was limited to those hours. After the first plane landed more planes came in. Five additional plane loads of wounded were taken out that afternoon. We would have gotten out more but an incoming plane, loaded with 105mm ammunition, collapsed its landing gear. The plane was too heavy, with its load, to push off the runway and we had to unload it, thus losing valuable time. (We attempted to have incoming planes loaded with ammunition and other needed supplies to supplement the air drop.) We had built up at Hagaru-ri a level of six days' rations and two units of fire."[3]

reprehensible. He viewed the presentation as cheapened when Almond himself accepted a DSC.[4]

The order of march for the 7th Marines in its attack south was, 2nd Battalion, with a tank platoon attached, astride the MSR, 1st Battalion echeloned right along the high ground flanking the MSR to the left rear, and an Army provisional battalion (31/7, survivors of the 31st Infantry Regiment that had been overrun on the eastern side of the Chosin Resevoir), under LtCol Berry K. Anderson (U.S. Army) echeloned to the left rear. 3rd Battalion was in reserve behind the regimental train, with one company along its flanks. Artillery units and Division train number one followed 3rd Battalion.

The division march order specified:

> Personnel of units in Division trains will be employed for close-in flank security of serial within trains by proceeding on foot to flanks of motor serials. All personnel except drivers, relief

drivers, radio operators, casualties and personnel specifically designated by RCT [regimental combat team] commanders will march on foot to flanks of motor serial. Vehicles breaking down will be pushed to side of road and if not fully operable by the time column has passed will be destroyed. Destruction of vehicles and equipment will be authorized only by RCT commanders, battalion commanders and train commanders. Perimeter defense of motor serials will be habitually established during halts.

The 5th Marines brought up the rear, acting as rear guard. Fortunately the road from Hagaru-ri to Koto-ri was relatively flat, with the mountains set back some distance, which made for easier going.

All excess material—office equipment, extra clothing and baggage, unserviceable weapons and apparatus that might hinder the withdrawal—was burned or destroyed.

At 0450 on 6 December, Company C left the perimeter to secure a long ridge that extended for almost 4,000 yards on the eastern side of the road. The remainder of the battalion followed Company C and reached the crest of the ridge without incident. "As my lead elements got to where we were supposed to be at daylight, they discovered an extra hill nob that we had not seen from our reconnaissance and it wasn't on the map," Davis explained. "When one of my patrols walked up there, they found the place just full of Chinese, but they were not alert. Our patrol was large, so they got themselves set and just shot all those Chinese before they could react. We would have been sitting ducks if those guys had been awake, because they were looking right down our throats ... we would have been hard pressed to get to them in a hurry."[5]

Davis' battalion continued to push ahead to the right of the MSR against continued enemy contact, but nothing serious enough to deploy the entire battalion. The three rifle companies kept the momentum going by leapfrogging one another. Lieutenant Owen remarked that, "From Hagaru-ri to Koto-ri, 1/7 had the right flank and that provisional Army battalion had the left. We constantly had to stop and wait for them to come up. We took casualties because our left flank was often in the air."[6]

LtCol Dowsett recalled, "About 4:00 p.m. Lieutenant Colonel Anderson came up to the jeep I was riding in and told me he had lost control of his Army provisional battalion, that he had no communications with any of his units, that he didn't know where any of his units were except that they were somewhere along the road, and that, because it was dark, it would be impossible to regain control of the battalion." The 3rd Battalion took over the Army's mission. Dowsett said, "We thought, let them follow along the road and get the hell out of the way."[7]

By dusk, about 5,000 yards had been covered but enemy resistance was stiffening. Aerial reconnaissance reported columns of Chinese coming in from the east to cut off the column. Davis recalled, "We detected a large force of Chinese deployed in a cross-corridor depression several hundred yards ahead of our leading elements on the road below. I agreed to spot fires for 81mm mortar crews as they adjusted on this lucrative target. We bracketed the target quickly and fired five rounds for effect from the three mortar tubes. Tragically, the rounds walked away from the enemy positions. We repeated the process with, again, similar results. It was then discovered that the mortar baseplates were not holding in the icy ground. We returned to single round adjustment and scored enough direct hits to cause the enemy to abandon the position. With this major opposition eliminated, the leading Marine forces moved out smartly toward Koto-ri."[8]

The advance guard on the road soon outdistanced 1/7 on the icy mountain trails and its security mission was canceled. "Litzenberg told me to come on down and join the force on the road. As we started down a finger in the moon light in the snow toward the main supply route," Davis related, "we were 'discovered' by a friendly tank that took us under fire. The cannon projectiles missed us by a wide margin, but the entire area was peppered by machine-gun fire. I personally observed a dozen rounds in the snow within a few yards of my command group. The firing stopped suddenly as my radio operator, Roy Pearl finally managed to shift to the tank's tactical frequency and he could hear this tanker bragging how he was cleaning up this attack on the hill. Pearl broke in and shouted, 'You are shooting at Marines, knock it off!' The response was: 'Oh, my God—CEASE FIRE! CEASE FIRE!' Pearl authenticated his call, and it was over. The tanker must have fired hundreds of rounds and we didn't have a single person hit. Roy Pearl was a true and fearless professional who always came through in crisis situations."[9]

Near the base of the mountain, the battalion encountered a 15-foot vertical drop and they had to post two men at the top to help lower others to the bottom. The snow was soon hard packed and became smooth as glass. The heavily laden men had to slide down the incline. Fortunately no one was hurt, but it cost time and some bruised egos.

As the men approached the road, several men in the column didn't get the word about a friendly unit climbing down the slopes and opened fire. "One bullet pierced my clothing and grazed my right hip," Davis recalled. Profane bellows got the errant shootings stopped and no one was hurt. "Once we reached the road, the walk into Koto-ri was uneventful.[10]

Pearl received a radio message for Davis. LtCol Dowsett had been wounded and he was to take his place as regimental executive officer. Major Webb D. "Buzz" Sawyer, second-in-command, would take over the battalion. "As we reentered Koto-ri from the north," Davis recalled, "it mentally brought me back to when we first entered it from the south in early November, a full month earlier."[11]

The advance guard, 2/7, was the first to reach Koto-ri and, by 1700 Thursday, 7 December, the entire 7th Marines were inside the perimeter. Lieutenant Owen recalled, "By the time we reached Koto-ri, we were beat. They had warming tents for us. It was a big deal. They destroyed us—everyone just completely relaxed. All the company officers were in one tent. Jeez, someone came in to get us out. The warmth was wonderful. I couldn't move. The guys coming around getting us out were tough. One of them said, 'Get out, you sumbitches, or we'll shoot you.' Hank Kiser was so sick, we literally had to pull him off the deck. It was tough to get moving that day."[12]

After giving Sawyer the reins of the battalion, Davis assumed the duties as 7th Marines executive officer under "Litz the Blitz," Litzenberg. Roy Pearl remained behind as Sawyer's radioman. "We had been through a lot together, Colonel Davis and me," he lamented.[13]

Davis remarked about his relationship with Litzenberg. "He and I seemed to have developed a deep mutual respect by this time," Davis said. "I knew his tactics were well-considered and solid, and that he would see them through with whatever support was required. He would listen to reasonable suggestions or ideas. When I got orders from the commanding officer, 7th Marines, they were accepted without question. If the situation changed, I knew I could get a full hearing if I wanted to change instructions."[14]

Davis' immediate assignment was to displace the regimental command post to the outskirts of Koto-ri in preparation for the continuation of the attack south. The 7th Marines was assigned to seize the site of a bridge the Chinese had destroyed about three-and-a-half-miles south of Koto-ri. 1st Battalion, now Sawyer's, 7th Marines jumped off southward after receiving the message, "take Moses down the mountain," codenamed after an engineer named Moses, who was involved with replacing the missing bridge. "We moved out on the morning of the 8th in a snow-storm, which by the afternoon was blinding," Litzenberg noted.[15]

The Chinese had blown out a 29-foot section of a bridge about a third of the way down the mountain. They could not have picked a better spot to cause the Division serious trouble. At this point four large pipes, carrying water to the turbines of the power plant in the valley below, crossed the road. A sort of concrete substation was built over the pipes on the uphill side of the road. A one-way concrete bridge went around the substation. The drop down the mountainside was sheer. It was a section of this bridge which was blown. There was no possibility of a by-pass. The integrity of this bridge was vital, for without it the Division would have been unable to get out its vehicles, tanks, and guns.

"We sent a patrol from the 1st Battalion to the bridge site," Litzenberg said. "This patrol passed on beyond the bridge site and continued down the road to make contact with the battalion of the 1st Marines which was fighting its way up the mountain side from Chinhung-ni to meet us." Lieutenant Colonel John R. Partridge, 1st Engineer Battalion and several of his officers accompanied the patrol to get a firsthand look at the site and figure out how to bridge the gap.[16]

Partridge decided that the only way to bridge the 29-foot gap was by airdropping 2,500-pound sections of an M-2 steel Treadway bridge. Smith was skeptical of the unprecedented plan and questioned the engineer in great detail about its feasibility. Partridge, "kind of a grouchy guy," Smith recalled, "finally got exasperated and exclaimed, 'I got you across the Han River! I got you the airfield! And I'll get you a bridge!'" Smith laughed off the engineer's coarseness and told him to proceed.[17]

On the morning of 7 December, a detachment of the Air Force's 314th Troop Carrier Wing at Yonpo loaded eight separate 22-foot, 2,500-pound spans into C-119 "flying box cars" and airdropped them into an unmarked drop zone at Koto-ri. Two huge 48-foot G-5 parachutes hitched to each end of the span lowered them "gently" to the ground. One of the spans fell into Chinese hands and another was damaged, but the other six were serviceable.

Four U.S. Army heavy-duty Brockway B666 six-ton bridge-erector trucks from the 58th Engineer Treadway Bridge Company stranded at Koto-ri loaded four sections, together with additional wooden extensions, and moved them forward to within range of the bridge site. "Along about mid-afternoon we took some incoming mortar rounds near the Brockways," Partridge recalled. "The trucks ... were vulnerable items of essential equipment; we had to get them out of there." The trucks were taken back out of mortar range while the engineers worked on a solution to a new problem: the Treadway spans were 22 feet from end to end and the gap in the roadway was 29 feet, seven feet too short![18]

First Lieutenant David Peppin, Company D, 1st Engineer Battalion, was given responsibility for laying the Treadway spans across the extended gap. "One of my sergeants pointed to a pile of railroad ties and suggested building a 'crib' to extend the Treadway and make it fit."[19]

"As the airdropped bridge spans were put into place and the truck column started to roll," Davis explained, "my personal mission became one of expediter, to keep the column moving. I was aware from other operations that some truck drivers were not as aggressive or innovative as they might be and were just content to sit back and wait. This meant that no delays could be tolerated." At one point a truck broke an axle and had to be pushed over a cliff. Other stalled vehicles were simply pushed out of the way, "nothing was allowed to delay the column."[20]

When Partridge verified that the Division reconnaissance company was the last unit to cross the bridge, he ordered it to be blown up. "I had a sense of well-being after everyone had crossed over and I'd blown the bridge." Chief Warrant Officer Willie Harrison set off an 800-pound charge of TNT that dropped the Treadway into the chasm. The time was 0230, 11 December 1950.[21]

The Division column reached Chinhung-ni after fighting through occasional Chinese ambushes. "We got down through the pass to a little place called Chinhung-ni," Davis explained. "There was a railroad depot where the troops were to be loaded on a train that would shuttle them to the twin cities of Hungnam and Hamhung on the coast about 20 miles away. The vehicles were to continue driving. The separation of the vehicles from the foot column disrupted unit organization, particularly when command vehicles were involved. It was a totally disorganized effort."[22]

Davis was collared by Colonel Edward W. Snedeker, Deputy Chief of Staff. "Davis," he said, "I'm having trouble getting those cars loaded. Will you get some people and get those cars loaded because everybody on foot is going to ride the train. Those on the vehicles will go on down the road."[23]

"I walked among the troops looking at ice-covered faces under the parka hoods until I found enough officers and non-commissioned officers I knew to post one on each railcar to get it loaded. I was beginning to get the situation sorted out when over on one side of the train a soldier uncovered a large stockpile of sweets that had been hidden by a canvas covering. He yelled out for everyone to head, 'Anybody want candy? Come over and get some.' He was instantly stormed by half-starved troops. The candy, 4-inch Tootsie Rolls, was grabbed by the handful. For a while we lost control. Here were piles of boxes of candy, and for the first time I realized how starved we were." Time was of the essence. The train had to get underway before dark because it was expected the Chinese would launch night attacks.[24]

"I quickly found a few Marines I knew and took them to the back side of the tent. We made a hole large enough to get out several boxes of Tootsie Rolls, gave them to my men who held them aloft and called out: 'Anyone who wants candy get on the train!' In short order we were loaded and rolling toward Hamhung. During the train ride, to my amazement, I ate five or six of these large Tootsie Rolls. I have told that story so many times that when we have reunions, the Tootsie Roll Company will send us boxes of the candy."[25]

Hungnam

General Smith noted, "It never occurred to me and I don't think it occurred to any man in the division, that we wouldn't get out. The only time I was concerned was when the 5th and 7th Marines were fighting their way out of Yudam-ni and around midnight I received a dispatch from Litzenberg: 'Situation grave.' I didn't like that at all. It was followed within the hour with another that reported the situation was in hand."[26]

Special Action Report, 1st Battalion, 5th Marines, noted: "When the train arrived at Hungnam, troops were disembarked and placed aboard Army trucks for movement to the regimental bivouac area, Yonpo Airfield. All personnel were billeted in the bivouac area … with tents, stoves, galleys with hot food, water, and a security guard." Davis recalled, "In two hours I ate something like seven or eight enormous pancakes." The remainder of the day and the morning of the following day personnel spent time resting, reading mail, and making preparations for going aboard the ship.[27]

Smith recalled, "Our first mission was to go into assembly area around Hungnam and defend the place. Then we got the orders to go aboard the ship and sailed on 13 December." Eventually, some 17,000 vehicles, 100,000 refugees, and 100,000 troops came out of the port. The 7th Marines boarded the MSTS (Military Sea Transportation Service) *Daniel I. Sultan*.[28]

While aboard the ship, Davis received surprising news. "I drafted a recommendation for the award of the Medal of Honor for Colonel Litzenberg, since I felt that his was the main effort in extricating our forces from the Chosin threat. He said, 'No! It was an all-hands effort! But here is one that will fly!' He handed me a draft with my name on it. That was my first hint that 1st Battalion, 7th Marines, had earned for me a recommendation for the Medal of Honor! I was speechless as he insisted, 'Don't you agree?' These original papers were lost in a division headquarters fire, but were reconstructed a year later, largely through the personal efforts of General V. H. 'Brute' Krulak."[29]

On 15 December, the Division unloaded at Masan and bivouacked in tents at the "Bean Patch," a location familiar to many of the men who had fought in the battle of the Naktong with the 1st Provisional Marine Brigade. "It was cold in the Bean Patch, but nothing like up north," Davis recalled. "We were in tents with oil heat. We were getting reorganized and doing a lot of patrol work, as much for training as anything else."[30]

"As with other Marines units, the 7th Regiment had to be rebuilt," Davis said. "Our losses were beyond belief. Personnel replacements and weapons and equipment arrived and retraining was quickly underway. Units were assigned security missions in conjunction with their training. After a series of field exercises, we were ready to return to combat. Our area of operations was to become the central front east of Seoul."[31]

"I am understandably proud of the performance of this Division. The officers and men were magnificent. They came down the mountains bearded, footsore, and physically exhausted, but their spirits were high. They were still a fighting division. Just a miraculous performance, again demonstrating that these fine young Americans can do anything when they have to."[32]

CHAPTER 29

The Great Pohang Guerrilla Hunt

In mid-January, the 1st Marine Division was assigned to clear out the remnants of the 10th North Korean Division that had infiltrated through the lines. It was little more than a guerrilla force of about 2,500 to 2,600 men located in a sector north and northwest of Pohang. "We went into a large, rural mountain area near Pohang, on the east coast, which was experiencing a lot of guerrilla activity," Davis explained. "An all-out 'guerrilla hunt' was conducted over a period of three weeks. Blocking positions were established and units were moved rapidly in response to reported activity. It was great training, but few guerrillas were caught." Litzenberg described the operation as a "great game." "We would find them about 1400 in the afternoon, get our artillery on them, air on them; and then they would disappear. The next day we would have to find them again." Litzenberg thought that in the three-week operation the North Korean force was reduced by 1,600 men, mostly through desertions rather than battle casualties. O. P. Smith said, "We drove those North Korean devils crazy. The North Korean commander had a nervous breakdown ... we just made life miserable for them."[1]

Chungju, Operation *Killer*

On 12 February, the 1st Marine Division received a warning order to pack up and go to Chungju, in the center of the United Nations line to participate in Operation *Killer*, which was scheduled to jump off on the 21st to forestall a Chinese counter-attack. The Division came under the operational control of the IX Corps, with the 7th Infantry Division on right flank and the 6th ROK Division on the left flank.

The 7th Marines, the last regiment to arrive from Pohang, tied in with 6th ROK Division on left and 1st Marines on the right. "We moved to our new operating area in the central front of South Korea below the 38th Parallel," Davis explained. "With divisions abreast we moved north across the entire central front. Our patrols soon found enemy defenders on the high ground ahead. They would then withdraw to a safe position while we applied artillery fire and air bombardment on the enemy. After several such encounters, we concluded that if the defenders were North Korean

Army units, they would hold their positions; if Chinese, they would withdraw. Vigorous infantry assaults were necessary to dislodge the Koreans."[2]

"In early March 1951, I participated in maneuvering the regiment next to an ROK division. The Chinese would gang up on the ROK troops and break through, and they would pull us all back. We dispatched a liaison officer to serve with the South Korean Army division. From his reports we came to anticipate when trouble was coming. Korean units were loosely controlled, at times outdistancing the range of their supporting artillery, and losing contact with one another. The Chinese seemed to detect this and would launch a human wave attack against them."[3]

"Caught with 'both feet in the air,' so to speak, the Korean units rapidly withdrew and at times fled to the rear. We quickly positioned units to protect our flanks, and almost invariably received orders to move back in order to reestablish the broken front lines. After very few miles, the Chinese units stopped. It became apparent that they had outdistanced their supporting weapons, had lost communications with higher headquarters, had run out of supplies, and found their units intermingled and disorganized. These problems were confirmed by prisoners we captured. Our application of massive artillery fire and air bombardment caused them to flee in great disorder. Then we would attack and retake the high ground—the Chinese under our attack usually withdrew quickly, whereas vigorous assaults were necessary to dislodge the North Koreans. I called it Operation Yo-Yo, because this happened two or three times. Then we went into a mass-fire phase. The UN command would put tanks on ramps and give the artillery a quota of ammunition to fire each day. They were firing 70 truckloads of ammunition a day; after a few days, they sent out patrols, only to find that there was nobody there."[4]

"Later, as we moved forward again, we found many cross ridges with high passes through them. Enemy units would protect these passes by defending the high ground on either side of the pass. Our assault units had great difficulty in dislodging the defenders. Their only reasonable approach was along the narrow ridge top. Detecting this pattern, we designed an innovative plan which came to be called 'busting through the middle.' As our ridge top assault units pinned down the defenders, we launched a tank-infantry (tank heavy) force up the road toward the pass. Invariably the defenders would withdraw under this double threat and we could move quickly through the pass area."[5]

"Another somewhat strange employment of our forces was the establishment of a 'protective screen of fire.' Orders were received that each artillery piece would fire a minimum number of rounds per hour for 24 hours per day. All tanks would be put on to dirt inclines to increase the elevation of their guns and thereby add range; they too were assigned a minimum quota of rounds per hour."[6]

"On occasion we would request a ceasefire in order to send out patrols to make sure no enemy was being assembled to threaten us. Our patrols brought back pleas from farmers that we stop the 'shoot-out' so that they could attend to their crops."[7]

"The main result of this 'screen of fire' was to drain every ammunition supply depot west of Denver, Colorado, and create a serious shortage in the national stockpile. Possibly the weakened Republic of Korea divisions were made more secure, but our infantry regiment was only hurt by it: gun tubes were worn, crews exhausted, nearby units unable to sleep, limited ability to patrol to our front, ammunition shortages generated. In June 1951, my time in Korea ran out during this central front campaign, and I soon returned to the States. We started moving forward again in April; then I was relieved and was pulled out of Korea."[8]

"I took some leave and moved on to Headquarters Marine Corps in the Navy Annex, Washington, D.C. I reported to the Operations Subsection, G-3, Division of Plans and Policies. I initially went into the G-3's Training Section, where I set up all the training directives for all the schools throughout the Corps."[9]

CHAPTER 30

Above and Beyond

One of the first questions Davis was asked upon reporting to headquarters was if he knew that he had been recommended for the Medal of Honor. "I knew down at the Bean Patch that Litzenberg had written it up, but it was among things that were burned in a big fire. I heard nothing more about it until 1952."[1]

The Medal of Honor award was, "A different kind of citation in that they [the awards board] weren't accustomed to awarding for a 'command performance,' so to speak. Most Medal of Honor awards were based on an individual suicidal type of act or a totally personal heroic exposure. I was told that mine took a lot of effort to convince [the board] and others that a sustained heroic performance over several days was worthy."[2]

"On the other hand, there were others where this had happened before: Merritt 'Red Mike' Edson's was a heroic leadership award, at Guadalcanal along with General Vandegrift; then Dave Shoup at Tarawa; so there was precedence for it. In retrospect, it doesn't seem valid now that such a concern would have come up unless it was at a time when every award was for heroic acts. Mine was the first recommendation for a Medal of Honor for unit leadership over a period of time."[3]

The award was announced when Davis was in Istanbul during a trip to Europe to observe maneuvers. "I was surprised and in some disbelief since I had not heard anything for more than a year." The trip back to the United States in time for the ceremony became an interesting challenge for the Marine Headquarters Personnel Department. "Our party was going back to Paris where I was supposed to fly in time for the White House presentation; a very tight schedule. But, as we flew over to Paris, heavy snowfall covered the runway, which sent us on to London. As usual, money was tight in the Corps and they were not going to pay commercially to get me back. Since there was no scheduled military flights, messages went back and forth between Navy Headquarters in London and Washington about getting me back by a certain time and date to guarantee my appearance at the White House as scheduled."[4]

A small plane picked Davis up in Prestwick, Scotland, just in time to take him to Frankfurt, Germany, for a military flight to Washington. "The naval authorities had discovered a flight to Prestwick and they held a space for me. I made it back in time but everybody in Marine Corps Headquarters was annoyed with me and concerned that I hadn't responded more smartly. This was before jets, and with an old prop job, it was a long, long trip."[5]

The Medal of Honor ceremony was conducted by President Harry Truman at the White House on 24 November 1952. Knox and the three children were also present; Willa, aged two, Gilbert aged nine and Miles aged six. Two other Marines—PFC Hector C. Cafferata (Ret) and T/Sgt Robert S. Kennemore (Ret) (both men were medically retired because of wounds)—also received the award for their heroism during the Chosin Campaign. T/Sgt Kennemore said that immediately after the ceremony, President Truman said to him, "I would rather have earned this Medal of Honor than to be President of the United States."[6]

Davis was often asked if the Medal of Honor affected his career. "My attitude towards it is one of great humility. I fully recognize the gallant efforts and sacrifices of those many young Marines, those young troopers who put out, who did the job, who made it all possible. It wasn't totally my doings ... the 'Medal' itself was no guarantee of any kind or that I was supposed to get any special recognition. Certainly it made me work harder to live up to what it represents."[7]

Davis' Medal of Honor Citation

For conspicuous gallantry and intrepidity at the risk of his life above and beyond the call of duty as Commanding Officer of the First Battalion, Seventh Marines, First Marine Division (Reinforced), in action against enemy aggressor forces in Korea from 1 through 4 December 1950.

Although keenly aware that the operation involved breaking through a surrounding enemy and advancing eight miles along primitive icy trails in the bitter cold with every passage disputed by a savage and determined foe, Lieutenant Colonel Davis boldly led his battalion into the attack in a daring attempt to relieve a beleaguered rifle company and to seize, hold and defend a vital mountain pass controlling the only route available for two Marine regiments in danger of being cut off by numerically superior hostile forces during their redeployment to the port of Hungnam.

When the battalion immediately encountered strong opposition from entrenched enemy forces commanding high ground in the path of the advance, he promptly spearheaded his unit in a fierce attack up the steep, ice-covered slopes in the face of withering fire, and, personally leading the assault groups in a hand-to-hand encounter, drove the hostile troops from their positions, rested his men and reconnoitered the area under enemy fire to determine the best route for continuing the mission.

Always in the thick of the fighting, Lieutenant Colonel Davis led his battalion over three successive ridges in the deep snow in continuous attacks against the enemy and, constantly inspiring and encouraging his men throughout the night, brought his unit to a point within 1500 yards of the surrounded rifle company by daybreak. Although knocked to the ground when a shell fragment struck his helmet and two bullets pierced his clothing, he arose and fought his way forward at the head of his men until he reached the isolated Marines.

On the following morning, he bravely led his battalion in securing the vital mountain pass from a strongly entrenched and numerically superior hostile force, carrying all his wounded with him, including 22 litter cases and numerous ambulatory patients. Despite repeated savage and heavy assaults by the enemy, he stubbornly held the vital terrain until the two regiments of the Division had deployed through the pass and, on the morning of 4 December, led his battalion into Hagaru-ri intact.

By his superb leadership, outstanding courage and brilliant tactical ability, Lieutenant Colonel Davis was directly instrumental in saving the beleaguered rifle company from complete annihilation and enabled the two Marine regiments to escape possible destruction. His valiant devotion to duty and unyielding fighting spirit in the face of almost insurmountable odds enhance and sustain the highest traditions of the United States Naval Service.

CHAPTER 31

Peacetime

In February 1952, Davis was assigned to the G-3 Training Section and in April 1953, he was promoted to colonel and became Head of Operations and Training Branch, G-3 Division. "In the Operations and Training Branch we prepared the tables of organization [T/Os] and the training directives for the Corps, as well as plans for deployment. In addition we promoted operations and training support necessary from the Washington level for the Fleet Marine Force, plus bases, barracks and detachments."[1]

One of the issues Davis faced was introducing a training syllabus that reflected both the World War II and Korean War experiences. "World War II was shoulder-to-shoulder movement forward. You didn't dare let the Japanese find a space between units, because they were masters at exploiting it to wind up in your backyard. Heavily defended positions were commonplace. In Korea, it was more a war of maneuver on foot ... there were no shoulder-to-shoulder operations ... until late in the war when peace negotiations began and we got into fixed positions."[2]

During the Korean War, a large segment of the Corps had little or no experience in amphibious warfare. "Our training directives later reflected the need for landing exercises and follow-on maneuvers ashore. Between wars, we quickly moved to reestablish our capability as the nation's force from the sea. Also, we trained in the area of airlift."[3]

The young Davis family enjoyed their time in the Washington area. Ray was able to take them on tours of the scenic tourist attractions and participate in youth activities. There were also military social activities that the couple was expected to attend. Knox was put off by the attitude of many of the senior officer's wives. "Washington had many high society ways and I detected a bit of a cast system based somewhat on rank. Ray's decorations moved us up a bit at times which gave me a better feel for the social status concerns. Many wives who had long, broad experience had much to offer less experienced wives, but seemed loath to do so. This was a lesson for me. Thereafter I made sure that I maintained good communications with more junior wives."[4]

Ray said, "There was some good to come of Knox's experience with some of the older, veteran wives. The adversity she felt generated a deep-seated determination to better the status of younger wives. She developed an acute sensitivity for the needs, concerns and aspirations of younger officers and their families. It became a persistent pattern that opportunities would present themselves to do special things for young families. An aide or junior staff member's wife would be given a baby shower in our quarters with two or three dozen of her friends in attendance. Knox also played a key role in our free-wheeling meetings with junior officers and their wives."[5]

Ray characterized Knox as "a very successful military wife because her approach is realistic. She says what she thinks, not to hurt anybody, but tell it the way it is. She works hard, as opposed to some wives who just tried to look around to see precisely what had to be done to get their husbands ahead."[6]

In July 1954, Davis was scheduled for assignment. His relief reported early, which gave Davis an opportunity attend the six-week Special Weapons Employment Course, Fleet Training Center, Norfolk, Virginia, where he received an in-depth exposure to nuclear weapons. "The essential reason was that atomic weapons instruction at Quantico [where he was slated to go after completing the Senior Course at Quantico] was to be upgraded."[7]

In September he entered the Senior Course, Marine Corps Schools, Quantico. Upon completing the course in June 1955, he served consecutively as Assistant Director and, later, Director of the Senior School. "At that time, the emphasis in the Senior Course curriculum was staff and command in general, and very broad in scope, since the students were lieutenant colonels and colonels, Division staff and regimental command were the focal points. The development of the helicopter concept [high mobility] and tactical use of nuclear weapons 'with a Marine Corps flavor' were at hand in the schools."[8]

One of the changes Davis implemented at the Senior School was to reduce the syllabus to a more manageable number of instructional hours. The "seminar" conference-type instruction was also introduced into the curriculum. The changes were not well received by the senior leadership of the Corps. Brigadier General Victor H. Krulak was assigned to the Education Center with instruction "to get back there and straighten out that mess ... get rid of that mess." Davis remarked, "Unfortunately even though the corrections had already been made, the concept was disapproved and pretty much killed. My resistance to those who destroyed the conference instruction got me an 'early move' out of Quantico."[9]

In October 1957, Davis was again transferred to Washington, D.C., where he served as Assistant G-2, Headquarters Marine Corps, until August 1959. "One of my early jobs was to chair a very broad committee of experts on the development of a Marine Corps doctrine for Communications Intelligence (COMIT) and Electronic Intelligence (ELINT), to guide Marine Corps units in working in these areas in our field forces. Also, we concentrated on air and ground reconnaissance, including their training and equipment."[10]

The Headquarters G-2 reviewed all the intelligence that flowed through the Division and extracted any material that potentially reflected on the Marine Corps. In addition, the commandant was briefed on the world situation that affected the Corps.

"When I arrived, I recognized that this was a good place to be … the longer I was there, the more I was immersed in the total effort of the intelligence game. As I found out later in Vietnam, I would have been much more reluctant to deliberately launch some widespread, very bold operations, if I had not previously been immersed deeply in the intelligence business."[11]

During his tour in Washington there was a major effort by the Defense Department and Congress to downgrade the Marine Corps. "An informal group [Chowder Society] was formed to prepare a counter-attack and solicit support from the entire Marine Corps 'family.' Position papers were prepared, key Marine staff and liaison officers everywhere throughout the top echelons of government were briefed. Inactive Marines were utilized as messengers to friendly Congressmen, particularly those on the Armed Services committees."[12]

"Papers were prepared and distributed to generate support. One chore of mine was to maintain a file with a friend in a remote office of the Headquarters; he was not privy to their contents. In this way no hard evidence of our activities would be surfaced if we were 'caught.' Active duty Marines were not permitted in the hearing rooms of Congress, so Nancy Walt [wife of Marine General Lewis W. Walt] and Knox Davis became our 'spies.' They were spoken to and greeted from time to time by Congressmen at the hearings, but never challenged. Our efforts won the day!"[13]

Davis' tour at Headquarters was shortened to two years so he could attend the National War College in Washington. "It had long been my desire to attend the National War College. I had requested it in fitness reports. Many of the instructors who taught at the College were the most knowledgeable people in and out of government. The College is much sought after by senior officers of all services, as well as most government agencies." Davis became friends with Colonel William Rosson, U.S. Army, who later became his boss when he became deputy of Provisional Corps Vietnam.[14]

Students were required to write an Individual Research Project (IRP). "I wrote about abuses in the centralization of authority. My study of the organizational structure of General Motors versus the U.S. Government led to the conclusion that the concentration of authority was counter-productive. At a time when Pentagon leaders were attempting to centralize authority in the Joint Chiefs, my report was an attack on the centralization of authority. It was not a very popular paper, but I am convinced that my conclusions were correct."[15]

"A great advantage of the National War College is that you meet so many people … you are close together for the better part of a year, arguing with one another, discussing things, making trips around to the various parts of the world. It's a very fine relationship, I thought, and that is a big gain out of the time spent there."[16]

Upon graduation in July 1960, Davis was assigned as Chief, Intelligence, Analysis Branch, J-2, Staff of the Commander-in-Chief, European Command, Paris, France. His family was overjoyed with the assignment, which gave Knox and the children an opportunity for travel throughout the continent. As a family, they were able to visit Norway, Austria, Italy and Spain.

The assignment was an interesting and exciting time for Davis. It was the time of the Berlin Crisis, the Middle East Crisis, and the Cuban Missile Crisis. "One crisis came when we were completely duped by the Russians during a period of no test agreement. Those rascals saved up for a massive effort, then suddenly violated the agreement. Starting one night for a very short period they fired over 100 massive tests, many of which were 100 megatons in size. It completely shocked us and demonstrated the futility of any kind of agreement with those people." At the end of his tour, he was selected to be a general officer. "I was actually promoted on the ship coming home."[17]

Brigadier General Davis' next assignment was in the Far East where he served as Assistant Division Commander (ADC) 3rd Marine Division, Fleet Marine Force, on Okinawa, from October 1963 to November 1964. During this period, he also performed additional duty as Commanding General, SEATO Expeditionary Brigade in the Philippines during June 1964; and as Commanding General, 9th Marine Expeditionary Brigade (9th MEB), in China Sea Contingency Operations, from 2 August to 16 October 1964.

His primary responsibility as the assistant Division commander included training and infantry inspector, and readiness coordinator. "My favorite challenge had to do with readiness. My time was spent in two primary areas: advance combat training and effective emergency response time. I accompanied units to remote training areas and went through the training with them: firing exercises, movement, bivouac, rappelling, cable slide—the works. I was chagrined to find, very infrequently, a company grade officer or non-commissioned officer who would not participate fully in the training, sending their Marines through the rough events, but not going themselves. This situation was quickly remedied when the word got out that the assistant Division commander was going all out with the troops, and that he was ferreting out leaders who were doing less."[18]

"In my time there [9th MEB] I made a trip with one of the Marine C-130s over to Thailand, and disturbed the whole countryside, because we flew five hours at treetop level exploring roads and passes and everything on that side of Cambodia—we couldn't go into Cambodia—as part of an overview to possible deployment to Vietnam. The few days I was ashore in Vietnam with my staff, [we] checked out landing beaches and worked out plans for putting troops ashore. In fact, when they [Marines] finally went ashore in '65, they went over the exact same beaches."[19]

"We were in and out of Vietnam a number of times," Davis admitted. "I flew directly to Da Nang [with several members of his brigade headquarters] and went ashore, uninvited. However, General Westmoreland got a little concerned about having an uninvited brigade headquarters at Da Nang, and I was invited to get back on ship. I couldn't go back on the ships immediately because they were off the Philippines. Finally the ships came over the horizon we were able to get back aboard."[20]

In December 1964, Davis was assigned to Headquarters Marine Corps, where he served as Assistant Director of Personnel until March 1965, then served as Assistant Chief of Staff, G-1, until March 1968. "I jokingly said to some of my bosses in Washington that they were trying to find something I can do, because you had me up here in the G-2, and the G-3, and I've been a G-4; I've never been a G-1! But I really enjoyed that."[21]

Manpower support for the Marine effort for the war in Vietnam became Davis' primary focus. "As the Vietnam War started, $11 billion was needed for Department of Defense supplementary budget to pay for mobilization and deployment, but we were going to get only $1.7 billion. This meant that everything had to be gouged deeply and cut to try to keep the cost down, and the major cost is always manpower. We had a terrible time selling the needs for an adequate training, travel and casualty pipeline. We could not convince the bureaucrats in the Pentagon that we are going to have X amount of casualties, this size of pipeline, this training cost … the inexperienced civilians in charge were not convinced."[22]

At one time Davis sat across from Paul Nitze, Secretary of the Navy, who questioned him on the Corps' estimated casualty figures. Nitze accepted the data, but responded that, in his authority as Secretary of the Navy, he was going to cut the figure by 20 per cent. "That happened on all parts of it [casualty projections]; the training base was chopped, the pipeline was chopped, the casualty estimates were chopped, and that's the reason we had such a difficult time maintaining our rifle strength …."[23]

Davis was concerned about the lack of communication and some mismanagement involved between Marine Corps Headquarters and Fleet Marine Force Pacific headquarters in Hawaii. "When there was a shortage in the rifle units in Vietnam, the command in Hawaii would set up special training programs and grab people out of the pipeline in various basic skills and transfer them over to another which required retraining. Our Personnel Department was over a barrel as their training outputs were being warped."[24]

Davis led a team from headquarters to the Pacific for six weeks to examine the manpower problems. The team came up with several recommendations. The most serious issue they discovered was there a communication problem between Hawaii and Headquarters. "It could have been better handled if Washington and Da Nang had the main effort, with Hawaii doing more monitoring than managing." Upon their return, the team stopped off in Hawaii to give Lieutenant General Victor Krulak a courtesy brief before returning to Washington.[25]

Davis thought that the antiquated manpower system needed to be computerized because the system was totally inadequate. Under his leadership, Headquarters developed a manpower management computer system for which he was recognized with a Legion of Merit (his second award). The citation noted:

> Major General Davis devoted countless hours to the development of sophisticated automated data models and processes to obtain ever improving managerial tools to exploit the modern computer in the achievement of optimal use of manpower assets during this period of turbulent growth.

Davis was promoted to major general in November 1966.

In March 1968, a request came to Headquarters to provide a senior officer for assignment as the Deputy Commanding General of the Provisional Corps, Vietnam (PCV). Davis immediately went to see the Commandant Leonard F. Chapman, Jr. "I told General Chapman I had the ideal man for the job, Raymond G. Davis." Chapman informally floated his name through channels and found that the Army, particularly Lieutenant General William B. Rosson, the current commanding general of PCV, approved. The approval was a mere formality because Davis and Rosson had attended the National War College together and were close friends. Davis thought highly of the Army commander. "Bill was, in my view, the ideal type of commander who was really out with the troops, getting the most out of his forces all the time, day and night."[26]

Part Six

Vietnam

CHAPTER 32

Provisional Corps Vietnam (PCV)

Just before Davis arrived in Vietnam, the Commander U.S. Military Assistance Command, Vietnam (COMUSMACV), General William C. Westmoreland, directed the establishment of a tactical Corps headquarters. Designated Provisional Corps Vietnam, it was set up in the Hue-Phu Bai area under the command of Lieutenant General William B. Rosson. This command was subordinate to the III Marine Amphibious Corps (MAF) located at Da Nang.

In addition to the Corps headquarters, the Army sent two of its highly mobile divisions north, the 1st Cavalry Division, which was often called the 1st Air Cav because it was an airmobile division, and the 101st Airborne Division, including the 3rd brigade of the 82nd Airborne Division. ("The Screaming Eagles" of the 101st was also a helicopter-heavy airmobile division.) The PCV headquarters was activated on 29 January 1968, just in time for the nationwide 1968 North Vietnamese Tet Offensive.

The complex command structure between III Marine Amphibious Force and PVC was a source of contention. While PCV was subordinate to III MAF, the two Army divisions that were assigned to the Army Corps were not directly under the command of the III MAF commanding general or the "control" of the III MAF staff, as were the 1st and 3rd Marine divisions. PCV had its own staff and was commanded by its own Army three-star general.

Major General Rathvon McClure Tompkins, commander of the 3rd Marine Division, deeply resented the establishment of MACV (Military Assistance Command, Vietnam) (Forward) "unless you're very, very, very worried about the local commander … it's tantamount to … the relief of a commander." The issue remained a serious bone of contention, even with Westmoreland's Letter of Instruction, which outlined specific responsibilities for the two headquarters. III MAF headquarters never completely trusted the arrangement.[1]

Davis, however, said he was not concerned. "I did not see having a senior Army command in the Marine zone as a vote of no confidence … vis-à-vis Marines at Da Nang [III MAF headquarters]. The Army had put its best and most important forces forward ... so I can see how the Army would be ticklish about turning them over to the Marines." General Davis' aide-de-camp, agreed saying, "The Army did not want direct Marine control of its elite units. And I can understand that, after seeing the caliber of some of the Marine commanders ... until General Davis arrived." Other senior Marine commanders were not convinced.[2]

The deployment of the 1st Cavalry Division seemed to justify the Army's concern when the Division commander complained that the Marines were not providing enough air support. General Westmoreland "blew his top" and moved to centralize control of air operations under a single manager, the Seventh Air Force—an anathema for the Marine Corps, which considered its aviation assets to be an integral part of its air-ground team. The fight intensified when General William W. Momyer, who commanded the Seventh Air Force, called upon General Rosson to solicit support for the concept. Rosson was well aware of Marine sensitivity and, unknown to Momyer, invited Davis to sit in on the meeting. To say that the Air Force officer was disconcerted upon seeing the Marine general in the office would be an understatement.

The two Army divisions, particularly the 1st Cavalry, were organized on the concept of high mobility, using helicopters as their primary mode of transportation. Infantry, artillery, aviation, and engineers were molded into a finely tuned, highly mobile force that added a new dimension to the war in the northern I Corps Tactical Zone (ICTZ).

The Army was critical of how the Marines used helicopters, according to Davis. "We had our operations usually tied to selecting an ideal place for a helicopter to sit down as opposed to sitting down where you can best defeat the enemy. Being oriented towards helicopters already and watching this with Rosson, I learned the lesson of operating with helicopters on high ground as opposed to the way the Marines had been doing it in the flat landing zones."[3]

Lieutenant General Rosson welcomed Davis as an old friend, treating him with respect and courtesy and ensuring that his staff extended the same consideration. Of course, Davis immediately won the staff over by his outgoing personality and professional approach to the assignment. He made no secret that he was there to learn. There was none of the fractious Marine vs Army relationships that seemed to be so prevalent at the senior command level.

Rosson immediately invited Davis to accompany him as he toured the Corps' area of operation. On these orientation trips, Davis met the principal Army commanders in PCV—Major General John J. "Jack" Tolson III of the "Cav," the 101st Airborne's Major General Olinto M. Barsanti, General Rathvon Tompkins of the 3rd Marine Division—and established not only a professional working rapport, but a personal, first-name-basis friendship. The author noted a marked difference between the two spirited Army generals and the Marine Division commander. Tolson and Barsonanti were vibrant, enthusiastic troop leaders. Tompkins, however, seemed worn out, the weight of command seemed to rest heavily on his shoulders. I believed he had been at war too long.

Rosson also provided Davis with a helicopter on a daily basis to visit the Corps' area of operations, which included the two northern provinces. "It was an ideal way to get oriented and attuned to the entire situation in terms of evaluating the readiness and effectiveness of [our] forces," Davis stated. One PCV officer commented that senior officers of Rosson's staff would "take turns having dinner with him [Davis] every night in the headquarters mess, giving him our ideas on mobile warfare, and during the day we flew around with him."[4]

The most important tactical lesson Davis learned while observing the Corps' units in action was exploiting the mobility of their helicopters, combined with air power, artillery, reconnaissance, and engineering equipment. In the mountainous terrain in the western part of Vietnam, the Army started knocking the tops off hills, emplacing artillery, and "air assaulting" infantry into these hilltop positions to scour the surrounding area for the North Vietnamese. After securing the immediate area, follow-on troops arrived to prepare command-and-control bunkers, artillery positions, and ammunition and supply dumps. Often a small bulldozer was heli-lifted in to assist with the preparations. The entire evolution was sometimes completed in a matter of hours, depending on the scale of the operation. The concept became known as Fire Support Bases and was used very effectively during Operation *Pegasus*, the relief of Khe Sanh by the 1st Air Cavalry.

Davis noted, "Operation *Pegasus* demonstrated the decisiveness of high-mobility operations. The Air Cavalry applied forces directly responsive to the enemy's disposition and forgot about real estate—forgetting about bases, going after the enemy in key areas—this punished the enemy most."[5]

From the very first, Davis started a routine that became standard throughout his tour in Vietnam—up at dawn, short situation brief, followed by helicopter visits to units in the field, returning late in the afternoon. In this manner, he was able to keep his finger on the tactical pulse of the units, as well as gain insight into the abilities of his commanders.

The Army Division commanders encouraged Davis to attend briefings and participate in their high-mobility operations. On one momentous occasion, Davis observed the 1st Air Cavalry air assault into the notorious A Shau Valley, a vital corridor the North Vietnamese used for moving supplies and personnel down the Ho Chi Minh Trail, and a staging area for attacks in Northern I Corps.

The NVA had taken control of the A Shau Valley in March 1966, after overrunning the isolated Special Forces camp located there. The North Vietnamese considered A Shau Valley to be their turf and had fortified it with powerful crew-served 37mm and rapid-firing twin-barreled 23mm antiaircraft guns, scores of 12.7mm heavy machine guns, a warren of underground bunkers and tunnels, and even tanks.

In mid-April, the "Cav" was ordered to air assault into the A Shau and clean it out. Davis was invited to observe the high-mobility operation. He flew into the valley in an Air Cavalry helicopter, a UH-1H Huey, piloted by the 52-year-old Jack Tolson, the Division commander. As the lead troop aircraft approached the landing zone, black puffs of 37mm antiaircraft fire darkened the sky. The NVA gunners shot down a Sikorsky CH-54 flying crane, ferrying an externally loaded bulldozer, two CH-47s and nearly two dozen Hueys. Tolson described the NVA's defenses as "very sophisticated and damn good antiaircraft forces … by far the hottest place we've ever gone into, and the most losses we've taken in a single day."[6]

The Cav lost nearly 30 helicopters the first day of the operation, codenamed "Delaware." The author remembers, "The sky was literally filled with helicopters, as wave after wave of 'sky troopers' entered the valley, in a carefully choreographed air-assault. The general's [Tolson's] aircraft flew at 10,000 feet, which allowed us to see the entire operation. It was unlike anything I have ever seen—quite beyond the capability of the Marine Corps at the time."[7]

Despite the helicopter losses, the operation was deemed a success because a huge amount of weapons and ammunition was captured or destroyed, and the flow of supplies was disrupted for months. When Davis landed in the valley, the first thing he saw were "Sky troopers" driving Russian-made trucks filled with NVA weapons. Several 37mm antiaircraft guns were captured and one was prominently displayed outside the Air Cavalry Division headquarters.

Davis was extremely interested in the high-mobility operations of the Air Cavalry. "This was an entirely different concept [of operations] and I picked it up immediately." He went so far as to author an article, with his aide, for the *Marine Corps Gazette* as an illustrative example of a Marine regiment in a heliborne assault. The article, titled "Marines in Assault by Helicopter," combined Army and Marine helicopter tactics into a lessons-learned format.[8]

A month after submitting the high-mobility article, Davis received a travel-worn package from the editor of the *Marine Corps Gazette*. It contained the article, along with a rejection slip. The accompanying note simply stated that, "As the article did not contain anything new in the way of innovative tactics, the *Gazette* did not feel it was worthy of publication." The editor was savvy enough to include the comments of the editorial board, some of whom were senior aviators. One rather terse comment simply stated, "Nothing new here, the Corps has been doing this for years." Davis was upset. "I called Lieutenant General Bill Van Ryzin, chief of staff at Marine Corps Headquarters, who had just returned from Vietnam, and said, 'Bill, you know what's real; those guys don't.'" The article was published.[9]

Clearly Davis wanted the article to be a guide for future Marine Corps' operations, because Marine mobility in I Corps was severely limited. "It became the bible for the first few months of my oncoming 3rd Marine Division command." A prime example of this occurred in late April when the Marine Special Landing Force, Battalion Landing Team 2/4, engaged elements of the 320th NVA Division near Dai Do, just north of the 3rd Marine Division Headquarters at Dong Ha. Rosson and Davis happened to be on a routine visit. General Tompkins gave them a brief on the Division's activities. He barely mentioned Dai Do and did not seem particularly concerned about the action.[10]

The two general officers returned to Dong Ha the following day. As the helicopter approached the base, evidence of heavy fighting could be seen around Dai Do. Plumes of greyish smoke marked bomb and artillery strikes. Supply and medical evacuation helicopters busily scurried back and forth. They could see the occasional flash of sunlight reflecting off a diving aircraft. By now it was obvious that 2/4 was in heavy combat with a major enemy force—and yet, as they found out later, Tompkins did not reinforce BLT 2/4.

In fact, the battalion fought alone until the NVA withdrew across the DMZ (Demilitarized Zone) to lick its wounds. To this day, Brigadier General William Weise, who was the battalion commander at Dai Do, blames Tompkins for not properly supporting his battalion. Davis said that Rosson "was disappointed with the Marines because they didn't apply all their forces to the situation ... and I agreed with that. I tried to understand that when forced into a defensive situation involving the manning of strong points for so long a period, one can become less aggressive in the pursuit and destruction of the enemy."[11] General Rosson's aide told the author that if the 3rd Marine Division's commanding general had been a soldier, he would have relieved him. The comment referred to the "Smith vs. Smith" brouhaha in World War II when Marine Lieutenant General Holland M. "Howlin Mad" Smith relieved Army Major General Ralph C. Smith during the battle of Saipan.

The III MAF Command Chronology for May 1968 noted: "In eastern Quang Tri, the enemy launched his most ambitious effort for the period, a multi-battalion attack by the 320th NVA Division aimed at Dong Ha. The main enemy force occupied the village of Dai Do, one-mile northeast of Dong Ha. Here they were met by the four understrength companies of the 2nd Battalion, 4th Marine Regiment reinforced by B/1/3. In three days of extremely heavy fighting the outnumbered Marines supported by air strikes, artillery, and naval gun fire stymied the enemy's attacks and inflicted extremely heavy troop and material losses on the 320th NVA Division."

On 28 April, shortly after the battle of Dai Do, the 2nd Brigade, 101st Airborne Division, in coordination with the 1st ARVN Division's "Black Panther," a Regional Force (RF) company, trapped a North Vietnamese battalion near a small village of Phuoc Yen, two miles northwest of Hue. A little after noon, General Barsanti asked the Corps commander to meet him and take a look at the results. General Rosson was absent, so Davis stepped in.

Davis met General Barsanti at the brigade headquarters and, after a briefing, flew to the scene of the action. They were met by a very excited paratroop commander, who escorted them around the battlefield. "Bomb and artillery craters covered almost every square foot of ground; bunkers were demolished; trench lines destroyed; and the area littered with the remains of the 8th Battalion of the 90th NVA Regiment. The group had to jump over a trench that ran through the center of the enemy defensive position. Fifteen dead NVA lay crumpled along its sides, the smell of death poisoned the air."

The official party, including the two generals, aides, and paratroopers, numbered more than a dozen. As they approached a small stream, one of the Black Panthers leaned over the bank and fired his carbine on full automatic. The firing caused quite a stir among the aides, who, alongside other jobs, provided protection for their bosses. A collection of pistols and various other weapons immediately materialized—pointing directly at the bemused Black Panther. The two old "war-horses," Davis and Barsanti, did not bat an eyelid. Several excited South Vietnamese jumped into the water, reached into the stream bank and pulled two "newly shot" enemy soldiers from their camouflaged hideaway. One quivered and gagged as blood poured from his mouth in the final throes of death.[12]

The operation was a classic encirclement operation, employing the rapid deployment of infantry by helicopter. Radio intercepts told of frantic NVA radio traffic trying to contact this "lost" battalion. The paratroopers counted over 300 enemy dead and more than 100 prisoners, up to that time the largest number captured during a single engagement.

Three days after the battle, at the behest of Barsanti, Generals Rosson and Davis returned to the battlefield. Barsanti was so proud of his paratroopers that he wanted the Corps commander to see what they had accomplished. One could smell the sickly odor of decay even as the helicopters flew over the site. Several decomposing bodies still lined the trench. The smell was overpowering, causing more than one onlooker to retch. Local Vietnamese were eventually hired to bury the remains. While the battlefield was gruesome, the three veteran general officers knew that this tactical victory was necessary if the North Vietnamese were to be defeated.

The Dai Do, A Shau Valley, and Phuoc Yen operations firmly convinced Davis that the Marines had to revise their tactics. "The way to get it done was to get out of those fixed positions and get mobility, to go and destroy the enemy on our terms—not sit there and absorb the shot and shell and frequent penetrations that the NVA were able to mount." He went on to say that, "The Marines 'invented' the troop-carrying helicopter, but we failed to exploit it. The Army came along … and had greater mobility."[13]

Davis closely observed the Army's high mobility for two months, particularly Operation *Pegasus*, the relief of Khe Sanh. "The Army applied forces directly responsive to the enemy's dispositions and forgot about real estate … forgetting about bases, going after the enemy in key areas … this punished the enemy most. Pegasus demonstrated the complete decisiveness of high-mobility operations."[14]

Davis developed such a professional rapport with Rosson and the other commanders that he had total confidence that he would be supported. "Rosson … guaranteed me that when we'd go into tactical operations, I never needed to look over my shoulder a single time and wonder if I was going to be supported. I knew that they were going to give me the helicopters I needed."[15]

CHAPTER 33

Taking Command, 3rd Marine Division

Thirty days later, Davis received orders to take command of the 3rd Marine Division at Dong Ha. He looked back at his time with PCV as extremely valuable in preparing to take over the Division. "I served with Rosson for the better part of two months—out with him every day, directly involved and actually participating in high-mobility operations that the Air Cavalry and the airborne division were conducting. The assignment as Marine deputy in Provisional Corps Vietnam allowed me to do something I had never done before or since, and that was to move in, prepared in the first hours to completely turn the command upside down."[1]

Upon his departure from PCV, Davis received a fitness report. Lieutenant General Rosson rated his Marine deputy outstanding in all respects and noted:

> In Major General Davis the United States Marine Corps possesses a future Commandant. As my deputy and alter ego he has performed with conspicuously outstanding effectiveness in active combat in Northern I Corps Tactical Zone, Republic of Vietnam. Of all general/flag officers known to me none surpasses him in unvarnished professionalism, proven leadership ability and potential for assumption of highest level command and staff responsibilities. Rock-like integrity, unswerving loyalty, pursuit of optimum standards, originality of thought and zeal for accomplishment stand out among other of his personal assets. Not only is he thoroughly at home and highly productive in the joint environment, but he has manifested uncommon talent for working with indigenous military forces and civilian agencies, by all of whom he is held in high esteem. He is superbly qualified to command a division in combat, and is certain to fulfill the duties entrusted to him in keeping with the highest and best traditions of the Marine Corps. Upon completion of his tour as division commander, I urge that he be promoted to lieutenant general ahead of his contemporaries.

LtGen H. W. Buse, Jr., Commanding General Fleet Marine Force (FMF), Pacific, the reviewing officer rated Davis as a "superb tactician and combat leader."

At 1100 on 21 May 1968, a small group of onlookers, mostly off-duty staff and a small contingent of troops, gathered around the landing zone in the center of the Division headquarters area at the Dong Ha Combat Base. Davis and Tompkins stood in front of a line of staff officers. The colors were brought forward by the Division

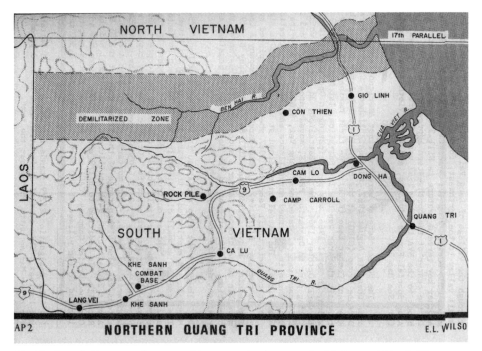

The Northern I Corps was the scene of heavy combat between the Marines and North Vietnamese regulars who used the DMZ to infiltrate men and supplies into South Vietnam. (U.S. Marine Corps)

sergeant major and presented to General Tompkins, who turned and presented them to General Davis, signifying the formal change of command. The two exchanged places—Davis on the right, the commander's position. The two officers spoke briefly, and then General Rosson stepped forward. He ended the ceremony by praising the abilities of both men and the 3rd Marine Division.

"The mission of the division." Davis explained, "was primarily the destruction of North Vietnamese and local forces in Quang Tri Province, secondarily, maintain fixed certain positions along the DMZ, and major bases throughout the province, and finally in close coordination with ARVN forces, to carry out the above specific missions."[2]

Immediately after the change of command, all key staff officers and regimental commanders were assembled in the Division conference room. Davis started the meeting by waving a copy of his "yet to be published high-mobility article." He announced, "From this point on, the Division will use it as a guide." He told them that no longer would the Division guard fixed installations. "I didn't ask or plead with them. I ordered: 'Before dark, these things will happen.' I laid out my scheme, what were later called my 'before-dark dictates.'"[3]

After he departed the conference room, several of the more senior officers groused about these new precepts. "Who does he think he is?" "Wait until he finds out what

3rd Marine Division, May 1968

When Davis took command of the 3rd Marine Division it was organized into three infantry regiments, one artillery regiment, and supporting elements, with the 2nd ARVN Regiment, 1st ARVN Division in a reinforcement role. His headquarters was located at the Dong Ha Combat Base 12 kilometers south of the DMZ, a no-man's land that cut across the northern part of the country separating North Vietnam from South Vietnam.

The maneuver elements of the Division were generally occupying fixed positions in four operational areas centered on the Demilitarized Zone from Cua Viet to Khe Sanh:

- The 3rd Marines headquarters and the 1st Amphibian Tractor Battalion were located at Camp Kistler at the Cua Viet's port facilities in the coastal lowlands. The 1st and 3rd Battalion, 3rd Marines and the 1st Battalion, 9th Marines conducted periodic sweeps of the nearby area. Units of the Tractor Battalion occupied the C-4 strongpoint, as well as conducting sweeps of the immediate area. This area was designated the Napoleon-Saline area of operations.
- The 9th Marines headquarters, located at Dong Ha near the Division COC, provided company-sized units for security of the outposts from Gio Linh to Cam Lo, as well as major line of communications, Routes 1, 9, and 561. The 2nd Battalion, 26th Marines secured the strongpoints at Con Thien, A-3, C-2, and C-2 bridge all strung along Route 561, the main north-south provincial road stretching from the Demilitarized Zone to Cam Lo. The area of operation for the 9th Marines was designated Kentucky.
- The 4th Marines headquartered at Camp Carroll in the Lancaster II area of operations had a battalion of the 9th Marines under its operational control. The 1st and 2nd Battalions, 4th Marines, the latter organized as a battalion landing team (BLT), and the 2nd Battalion, 9th Marines secured combat bases at Camp Carroll, Thon Son Lam, and Ca Lu, all centered on Route 9. The 3rd Battalion, 1st Marines was also located at Ca Lu.
- Task Force H, a multi-battalion task force headquartered at Khe Sanh, consisted of two battalions of the 1st Marines and the 2nd Battalion, 3rd Marines. The area of operations designated Scotland II was the largest of the four operational areas encompassing the western third of Quang Tri Province. The Task Force's three battalions were assigned the task of maintaining the defense of the Khe Sanh Combat Base and the surrounding outposts on Hills 881, 861, 950 and other prominent terrain features. In addition, troops of the task force secured Route 9, the vital overland resupply route for the Division's western-most fortified positions, from Landing Zone Stud and Ca Lu to Khe Sanh.
- The 12th Marines four organic artillery battalions provided a battery in every combat base and strongpoint to support the maneuver battalions.

it's really like." I [author] observed that it did not take the staff long to understand that Davis meant exactly what he said. He never raised his voice and was always courteous. I never heard him swear. However, his strength of character, powerful intellect, and tactical mastery communicated a determination that did not brook opposition.

The next day during the morning intelligence brief, a South Vietnamese Army (ARVN) officer pointed out the location of two major groups of North Vietnamese on the map that covered one wall of the general's plywood office. The officer started to move on, when Davis interrupted with several questions. The ARVN officer was stunned; no one had ever asked a question during any of his previous briefs. His information was always treated perfunctorily. It took a moment for him to gather his thoughts before answering. He traced a line on the map east of Route 1, along the Cua Viet River toward Dong Ha. Davis listened intently and nodded, as if to say, now I have an opportunity to take on the Division's old nemesis who escaped earlier in May at Dai Do (Davis had a habit of indicating acceptance by nodding his head). He was such a quick study that often he had formulated a plan by the time of the acknowledgement.

Davis turned to his aide and told him to order up his helicopter for a flight to the 2nd ARVN regimental headquarters. Twenty-five minutes later, he landed in their command post, completely unannounced. The compound exploded as frenzied Vietnamese rushed to greet the two-star visitor. Lieutenant Colonel Vu Van Giai, the regimental commander, met Davis, and, after being informed of the purpose of the visit, confirmed and upgraded the intelligence reports. Davis then asked Giai if he could support a multi-battalion plan to encircle the NVA. Without hesitation the Vietnamese officer indicated that he could provide two battalions that afternoon.

Colonel Giai was an impressive officer with a good command of English. He was a slender, wiry Vietnamese soldier who had a well-documented record of bravery. One story had him leaping from a helicopter in the DMZ to grab weapons and equipment of NVA soldiers he had just killed. He was tough, combat hardened, and respected by Davis for his tactical and leadership skills. Giai was eventually promoted to major general and placed in command of the 1st ARVN Division. During the 1972 NVA offensive, his division was routed and defeated. Giai escaped to the United States upon the fall of South Vietnam.

"I asked Lieutenant Colonel Giai which force the Marines could have," Davis explained. "We agreed that the Marines would attack the northern one immediately. This was the largest and possibly the command element of the 52nd Regiment, 320th North Vietnamese Division. Giai and his regiment would assault the force posing the more immediate threat to the Cua Viet waterway." Unit boundaries, exchange of liaison officers, general timing and support were arranged. The units were then set in motion, and the staffs went to work on the details. Within minutes Davis was airborne on the way to the 9th Marines headquarters, which was located a short distance from the Division helipad.[4]

The 9th Marines "owned" the "Square" area, but never had more than a bob-tailed battalion to operate in the area, as the rest of the regiment guarded base camps. The regimental CP was located in a large sandbagged bunker less than 100 meters from the 3rd Division CP. The aide remembers how he and Davis walked over and entered the CP, unannounced, surprising the hell out of the regimental commander. It was the author's job as Davis' aide to ensure this did not happen. The colonel was not happy and, if looks could kill, he would have been a dead man!

After greeting everyone, Davis immediately stepped to the tactical map that covered one wall. In typical fashion, he pointed to the suspected enemy location and quickly briefed the commander, Colonel Richard B. Smith, ordering him to coordinate an attack on the enemy force. The quizzical look on the officer's face spoke volumes—"Where the hell am I going to find an extra Marine?" Smith believed that his Marines were "sitting in defensive positions up there playing strictly defensive combat. Marines are always supposed to be in an assault over a beach, but this just isn't the name of the game out there."

The stunned look was quickly replaced with astonishment as Davis informed him that two battalions of ARVN soldiers would be placed in operational control of his command within an hour, a Marine battalion was flying in from Khe Sanh, and another was force-marching to join him at that very moment. The look on Colonel Smith's face was one of total amazement. Within hours four battalions encircled the unsuspecting NVA force and pounded it with massive supporting arms.

The 9th Marine Command Chronology noted, "On one occasion, the encircled enemy attempted to escape across the trace; however, artillery ... gunships, fixed wing [aircraft], and tanks were brought to bear ... with devastating effect." The two-day fight was bloody—23 Marines killed in action and 75 wounded, while the NVA lost 161 dead and 26 prisoners, 87 individual weapons, 29 crew-served weapons captured, including an entire battery of 12.7mm machine guns. Unfortunately, many of the NVA escaped because the Marines were slow in completing the encirclement. However, Davis was pleased with the results because the operation introduced the concept of generating overwhelming Marine force by stripping the fixed position of their infantry.[5]

McNamara's Barrier System

During his two months at PCV, Davis participated in discussions with Rosson and Westmoreland regarding the tactical mobility of the 3rd Marine Division. In essence, many of the Division's infantry battalions were tied down, because of a political decision, to a series of strong points and base camps south of the DMZ in Quang Tri Province. "We had something like two dozen battalions up there all tied down (with limited exception) … and the situation didn't demand it," Davis said. "The way to get it done [fight the enemy] was to get out of these fixed positions and get mobility, to go and destroy the enemy, not sit there and absorb the shot and shell and frequent penetrations that the enemy was able to mount."[6]

The $6 billion McNamara barrier system, or the "Trace" as it was called, deployed a series of strong points spread across the top of South Vietnam. It consisted of three 600-meter-wide clearings lined with barbed wire, electronic and acoustical intrusion devices, and personnel minefields. The first section of the barrier was a linear-manned obstacle system which extended along the eastern portion of the DMZ some 20 miles to the South China Sea. Another section, also a series of strong points, was located along obvious avenues of approach across the western portion of the DMZ adjacent to the Laotian border. These strong points were anchored by numerous combat bases, Khe Sanh being the most western base. The last section was a scattering of sensors inside Laos along suspected routes of North Vietnamese infiltration branching from the Ho Chi Minh trail.[7]

"McNamara's brain trust had come up with a defensive concept of putting manned strong points across the DMZ, with all these megabuck sensors in between, to keep the guerrillas out," Davis commented. "This strong-point defense was faulty. We weren't fighting guerrillas; we were fighting North Vietnamese Army (NVA) units. The strong points were too far apart to protect the line, and it was tying down our forces." The freedom to maneuver belonged to the NVA, who regularly ventured south across the DMZ to attack specific targets along the barrier and then withdrew north to rest and refit. The McNamara Line policy gave the initiative to the enemy by keeping Marine infantry inside fixed installations. Defense became the name of the game, and with it came a corresponding loss of offensive spirit.[8]

In the "Leatherneck Square," a quadrangle bounded by Con Thien, Gio Linh, Cam Lo, and Dong Ha, it was commonplace for a single battalion to operate all alone because of the need to man the barrier positions. Given the mission to conduct sweep operations to locate and disrupt the infiltrating NVA, the Marine unit would often make contact with the superbly camouflaged and entrenched enemy whose strategy was to let the lead elements in close before initiating contact. The opening burst of fire was designed to cause casualties close to their position to nullify American artillery and close-air support. This placed the unit commander on the horns of a dilemma: either attack head on into prepared lanes of fire to rescue the wounded or withdraw to call in fire, leaving the casualties to fend for themselves. The outcome was often numbing: heavy casualties with little to show for the effort. No exploitation of the contact, no pursuit, no overwhelming concentration of force, just "soldier on," day after day, contact after contact, until relieved by another one of the strong-point battalions. Battalion after battalion rotated through this "meat grinder."

Morale within the infantry battalions dropped precipitously as casualties and frustrations mounted. In 1967, 5,000 Marines were killed or wounded, with almost

1,000 in September alone, in and around the DMZ, including the Leatherneck Square area. One long-suffering unit, 1st Battalion, 9th Marines, which was intimately familiar with combat in the Leatherneck Square, earned the macabre nickname, "Walking Dead." Continued heavy fighting promised more of the same. In the first three months of the New Year, the 3rd Marine Division averaged 170 marines killed and almost 1,200 wounded a month.

The 3rd Marine Division G-2 (intelligence) estimated that, at one time or another, elements of five NVA divisions operated against the Marines: the 324th, 325th, 308th, 307th, and 320th divisions, together with several separate battalions—some 20,000 men. A "front" headquarters was located north of the DMZ to control these forces. It maintained pressure on the Marine positions by direct infantry attack and by indirect fire from artillery, rockets, and mortars. All the major Marine bases in the central and eastern DMZ could be hit by NVA artillery located north of the Ben Hai River.

The NVA's 1968 Tet Offensive throughout South Vietnam marked a renewed effort to win the war. The U.S. news media were filled with accounts of the fighting, including the dramatic sapper attack on the U.S. Embassy in Saigon. In the north, the battles of Hue City and the siege of Khe Sanh captured the public's attention.

Davis looked at the situation as "kind of a desperate suicidal effort on the part of the NVA and they were punished severely. Our forces held and there was no permanent loss of positions anywhere. Some severe setbacks, but it really resulted in more pluses on our side than on theirs because they had made their maximum effort and they failed. It didn't get that treatment in the press. It was a total condemnation of our effort by the news media, and I don't think that we ever outlived it. I don't think we ever again were trusted and given credit for what we did … it had a devastating effect on us here in the United States."[9]

With the success of the first operation, Davis "directed that each of the four or five forward positions where there was a battalion holed up … or hiding out, as someone coined … would now have only one company, and the other three rifle companies and the headquarters would deploy as a mobile force to seek out the enemy." He reversed the Division's tactical disposition to take the fight to the enemy. Lieutenant Colonel Max McQuown, Battalion Landing Team 3/1, stated that prior to Davis taking command there were "a myriad of static defensive positions of little tactical value. These positions and the rigid control the Division exercised over every combat unit, fragmented battalions reduced their combat capability, and severely limited their freedom of action … The initiative passed to the NVA by default." Tompkins' defenders pointed out, however, that Khe Sanh had been the Division's main focus of attention. In addition, he was hamstrung by the requirement to maintain and man the McNamara line.[10]

However, some of the infantry battalions had leadership problems. Soon after taking command, Davis stood on a ridge reviewing the next day's helicopter assault with a battalion commander. He pointed at the objective and said, "I want you to sweep that entire area with artillery before you land." The next day, the lead company was shot out of a hot zone. One helicopter, carrying a dozen Marines, crashed and tumbled down the slope of a hill, killing everyone onboard. The day after the aborted assault, Davis called me into his office and asked me to verify his order (to use artillery) to the battalion commander. "I remember [General Davis] watching me intently as I recited the conversation. After finishing, he nodded and said, 'He killed my Marines.' I found out later that [Davis] relieved the battalion commander."

Davis believed that Vietnam "demanded superior quality commanders, even more than Korea and World War II. There were just too many near impossible things that had to be done. In other words, the very good to excellent officer can perform most things, but when you've got Marines' lives at stake, you need an officer who can ensure that the task gets done with the least casualties. I guess I relieved as many battalion commanders as anybody ... but it was never because of any flush, immediate judgement. It was because of performance over a period where they were getting too many Marines killed, not responding to the kind of operation that we wanted to conduct, or some other good, substantial reason."[11]

One of the difficulties Davis encountered was the constant rotation of battalions among regiments. This system broke down the traditional relationship between a battalion and its parent regiment. One commander described its shortfall. "The regiment had little interest in the logistics, personnel, supply, and maintenance fields of the battalion." On the other hand, "Battalions felt ... they were commanded by strangers." Colonel Robert H. Barrow (later Commandant of the Marine Corps) was equally concerned. "Every unit has a kind of personality all its own, often reflecting the personality of the commander, so you never got to know who did what best, or who you would give this mission to." Davis reorganized the Division so that regiments controlled their own organic battalions. He felt this restructuring created "a greater awareness on the part of the staff officers in the regiment and their counterparts in the battalions about one another's capabilities and personalities. Unit integrity is essential for high-mobility mountain warfare—very complex, very fast-moving operations where you must depend on people knowing each other and being able to respond. It was crucial in the kind of war I wanted to fight."[12]

CHAPTER 34

Assault from the Sky

Davis' operational success depended on the exploitation of intelligence, employment of highly mobile infantry utilizing helicopters, and backed by aircraft and artillery support. The first part of the Davis mobility strategy was implemented by the closure of the Khe Sanh Combat Base, which generated three infantry battalions and greatly reduced the logistical requirement of the Division to support the combat base.

When the news leaked out, Davis was asked by several newsmen: "How can you abandon Khe Sanh after you paid so much for it?" He replied, "I can manage that whole area with a couple of mobile battalions better than it was managed with five fixed, in place, battalions." A news blackout was clamped over the closing to protect the lives of the remaining garrison. Major General Carl Hoffman's Task Force H began a quiet orderly withdrawal, until a correspondent broke the story. Hoffman blamed John S. Carroll of the *Baltimore Sun* for breaking the blackout. Along with Carroll's story, the *Baltimore Sun* published an aerial photo of the base, which showed the position of every trench, bunker, and installation. Immediately after the story was published, there was a dramatic increase in shelling, which cost the lives of several Marines. Although it was a small punishment considering the crime, Carroll's press credentials were suspended for six months.[1]

The second part of Davis' high-mobility strategy depended on helicopters. "Fortunately, I arrived at a time when our resources were fully generated; the new model of the CH-46 helicopter was available, with greater power and lift capacity … the old 46 would hardly pick up a squad. Soon we were knocking the tops off little mountain peaks, putting our forces up there to move down against the enemy [Fire Support Base concept]." Provisional Marine Air Group 39 (PROV MAG-39), comprising three squadrons of CH-46 helicopters, was formed to support the Division from Quang Tri.[2] Davis placed increasing demands on PROV MAG-39 to support his high-mobility concept. Much to Davis' chagrin, the group commander, a colonel, did not have the "horsepower" to change rigid operational procedures. On one particularly frustrating day, helicopters were actually in the air when they were called back to base because the pilots were about to exceed their daily flight hours. In another instance, Davis' scheduled daily helicopter failed to show. After repeated calls, a beat-up "hanger queen" arrived—no doors, oil leaks, and a flight crew that had not been briefed on the mission. An investigation discovered that the squadron commander, a lieutenant colonel, had taken the general's bird for his own personal use. It was the last time he made that mistake!

The MAG commander finally assigned Davis his own helicopter, a Huey UH-1E. Unfortunately, "it couldn't hack it" in the mountainous terrain of the Division's area of operations. It lacked the lift capability of the Army's H model, which Davis had used at PCV. An H model's increased power would have allowed him to get into "all of these out of the way places and these hilltops, and through all this weather." In the Marine bird he "got flopped two or three times." On one memorable occasion, the aircraft hit the ground at full power, tearing up shrubbery and creating a huge dust storm as it bounced over the landscape. When it finally stopped, Davis calmly unbuckled and exited the rocking aircraft—immediately followed by his frenzied aide (the author).

Davis "went to war" with the III MAF and 1st Marine Air Wing (MAW) in an effort to gain more helicopter mobility. "We suffered many, many times because we didn't have the air part of the air-ground team up north. The effort to run the air campaign from Da Nang just didn't work." This lack of support was particularly galling, because the 3rd Marine Division "established all kinds of records, in terms of helo lift, support, and utilization rates—but something is wrong with the system. It has led us to too many bad days." Davis thought the allocation of helicopters "was so centralized that you have got to work out in detail the day before exactly what you want and schedule it. There's no way a ground commander can work out a precise plan for the next day's operation unless the enemy is going to hold still." He wanted a system that was "totally flexible and responsive to the ground commander's needs."[3]

The system was partially fixed when Brigadier General Homer Dan Hill, assistant wing commander, came north to keep an eye on "that infantry ruffian," as one air officer stated. Hill turned out to be Davis' right-hand man—he was an aviator who made things happen. "Homer Dan," Davis said, "brought authority from the wing commander to not only offer professional advice to me, but to run our air operations. He gave us great flexibility." Hill commented that he had participated in about 75 "highly successful helicopter heli-borne assaults in and around the DMZ during the temporary assignment." Hill attended all Division briefings and went with Davis "on many of his helo rides to his units talking to our FACs [forward air controllers] and ALOs [air liaison officers] as well as regimental and battalion commanders."[4]

Unfortunately, Hill "was recalled down below the pass, and the longer he stayed away, the more problems were generated." Davis was forced to deal with officers who were not in a position to make decisions without going to Da Nang for approval. He viewed this as unworkable. Lieutenant Colonel Richard E. Carey, a staff officer with the MAW, said that while Hill was with Davis the relationship "was superior, simply because he spoke for the wing and worked so closely with the Division commander. [Hill] maintained a constant dialogue on both fixed-wing and helo support for the Division. It was not uncommon for him to be on the phone at all hours of the day and night working closely with us on the details of the required support. After he left, work had to be conducted through an intermediary, which really slowed down the decision process. We also lost the pulse of the dynamic fast-moving General Davis."[5]

The III MAF Chief of Staff, Brigadier General Earl E. Anderson, pushed back on Davis' requests for additional helicopter support. "Ray Davis has really been shot in the fanny with the Army helicopter system; although I frankly believe that it's more the result of the large numbers of helicopters available to the Army units, together with the fact that the ground officer has greater control over them than does the Marine commander." Davis fired back that this was exactly the problem. He complained that after the initial planning, the infantry commander played a secondary role. "The helicopter leader with this captive load of troops decides where, when, and even if the troops will land."[6]

The allocation of helicopters was never satisfactorily resolved and remained a constant source of irritation. The bottom line, as Davis told III MAF, was, "If I don't get this helicopter support that I'm asking for … from you, I'm going to get it from the Army. The devil take the hindmost!" Davis commented later, "I hope we never again try to run a Division-wing team with the air side of it absent."[7]

Reconnaissance Patrols

Davis explained that the Division's success was the result of the exploitation of intelligence; electronics collection; information from local villagers; sensors (the Division monitored 125 sensor and acoustical sensor strings); and the most reliable, four-to-six man reconnaissance patrols. "There was never a needle flicker in the sensor system that indicated activity that we didn't go out and find out what it was … we never found any indication that looked the least bit real that we didn't put [reconnaissance] Marines out there to check it. And when they found it was true, we went out and did something about it. So, it was this exploitation of intelligence that made success possible."[8]

All through the summer and into the fall, North Vietnamese attacks slacked off. However, it did not "smell" right. The Division G-2 reported increased enemy activity along the Laotian border, 35 miles due west of Hue City, the same area they used to stage for the 1968 Tet Offensive. There was some concern the North Vietnamese were going to launch another offensive, "Tet '69." Signal intelligence picked up increased radio traffic on the recently reopened Route 922, which ran from Laos toward the A Shau Valley. Reconnaissance aircraft sighted scores of trucks, sometimes as many as a thousand per day. The road was protected by 12.7mm, 35mm, and 37mm antiaircraft guns. In mid-January, a 37mm gun shot down an A-6 Intruder, with the loss of its two-man crew. The NVA definitely did not want aircraft nosing around.

Davis knew something was up and he "had to know what was going on in those mountains. The NVA logistics system was designed to support not only his [the NVA] main force … but also his local forces through prepositioned supplies. He [NVA] would start down through Laos or the DMZ and establish concealed bases about every ten miles. Each of these bases was prepared with bunkers, tunnels, and hideaways, so that his porters could leave their supplies and dodge our air attacks." Most enemy porters relied on guides instead of maps, and used well-marked, high-speed trails. "We came to realize," noted Davis, "that if we were able to keep Marines on these trails, even from time to time, and were able to clean out his way stations periodically, that we could severely limit his [NVA] activity."[9]

With the enemy playing a deadly game of hide and seek, Davis ordered reconnaissance teams into the mountain vastness—as many as 40 teams in operation at all times—to locate enemy base camps. He was deadly serious about this. "Every day at our staff briefing, my officers knew I would ask the same question: 'How many patrols do we have on the ground?' If we had less than twenty, they would have until noon to get at least twenty on the ground."[10]

The Division G-3, Colonel Alexander L. Michaux, said the mission of these teams was "not to call in fire or anything … just find them and tell us where they [the NVA] are." Davis emphasized that "Every indication of enemy activity from whatever means is explored by the insertion of reconnaissance teams … everywhere … on a continuing basis, a massive reconnaissance team effort is maintained. We knew with some precision where the enemy was located, and what he was doing. And just as important, where he was not. This meant that we could move our limited forces very quickly to areas of immediate interest without much concern over the resultant denuding of other areas in the process."[11]

The reconnaissance teams were inserted by helicopter, with enough food and water for several days. Stealth was their primary defense against the heavily armed North Vietnamese. When the reconnaissance teams discovered a "high speed trail," they would monitor it and if warranted, infantry would be deployed to interdict it.

However, stealth did not always protect them. One reconnaissance team, call sign "Amanda," ran into trouble immediately upon insertion. They heard movement and almost simultaneously began receiving a heavy volume of small arms and automatic weapons fire. The team returned fire and called for help. An aerial observer came up on station and directed air strikes. By this time, the hard-pressed recon team was trading hand grenades with the NVA, who were only 50 feet away. Air strikes were brought in close; dirt clods from a bomb explosion hit one of the team members. The situation was desperate; Amanda was in danger of being overrun and needed immediate extraction.

A last air strike was called in to clear a path to a landing zone 75-meters away. The team made a mad dash, as four helicopter gunships swooped in, guns blazing, to cover the extraction bird. The CH-46 touched down, the team scrambled on board, and the helicopter leaped back into the air, taking hits as it passed out of range. Team Amanda was lucky; they survived the experience. Ground troops were inserted to exploit the contact, in accordance with Davis' precepts. "Where we found activity we went in and smashed them …."[12]

The 3rd Marine Division "never launched an operation without acquiring clear definition of the targets and objectives through intelligence confirmed by recon patrols. High-mobility operations [were] too difficult and complex to come up empty or [end] in disaster."[13]

CHAPTER 35

Swing Force

Within weeks of taking command, Davis sketched out his concept for a dedicated force to exploit intelligence reports. Initially he identified 2nd Battalion, 9th Marines as his dedicated battalion. Lieutenant Colonel Frederic S. Knight related a conversation on the subject. "General Davis dropped in at my headquarters. 'Fred … I have decided to make you my swing battalion.' I asked him what a swing battalion was. He responded, 'Whenever anyone finds the enemy, I'm going to drop you right on top of them.'" Davis wanted the capability to commit up to a regiment, if necessary. After carefully screening the Division's regiments, he settled on the 26th Marines, who were just pulling out of the abandoned base at Khe Sanh. Unfortunately, before he could officially designate them, they were transferred to the 1st Marine Division.[1]

Davis received notice that III MAF intended to further reduce his forces. "It is obvious that a severe draw down on 3rd MarDiv capability at this time will seriously limit my ability to maintain the present flexible, mobile posture which I feel is necessary if I am to continue the effective suppression of enemy activity in this area." Lieutenant General Richard G. Stilwell, Rosson's replacement at PCV, took up the issue with III MAF and, after some hard bargaining, got a commitment from them to maintain 3rd Marine Division at 12 battalions, nine Marine and three Army. III MAF acquiesced after PCV, now XXIV Corps, proposed a boundary shift, which decreased the area of operation of the 1st Marine Division. With that commitment, Davis selected the 9th Marine Regiment as his swing force, but he needed a commander who could lead it.

Davis "wanted to bring back unit integrity. This whole business of rotating units in and out of fixed positions just served to disrupt the organization … The regimental commander didn't know his own regiment at all … half their battalions belonged to them and the other half were somewhere else." By reducing the fixed positions to company-sized units, Davis was able to generate a mobile force of several battalions and keep them together, along with their supporting units—artillery, engineers, and communications. He was convinced that "Unit integrity is essential for high-mobility mountain warfare—very complex, very fast-moving operations, where you must depend on people knowing each other…" The 9th Marine Regiment "Striking Ninth," was his swing force, and Bob Barrow was going to lead it.[2]

Bob Barrow recalled, "In the spring of 1968 I was told I was going to the 1st Marine Division as the G-3. It was a little bit of a disappointment because I would like to have a command, but orders are orders, so I reconciled myself to the staff assignment. At the time, all colonels and above going to Vietnam had to stop off in Hawaii for briefings and to pay a call on the FMF PAC commander, Lieutenant General Henry Buse. I knew him well. He has a delightful sense of humor, likes to tease people, but I was not prepared for it. He asked, 'Now, where are you going' and, 'What are you going to do?' I told him and he replied, much to my surprise, 'Well, you're not going there. I just visited Ray Davis. He spoke of what he planned to do … That is quite different from what his predecessors had been doing. He said, "I need a swing regiment and you have a fellow coming out here that I want to command that regiment—and that's Bob Barrow," so that's where you're going.'"[3]

Two days later Barrow reached the 3rd Marine Division Headquarters (Forward) at Dong Ha and reported to Ray Davis, who "immediately took me on an aerial reconnaissance all around the area." The tour gave Barrow an opportunity to see, first hand, what Davis had in store for the "Striking Ninth." Once Barrow was established with the regiment, this aerial tour became standard procedure for every new field-grade officer who reported to the Division. Davis would drop the officer off at the 9th Marines CP, where Barrow would take him in tow for a little chat. If the officer passed muster, he stayed; if not, he was loaded back aboard a helo and assigned elsewhere.[4]

Davis had great confidence in Barrow. He was the man for the job. Likewise, Barrow "knew Ray Davis. He was one of our great thinkers, a doer, a real hero, with a Medal of Honor, Navy Cross—a very distinguished record of service. He was also very aggressive and wanted to do things quickly." A day after Barrow arrived in Dong Ha, he took command of the 9th Marines. After a short, simple ceremony, he turned to the operations officer and said, "Saddle up the headquarters." The look on the officer's face was priceless. "Where to?" he asked incredulously. At that time, the regiment had almost a permanent base comp, with all the amenities of home. They had gotten comfortable or, as Barrow noted, "Even though they were good guys, they had lost touch with the men in the field. They were used to putting up antennas and staying in contact with subordinates—at some distance." Barrow responded, "We're going to C-2," an artillery position below the DMZ.[5]

Some hours later, they finally squeezed aboard the trucks for the motor march to C-2. One of Barrow's friends observed the evolution: "My God, Bob, they look like Cox's Army!" The men and truck were festooned with personal gear. Barrow replied, "After I move them three or four times, they'll get rid of that stuff." He also noted his boss watching. "Being the man that he was, Davis just smiled in his quiet, taciturn manner; he knew what the results would be." In the coming months, Barrow was true to his word. He displaced the command post 14 times, getting the relocation down to a fine science. "I'd say, 'Let's move this afternoon.' We'd get a couple of helos and, in no time at all, we'd be gone." The regiment flew to the sound of the guns.[6]

Dewey Canyon

In early January 1969, Davis ordered a pre-emptive strike into the A Shau Valley: Operation *Dewey Canyon*. Barrow's swing force was given the mission to interdict the enemy's supply route and capture and destroy his equipment. "In five days we conceived, planned, and launched a regimental-sized force, totally dependent on helicopter resupply, in and around the A Shau Valley, thirty miles from the nearest friendly force." A Shau was one of the strongest enemy bases in South Vietnam. It was located only six miles from the Laotian border near the Ho Chi Minh Trail network, the major enemy supply route that provided access into the two northern provinces.[7]

Hundreds of trucks convoyed supplies and equipment east, along Route 922, into the southern end of the valley, where it was stockpiled in camouflaged dumps. "No army fights without logistic support," Barrow declared. "The NVA laboriously and surreptitiously built-up its supplies in South Vietnam before its troops arrived. The [enemy's] first order of business was to move all the things of war; all their logistics forward from the sanctuaries of North Vietnam, just across the DMZ, or from Laos. We must do everything we can to find that stuff, wherever it exists, and obviously destroy it."[8]

A Shau itself was a deep valley 22-miles long, sandwiched between two heavily forested mountain ranges. Thousands of North Vietnamese porters and support troops maintained the road network and security. Battle-tested NVA of the 6th and 9th Regiments provided security. Three abandoned airstrips and remnants of an old Special Forces camp—overrun in a savage battle—bore mute testimony to the enemy's fighting capabilities. Barrow knew they were tough opponents, "The enemy bore no resemblance to the little fellow with black pajamas; they were really a first-class army."[9]

In the early morning hours of 22 January, artillery and air strikes pounded the 9th Marines' first objective, a hill mass three kilometers inside the A Shau Valley. Immediately following the prep fires, two companies of the 2nd Battalion conducted a heliborne assault onto the hill. Teams of engineers closely followed and began clearing trees to from a landing zone for a 105mm artillery battery. It was not an easy task—trees three to four feet in diameter had to be cut down. Bulldozers were heli-lifted in to help clear the area, as well as dig gun pits, ammunition berms, and command bunkers. Within 24 hours, Fire Support Base (FSB) Razor was up and running and prepared to support the next helicopter assault. Barrow recalled that FSB Razor was named after General Davis from a nickname given him in the early 1960s by Major General James N. Master, Sr., when both served on Okinawa: "The razor cuts to the root of the problem."

Without incident, Fire Support Base Cunningham, a 1,100-meter-long razorback ridge in the center of the regiment's area of operations, was opened next. The two FSBs were mutually supporting—within artillery range of each other. The concept required that FSBs be established no more than 8,000 meters from each other in order to provide mutual support—plus an additional 3,000-meter overlap, the range of North Vietnamese mortars.

Soon, five artillery batteries were in position to support infantry patrols into the surrounding jungle. Almost immediately, a company discovered a four-strand telephone line that ran for miles through the jungle, from Laos to Quang Tri Province. It was strung from tree-mounted insulators under the jungle canopy, effectively concealing it from air observation. A special fire-man army and Marine intelligence team tapped into the wire and monitored North Vietnamese transmissions.

Infantry patrols, operating under the protective artillery fans of the two FSBs, searched for signs of the enemy. Barrow described the effort. "Each battalion has four companies operating out of company operating bases, each separated from the other by about 2,000 to 3,000 meters. A company will spend, characteristically, two, three, or four days in one of these operating bases and conduct extensive patrolling by platoon or squads in all directions ... so that after three or four days the area extending in a radius of a couple of thousand meters out from the operating base has been covered. The operating base represents a place of resupply and for a patrol that has been out perhaps for two days to rest for a day, preparatory for renewing its patrolling activities."[10]

The patrols quickly ran into small groups of enemy soldiers. The deadly encounters were often at close range—a few meters in the dense foliage—and usually resulted in casualties on both sides. The enemy was trying to slow the Marine advance, so they could evacuate or conceal their supplies and facilities. It was not enough. One patrol discovered a complete field hospital, consisting of eight large wooden buildings capable of housing 150 patients. In addition, large quantities of Russian made surgical instruments and medical supplies were captured.

Enemy resistance stiffened as the swing force advanced toward the southern end of the valley. North Vietnamese Army 122mm artillery shelled Cunningham from inside Laos, killing and wounding ten Marines and temporarily disabling a 155mm howitzer. Counterbattery fire proved ineffective because the Marine guns were outranged. The only solution was to use air. Barrow noted, "counterbattery was simply always having an AO up." Failing to knock out Cunningham by indirect fire, the NVA tried another tactic. In the early hours of 16 February, elite sapper teams from the 812th Regiment attacked the fire support base.[11]

Under the cover of a thick blanket of fog and a heavy mortar barrage, three teams—50 sappers—breached the defensive wire and fought their way inside the perimeter. Chaplain David Brock was startled awake. "During the early moments of the attack, an NVA soldier stuck his head inside the tent ... but fortunately did not throw a grenade inside. A grenade was thrown into a small bunker a few feet away, killing two men." An officer crawled out of his partially collapsed bunker, to face an enemy soldier. He leaped on the surprised North Vietnamese and bludgeoned him to death with a hand grenade. The company gunnery sergeant killed several sappers, in hand-to-hand combat, with his K-Bar fighting knife.[12]

Dawn revealed a gruesome aftermath: dead sappers strewn amid shell-blasted bunkers and gun pits. The penetrating odor of cordite and smoke hung in the air. Another smell, a mixture of blood and decomposition, mingled with the stench, leaving a never-to-be forgotten memory for the survivors. Casualties totaled 37 North Vietnamese, four Marines killed in action, and 46 wounded. Barrow praised the actions of the Marine defenders: "They'll [NVA] probably think twice from here on out before taking on another Marine headquarters group. These lads did a fantastic job ... They were 100 percent professional fighting men; good Marines all the way."[13]

Bad weather accomplished what the NVA could not do: force Barrow to curtail operations. Heavy rains alternating with drizzle and dense fog grounded the helicopters. He ordered the infantry battalions to regroup near the two FSBs where there were supplies of food and ammunition. However, one company endured an extraordinarily grueling ordeal. Company G ran into a large enemy force and, in the ensuing firefight, lost five Marines killed and 17 wounded. Without helicopter evacuation, they were forced to carry them for three days through almost impassable terrain. The company commander, Captain Daniel A. Hitzelberger, described the ground: "At this time the stretcher cases were moving up and down slopes in excess of 70 degrees. We had to use six, eight, and at times, ten men to carry a stretcher and it would take us over thirty minutes to move one stretcher case over one bad area." At one point, they had to lower the stretchers on ropes down the face of a rock cliff.[14]

Company G finally reached a flat area. Two CH-46 medical evacuation helicopters, in a heroic display of airmanship, flew through the dense fog and enemy small arms fire to evacuate the company's wounded. A day later, their battalion commander watched the battered but unbroken company enter friendly lines. "They were smiling and laughing. Their clothes were torn, and in some cases completely off them, but they were ready for a fight." Barrow believed, "Well-trained, well-led men with character do what is expected, independent of orders, because they do not want to let their comrades down."[15]

The weather cleared and the 9th Marines pressed the attack. Enemy resistance stiffened, desperate to keep the Marines from advancing on Route 922. In one action, Company C fought through an NVA position and discovered two Russian-made

122mm field guns and a 5-ton, tracked prime mover. (General Davis could not find a legal way to ship one of the captured weapons back to Quantico, so he simply had it loaded aboard a Marine C-130 transport aircraft and directed a sergeant to make sure it arrived safely. The NCO successfully carried out his orders, and the weapon is on display at Quantico Marine Base.) First Lieutenant Wesley L. Fox's Company A continued the attack, seizing another truck and a large amount of artillery ammunition. Each day brought new discoveries, as Marines uncovered supply caches, weapons, and ammunition, often cleverly concealed in the bottom of bomb craters, caves, and jungle hideouts. The swing force was well on its way to completely interdict the NVA's supply network in South Vietnam. The enemy, however boldly continued to exploit its road network across the border.

The persistent shelling of Marine positions from Laos and continued heavy NVA traffic across the international border caused Davis to request a cross-border operation. "From the present position of the 9th Marines, a raid by a force of two battalions could be launched quickly and effectively to cut Road 922 and move rapidly back to the east, destroying artillery forces, and other forces and installations which threaten us." His request was denied. However, the rules of engagement permitted commanders to take "counteractions against VC/NVA forces in the exercise of self-defense and to defend their units against armed attacks with all means at their disposal."[16]

Barrow echoed Davis' request. "During the day the AOs were reporting fresh vehicle tracks, including vehicle tracks on the road. This was a pretty unacceptable situation, and it cried out for some sort of action to put a stop to it." Captain David F. Winecoff's Company H, 2nd Battalion, 9th Marines, watched an enemy convoy drive slowly down Route 992 on the Laotian side of the border. He called in several fire missions with unknown results. His troops wanted action. "The company was talking about let's get down on the road and do some ambushing. I don't think they really thought that they were going to let us go over into Laos."[17]

Winecoff's heart went into his throat. His radio operator had just deciphered a priority message from Barrow: "Ambush Route 922 tonight!" "No way," he thought. "We're not ready," and immediately requested a 24-hour delay. "No way," Barrow replied, "and by the way, be back in South Vietnam before 0630 tomorrow morning." Winecoff, with two platoons—one stayed behind to provide security—climbed down the steep slopes to their ambush position. After a harrowing four-hour trek through thick jungle foliage, they halted while a two-man reconnaissance team scouted a good ambush site. As they waited, six trucks and a tracked vehicle mounting a spotlight passed by, shining its light on both sides of the road. At one point, it played over the lead elements of the company but did not spot them. The recon team returned and led the company into position. Winecoff put the two platoons on line, in a hasty linear ambush. Several enemy vehicles passed by before they were finally ready.[18]

"I made a decision to ambush the road despite the rules of engagement (ROE) that prohibited the use of ground troops in Laos," Barrow explained. "I thought it was essential to protect the lives of my men and accomplish the mission." Winecoff's men were 500 meters inside Laos, when Barrow alerted his nominal boss at Task Force H—Davis was on R&R with his son, Miles, who was recovering from being wounded in action during Operation *Dewey Canyon*—over an encrypted radio.[19] "Where are they?" his superior exclaimed. "Are you crazy?" Then, more threateningly, "There were some of us who thought you had a future in the Marine Corps." Barrow would not back down. He took full responsibility for the decision—and waited for the axe to fall.[20]

Ambush

An NVA soldier strode into the ambush site aimlessly firing his AK-47 into the underbrush. He did not hit anyone and was allowed to pass by. At 0230, a line of trucks drove up and stopped, three of them in the kill zone. Fearing they would be discovered, Winecoff triggered a claymore mine, which detonated with a huge blast, sending hundreds of deadly steel balls into the second truck—killing its three occupants. The company opened fire with a vengeance: "Everybody had been waiting a long time and the excitement was keen!" Winecoff ordered a ceasefire and then swept through the zone, checking it for prisoners and anything of intelligence value. They discovered eight bodies and three destroyed trucks. There were no Marine casualties. Winecoff radioed a brief status report and "proceeded in column right back in the same direction we came."[21]

Every echelon in the chain of command seemed to be monitoring Winecoff's transmission. Regiment notified Division, who in turn, notified III MAF and on up the chain of command. The next morning, Barrow sent a formal request "stating why we had done what we had done, reiterating the success achieved, and then my final paragraph made an urgent request for authority to maneuver into Laos ...." Faced with a fait accompli, MACV acquiesced, letting Barrow off the hook. Davis found out about the ambush while on R&R. He responded "Great!" when asked what he thought of it. Barrow "had no concerns. I had great confidence in him [Davis] and definitely knew he would approve."[22]

Lieutenant Fox unknowingly triggered the last major firefight of Dewey Canyon, when he OK'd a working party to get water from a nearby stream. The 20-man water detail started filling their canteens. Suddenly, they came under heavy mortar and machine-gun fire. Fox ordered his first platoon to cover their withdrawal. It immediately ran into a buzz saw and started taking heavy casualties from a reinforced NVA company in a well-prepared, well-camouflaged, and heavily fortified bunker complex. The triple-canopy jungle and dense underbrush kept Fox from employing supporting arms, and he was forced to attack head on into the teeth of the enemy fire. As the Marines fought their way into the complex, a mortar round landed in the middle of the Company A command group, killing and wounding everyone, except one officer. Although painfully wounded, Fox continued to lead his casualty-riddled company through the bunker complex. At the end of the action, 11 Marines had been killed and 72 wounded. The North Vietnamese left 105 bodies on the battlefield.

"I had an announced 'law' that nobody could lose a skirmish with the enemy. Any time an outfit got chopped up pretty bad, the first question that I wanted to know from the battalion commander was how many rounds of artillery they fired; and if they didn't fire enough, then he was criticized." Davis ordered an investigation into Fox's bloody fight. It was determined that the officer's actions were fully justified, and he was subsequently awarded the Medal of Honor. Davis felt that, "When you've got Marines' lives at stake, you need an excellent to outstanding officer who can ensure that the task gets done with the least casualties." Davis relieved several battalion commanders for incompetence, "because of performance … where they were getting too many Marines killed."[23]

Operation *Dewey Canyon* marked the high point of Davis' high-mobility concept. He felt that "Bob Barrow and the 9th Marines worked together as a team, and it was just an absolutely superb performance …."[24]

By defeating the NVA, the local Vietcong guerrillas, who depended on them for support, were destroyed. Davis directed the 3rd Marine Division to "go into the villages and get the Vietcong out." He claimed, "Eventually we had total pacification," and issued a challenge to any visitor: "You can point anywhere in this province, day or night, and we'll be there and I'll take off my pistol and we'll walk around there alone." Davis claimed, "Quang Tri Province was much safer than the streets of most American cities."[25]

CHAPTER 36

Pacification: Winning Hearts and Minds

Davis thought winning the hearts and minds of the population was dependent on a foundation of overall military security by denying the enemy access to the population. He cautioned that "the periodic application of heavy combat forces in populated areas can quickly become counter-productive, particularly if they repeatedly sweep through villages. Except in extreme emergency, major military forces should enter populated areas only when they can either, (1) remain until the area is secure and friendly governmental presence is established, or (2) the population is evacuated to a secure area."[1]

"In Quang Tri Province, once major enemy forces were defeated," Davis explained, "We conducted an all-out village security effort over a period of sixty days." During this period, the 3rd Division closely coordinated with the 2nd ARVN Regiment, province and district chiefs and local forces to screen more than 85,000 Vietnamese. Of these, 1,600 were arrested for being members of the Viet Cong infrastructure.[2]

The operation commenced late at night (usually midnight) with Marines establishing a tight cordon around the area to be screened, while ARVN troops prepared a processing area inside the perimeter. On the first day, the people were informed of the plan for screening. On the following day, all draft age males were taken to the processing area where they were briefed, issued rations and guided single file through a row of small booths with peep slits that housed various intelligence agents. Any villager who was pointed out as either an enemy soldier or sympathizer was pulled out of line. The intelligence agent was required to write and sign a statement about his knowledge of the individual. This statement was used in the interrogation.

All draft age males who "survived" the screening received an offer to immediately volunteer to serve in the 2nd ARVN Regiment or be shipped off to a central draft center.

The remainder of the people were offered the opportunity to participate in a MedCap (Medical Civic Action Program) where they were processed through dental and medical facilities. Local officials were able to talk with the people while they listened to music by the Marine band or were entertained by Vietnamese performers. Finally, each individual was issued a certificate which indicated they had been processed. On subsequent days all remaining individuals were processed. The processing team ensured that some members of the family were permitted to stay in the home to protect its valuables. During the processing, Marines carefully searched the surrounding area for contraband.

"The result of these careful operations was remarkable," Davis boasted. "In one area north of Dong Ha there was daily sniper fire, assassinations, booby traps. After screening, there was not a shot fired in more than three weeks."[3]

In addition to the MedCap program, the 3rd Marine Division constructed schools, built a children's hospital, repaired roads, irrigation, opened markets, repaired homes and distributed 400 tons of captured rice.

As pacification progressed, a few areas of special interest were discovered. In a former Viet Cong stronghold, the initial screening netted absolutely nothing. The people were afraid of VC holdouts. Small Marine units were assigned on a full-time basis to operate with local Vietnamese security forces. They operated primarily at night to kill or capture VC leaders. Within three weeks most of the hard-core VC were eliminated.

Davis concluded that in counter-insurgency operations a complex set of actions are needed for success. The primary ingredient is the application of military force to provide security for the people but it is just one of a number of actions that provided the people with a greater incentive to support the government.

Davis was proud of the Division's accomplishments. By the end of 1968, Quang Tri Province had become one of the most secure. "From April through October, three North Vietnamese Army Divisions—the 304th, 308th, and 320th—had been decimated and their remnants driven from the province. With their elimination, it was found possible to reduce the number of U.S. maneuver battalions from 24 in May to a low of ten in December."

Lieutenant General Richard G. Stilwell, who had succeeded Rosson as Commanding General PCV (redesignated XXIV Corps), rated Davis' performance of duty as outstanding and noted in a written appraisal:

> It would be a massive understatement to say that General Davis' performance, during these past five and a half months, had confirmed my earlier high evaluation of his truly outstanding talents. For in that period, the 3rd Marine Division—under his dynamic, inspiring command—has attained new thresholds in combat worthiness and combat results.
>
> General Davis' overall accomplishments have been detailed in the recommendation I submitted for the Navy Distinguished Service Medal and in my further recommendation for an Army Distinguished Service Medal for spectacular achievement represented by Operation *Dewey Canyon*; both appraisals are incorporated herein by reference. To these, I need add only the briefest of commentary;
>
> —As a battle leader and directing genius of a division simultaneously engaged in conventional combat, anti-guerrilla operations and continuous support of the pacification process, General Davis has been incomparable;
>
> —As a man, magnificent in every dimension;

—His personal example, his tactical brilliance and his unique capacity to challenge by indirection will have enduring influence on a large cross section of Marines for the next two decades;

—He has no faults; only virtues.

General Davis has unlimited potential and is now eminently qualified for three- and four-star rank.

Lieutenant General Robert E. Cushman, Jr., Commanding General III MAF, echoed Stillwell's report: "General Davis had exhibited an outstanding flair for and grasp of mobile operations at the division level and has beaten soundly and destroyed enemy forces of superior numbers. His aggressiveness, decisiveness and flexible tactics have been the key ...." Cushman did rate him as only excellent in "cooperation," all the other areas were rated outstanding. The author believes this mark was the result of Davis' continued push for additional helicopter support.

Final Years of Service and Retirement

After completing the normal 13-month tour, Davis received orders to the Marine Corps Development and Education Command (MCDEC) in April 1969, to become the Director of the Education Center. "I was most enthusiastic!" he said passionately. "I welcomed it as a great challenge …." He viewed the assignment as an opportunity to educate Marines on the high mobility concept. "I was so enthused about this that it became my main theme, effort and concern—the development, selling and fostering the concept. That was my main interest at the Education Center."[1]

Davis was convinced that the high-mobility concept held great promise for the future of the Marine Corps because it would provide deployed forces with an ability to conduct operations from sea-based naval ships eliminating the need for a logistic base ashore. "There would not be any requirement to build major installations in the midst of a civilian population."[2]

Davis took his high-mobility show on the road to each of the Education Center's major schools—The Basic School, Amphibious War School and Command and Staff College. His three-hour presentation used maps to walk the students through his experience in Vietnam, followed by a discussion and question and answer session. He also introduced a program for junior officers—lieutenants, captains, and majors—to an informal forum where he presented his general views on Marine Corps' policies. This was his way of exposing ideas and communicating with people through key select groups of junior officers and their wives.

This was a time in the Corps when it was experiencing drug and race issues on an unprecedented scale and Davis wanted to confront them head on. "If we are going to be truly an elite Corps, we should be able to say to people, to parents, to everybody, 'If you want your son or daughter to be in an outfit where they are not going to get into drugs, join the Marine Corps.' We should be able to make statements that indicate that we are, in every respect, a different, totally elite Corps, and that includes no drugs. We need to get rid of alcoholics, we need to get rid of the drug addicts, and we need to get rid of the Ku Klux Klan types, the communist types, the racists. We should have some way of getting those who fail to meet high standards out of our system. They came out of society, let society rehabilitate them."[3]

Three months after taking over the Education Center, Davis was given command of MCDEC and appointed by the president to the rank of lieutenant general. Brigadier generals (one-star) and major generals (two-star) are selected by a board of officers at Headquarters, Marine Corps, but lieutenant generals (three-star) are appointed by the president after receiving recommendations from the Defense Department.

The tour of duty as commanding general of MCDEC lasted less than a year. However, it gave Davis an opportunity to oversee the education and development of the entire Corps. He continued to host young officers and their wives. For him it was an opportunity to "give more hard charging young officers a chance to deal face-to-face with a three-star general in semi-social settings."[4]

On 12 March 1971, Davis was nominated for a fourth star and upon confirmation by the Senate, became the assistant commandant of the Marine Corps. His mission at headquarters was to help build and sustain the Marine Corps' image through appearances, speeches, visits and inspections. When the commandant, General Leonard F. Chapman, was at headquarters, Davis hit the road to visit the troops and attend functions representing the Marine Corps. When Chapman was away from Washington, the assistant commandant took his place in the Joint Chiefs of Staff and Department of Defense.

Upon the retirement of Chapman, General Robert Cushman was selected to be the next commandant. Davis was advised privately that the Pentagon was recommending him for the position, but President Nixon chose Cushman because of their long-standing personal relationship. "The appointment proved my theory about 'cronyism' being bad medicine. The Corps took a downward spiral to become the worst of the military services in such things as unauthorized absences, brig population, drug and racial problems. Cushman was the only Marine Corps commandant in recent history who was not permitted to serve a four-year term as prescribed in the statutes."[5]

After 34 years of service, Davis was given a retirement ceremony in the band hall of the Marine Barracks in Southeast Washington. His wife, Knox Davis, remembered that at her husband's ceremony, she asked the band not to play "Auld Lang Syne" because, "I knew I could not get through it without crying." Instead they played, "Georgia on My Mind." "At least," she chuckled, "it wasn't 'Ramblin Wreck [from Georgia Tech]'!"[6]

When asked to sum up his three decades of service, Davis simply stated, "I wouldn't know how to do any better than I did. I went from a poor country boy in Georgia up to four stars in the most elite organization in the world. I gave it everything I had. I can't look back and see a single time when I took my pack off to coast."[7]

The retirement ceremony began at 1000 and by 1400 Davis started his new job in Atlanta as the Executive Vice President of the Georgia Chamber of Commerce.

Three years later he retired to Conyers, Georgia where he started RGMW, Inc., a family land development corporation.

In his long retirement, Davis worked tirelessly for veteran causes, including several trips to North Korea in an attempt to recover the remains of U.S. MIAs. His final legacy was the Korean War Veterans Memorial, in which he served as the vice chairman of the memorial's advisory board. During his tenure, he was able to steer the board committee through the very contentious selection process. His efforts paid off and today the memorial is a tribute to the veterans of the "Forgotten War."

Davis was the founder of the Georgia Marine Corps Coordinating Council in Atlanta, and was an active participant in the construction of a Georgia War Veterans Memorial Park in Rockdale Country. He was also appointed by Governor Roy Barnes to help coordinate the ceremony marking the 25th anniversary of the end of the Vietnam War.

On 3 September 2003, 88-year-old Ray Davis died peacefully in his sleep. His old friend Bob Barrow described him as "the finest man I've even known, a Marine's Marine."

"Above all, I see myself as a man of action. I never sit around and think about others doing this or that ... I am aware that as a holder of the Medal of Honor, I belong to this nation forever, because of a combat situation where literally thousands of men's lives depended on the actions I took when someone had to take action."

Bibliography

Personal Papers

Craig, General Edward. *Incidents of Service: 1917–1951*. Unpublished manuscript given to author, 1980.

Raymond G. Davis Collection (Coll/2079), Archives Branch: Personal Papers Collections, Marine Corps History Division, 1938–2003. Quantico, VA.

Personal account of Robert W. Fisher, USMC (Retired). Norcross, GA: Witness to War, Preserving the Oral Histories of Combat Veterans.

Oral Histories and Presentations

Bowser, Lieutenant General Alpha L., USMC (Retired). Interview by Benis M. Frank. Quantico, VA: Oral History Collection, Marine Corps Historical Center, 1970.

Bowser, Lieutenant General Alpha L., USMC (Retired). Oral History interview, National Museum of the Pacific War, Digital Archive, OH00859.

Brown, Lieutenant General Wilbur S., USMC (Retired). Interview by Benis M. Frank. Quantico, VA: Oral History Collection, Marine Corps Historical Center, 1967.

Davis, Raymond G., USMC (Retired). Interview at 7th Marines CP on 38th Parallel by Historical Division. Quantico, VA: Marine Corps Historical Center, 6 April 1951.

Davis, Raymond G., USMC (Retired). Interview conducted at Dong Ha Combat Base, Marine Corps History Division, 4 January 1969.

Davis, Raymond G., USMC (Retired). "High Mobility in the Northern I Corps Tactical Zone," brief to Amphibious Warfare School and Command and Staff College, Quantico, VA, 1969–1970.

Davis, Raymond G., USMC (Retired). Interview by Benis M. Frank. Oral history transcription. Quantico, VA: Marine Corps Historical Center, 1978.

Davis, Raymond G., USMC (Retired). Interview by Charles Stone at his home in McDonough, GA. Quantico, VA: Marine Corps Historical Center, 19 November 1979.

Davis, Raymond G., USMC (Retired). Oral History interview by Charles Stone, at his home in McDonough, GA. Quantico, VA: Marine Corps Historical Center, 29 November 1979.

Davis, Raymond G., USMC (Retired). Oral History interview by Marilyn Somers. Stockbridge, GA: Georgia Tech Living History, 13 August 1995.

Davis, Raymond G., USMC (Retired). Raymond G. Davis Collection (AFC/2001/001/22816), 2005 and (AFC/2001/001/89653), 2013. Veterans History Project, American Folklife Center, Library of Congress.

Dowsett, Colonel Fred, USMC (Retired). Oral History interview. Quantico, VA: Oral History Collection, Marine Corps History Division, 1951.

Fields, Lieutenant General, Lewis J. Oral History interview by Major Thomas E. Donnelly. Quantico, VA: Marine Corps History Division, 1971.

Georgia Tech Alumni Association. Living History Program, "Raymond Davis, Jr., CHE 1938," Georgia Tech History Digital Portal, accessed 29 December 2018, http://history library.gatechedu/items/show/3696.

Hayes, Lieutenant General Charles H., USMC (Retired). Oral History interview. Quantico, VA: Oral History Collection, Marine Corps History Division, 1970.

Litzenberg, Colonel Homer L., USMC (Retired). (Inchon Landing to CCF Counteroffensive). Oral History interview. Quantico, VA: Oral History Collection, Marine Corps History Division, 1951.

Litzenberg, Colonel Homer L. Commanding Officer, 7th Marines, 27–30 April and 10 July 1951, Inchon Landing to CCF Counteroffensive, 22 April 1951. Korean War Project Record: USMC-1036, RG 127. College Park, MD: National Archives and Records Administration, 1951.

Luckey, Lieutenant General Robert B., USMC (Retired). Interview by Benis M. Frank, at his home in Virginia Beach, VA, 15, 24, and 28 November 1969. Quantico, VA: Oral History Collection, Marine Corps History Division.

Mangrum, Lieutenant General Richard C., USMC (Retired). Interview by Benis M. Frank. Quantico, VA: Oral History Collection, Marine Corps History Division, 1971.

Selden, Lieutenant General John T., USMC (Retired). Interview by Benis M. Frank. Quantico, VA: Oral History Collection, Marine Corps History Division.

Silverthorn, Lieutenant General Merwin H. Silverthorn., USMC (Retired). Oral History interview by Benis M. Frank. Quantico, VA: Oral History Collection, Marine Corps History Division, 1973.

Smith, General Oliver P., USMC (Retired). Interview by Benis M. Frank, at his home in Los Altos Hills, CA, 9 and 11–12 June 1969.

Smith, General Oliver P., USMC (Retired). Interview by Benis M. Frank. Oral History transcription. Quantico, VA: Marine Corps Historical Center, 1973.

Thomas, General Gerald C. Interview by Benis M. Frank. Oral History transcription. Quantico, VA: Marine Corps Historical Center, 1966.

Twining, General Merrill B. Interview by Benis M. Frank. Oral History transcription. Quantico, VA: Marine Corps Historical Center, 1967.

Woods, Lieutenant General Louis E., USMC (Retired). Interview by Benis M. Frank. Quantico, VA: Oral History Collection, Marine Corps History Division, 1968.

Published Sources

Books

Blair, Clay. *The Forgotten War: America in Korea 1950–1953*. New York: Times Books, 1987.

Camp, Richard D. *Leatherneck Legends: Conversations with the Marine Corps' Old Breed*. Minneapolis, MN: Zenith Press, 2006.

Camp, Richard D. *Last Man Standing: The 1st Marine Regiment on Peleliu September 15–21, 1944*. Minneapolis, MN: Zenith Press, 2008.

Davis, Raymond G. *The Story of Ray Davis: General of Marines*. Varina, NC: Research Triangle Publishing, 1995.

Davis, Raymond G. with Colonel William J. Davis. *Protector of Freedom, The Story of Ray Davis, MOH, General of Marines*. San Diego, CA: Marine Books, 1990.

Frank, Richard B. *Guadalcanal: The Definitive Account of the Landmark Battle*. New York, NY: Random House, 1990.

Gailey, Harry. *Peleliu: 1944*. Mt Pleasant, SC: Nautical & Aviation Publishing Co. of America, 1983.

Garand, George W. and Truman R. Strobridge. *History of U.S. Marine Corps Operations in World War II: Western Pacific Operations, Volume IV.* Washington, D.C.: Historical Branch, Headquarters, U.S. Marine Corps, 1971.

Greer, Andrew. *The New Breed: The Story of the U.S. Marines in Korea.* New York, NY: Harper & Brothers, 1952.

Griffith, Samuel B. *The Battle for Guadalcanal.* Philadelphia, PA: J.B. Lippincott, 1963.

Hallas, James H. *The Devil's Anvil: The Assault on Peleliu.* Santa Barbara, CA: Praeger, 1994.

Hammel, Eric M. *Chosin: Heroic Ordeal of the Korean War.* New York, NY: The Vanguard Press, 1981.

Hoffman, Jon T. *Chesty: The Story of Lieutenant General Lewis B. Puller, USMC.* New York, NY: Random House, 2001.

Hough, Lieutenant Colonel Frank O., Major Verle E. Ludwig, USMC and Henry I. Shaw Jr. *Pearl Harbor to Guadalcanal: History of U.S. Marine Corps Operations in World War II, Volume I.* Washington, D.C.: Historical Branch, G-3 Division, Headquarters, U.S. Marine Corps, 1958.

Merillat, H. C. L. *Guadalcanal Remembered.* New York, NY: Mead and Company, 1982.

Millett, Allan R. *In Many a Strife: General Gerald C. Thomas and the U.S. Marine Corps, 1917–1956.* Annapolis, MD: Naval Institute Press, 1993.

Montross, Lynn and Captain Nicholas A. Canzona, USMC. *U.S. Marine Operations in Korea 1950–1953: Volume III, The Chosin Reservoir Campaign.* Washington, D.C.: Historical Branch, G-3, Headquarters U.S. Marine Corps, 1957.

Montross, Lynn, Major Hubard D. Kuokka, USMC and Major Norman W. Hicks, USMC. *U.S. Marine Corps Operations in Korea 1950–1953: Volume IV: The East-Central Front.* Washington, D.C.: Historical Branch, G-3, U.S. Marine Corps, 1962.

Shulimson, Jack. *U.S. Marines in Vietnam: The Defining Year, 1968.* Washington, D.C.: History and Museums Division HQMC, 1997.

Smith, Charles R. *U.S. Marines in Vietnam: High Mobility and Stand Down, 1969.* Washington D.C.: History and Museum Division, Headquarters Marine Corps, 1988.

Stanton, Shelby L. *America's Tenth Legion: X Corps in Korea, 1950.* Novato, CA: Presidio Press, 1989.

Toland, John. *In Mortal Combat: Korea, 1950–1953.* New York, NY: William Morrow and Company, Inc. 1991.

Vandegrift, Alexander A. *Once a Marine: The Memoirs of General A. A. Vandegrift, Commandant of the U.S. Marines in WWII.* New York, NY: Ballantine Books, 1964.

Zimmerman, Major John L., USMC Reserve. *The Guadalcanal Campaign.* Historical Division, Headquarters, U.S. Marine Corps, 1949.

Articles

Barrow, Robert H. "Operation Dewey Canyon." *Marine Corps Gazette*, November 1981, 84–89.

Camp, Richard D. "Cordon at Phuoc Yen." *Marine Corps Gazette*, February 1971, 28–31.

Camp, Richard D. "Taking Command: A Lesson in Leadership." *Marine Corps Gazette*, June 1999, 76–84.

Camp, Richard D. "Toktong Ridge Runners: 1st Battalion, 7th Marines." *Leatherneck, Magazine of the Marines*, December 2000, 40–46.

Davis, Gordon M. "Dewey Canyon: All Weather Classic." *Marine Corps Gazette*, July 1969, 32–40.

Davis, R. G. and Richard D. Camp. "Marines in Assault by Helicopter." *Marine Corps Gazette*, September 1968, 23–28.

Davis, R. G. and H. W. Brazier. "Defeat of the 320th." *Marine Corps Gazette*, March 1969, 22–30.

Davis, R. G. and J. L. Jones. "Employing the Recon Patrol." *Marine Corps Gazette*, May 1969, 40–45.

Davis, R. G. and S. W. Bell. "Combined Operations with ARVN." *Marine Corps Gazette*, October 1969, 18–29.
Owen, Joseph. "Chosin Reservoir Remembered." *Marine Corps Gazette,* December 1980, 52–55.
Winecoff, David. "Night Ambush." *Marine Corps Gazette*, January 1984, 47–52.

Unpublished Documents

Finding Aid. Solomon Islands: Guadalcanal, Bougainville. Quantico, VA: U.S. Marine Corps History Division Archives.
First Marine Division Commander's Final Report on Guadalcanal Operation. Phases I–IV, with appendices. In Finding Aid-Solomon Islands, Guadalcanal, Box 11, Folders 1–2. Quantico, VA: U.S. Marine Corps History Division Archives.
Georgia Tech Alumni Association. Living History Program, "Raymond Davis, Jr., CHE 1938." Georgia Tech History Digital Portal, accessed 29 December 2018. http://history library.gatechedu/items/show/3696.
Smith, O. P. Memorandum: *Action Report of Amphibious Operation to Capture Peleliu and Angaur,* 9 May 1945, 24.

Interviews by Author

Craig, Edward A. (LtGen, USMC, Retired)
Davis, Raymond G. (General, USMC, Retired)
Davis, Knox (Wife of General Raymond G. Davis)
Gayle, Gordon D. (BGen, USMC, Retired)

Statements to Support Medal of Honor Award

Sawyer, Lieutenant Colonel Webb D., USMC
Hovatter, Captain Eugenous M., USMC
Shea, First Lieutenant William E., USMC
Tighe, Major Thomas B., USMC

Endnotes

Preface

1   Major Loughran was later killed in action on a routine patrol when a booby trap exploded, and he died before he could be evacuated.

Chapter 1

1   Raymond G. Davis, *The Story of Ray Davis: General of Marines* (North Carolina: Research Triangle Publishing, 1995), 23.
2   Ibid.
3   Ibid, 29.
4   Ibid, 27–29.
5   Ibid, 29.
6   Raymond G. Davis, with Col. William J. Davis, *Protector of Freedom, Ray Davis MOH: General of Marines* (San Diego: Marine Books, 1990), 3–7.

Chapter 2

1   Davis, *The Story of Ray Davis*, 30.
2   General Raymond G. Davis, USMC (Retired). Oral History transcript (Quantico, VA: Oral History Collection, Marine Corps Historical Center, 1978). Hereafter Davis Oral History transcript.
3   Davis, *The Story of Ray Davis*, 31.
4   Davis Oral History transcript, 107.
5   Davis, *The Story of Ray Davis*, 32.
6   Ibid.
7   Ibid, 31.
8   Davis, *Protector of Freedom*, 5–1.
9   Davis, *The Story of Ray Davis*, 35.
10 Lieutenant General Wilburt S. Brown, USMC (Retired). Interview by Benis M. Frank (Quantico, VA: Oral History Collection, Marine Corps Historical Center, 1967).
11 Davis Oral History transcript, 111.
12 Davis, *The Story of Ray Davis*, 40.
13 Davis Oral History transcript, 112.

Chapter 3

1   Davis, *Protector of Freedom*, 7–2.
2   Davis Oral History transcript, 113.

3   Ibid.
4   Ibid.
5   Ibid, 114.
6   Davis, *The Story of Ray Davis*, 45.
7   LtGen Robert B. Luckey. Oral History transcript (Quantico, VA: Oral History Collection, Marine Corps Historical Center, 1969). Hereafter Luckey interview.
8   Davis, *The Story of Ray Davis*, 45.
9   Davis admired Jim Masters and held him in high regard. "Masters had a great deal of influence on my life in the Marines because he had a great capacity for taking a big problem and just getting his arms around it and moving it in the direction he wants to go. Some great lessons learned from sitting at his knee from time to time." Davis, *Protector of Freedom*, 7–5.
10 Davis Oral History transcript, 117.
11 Davis, *The Story of Ray Davis*, 46.
12 Ibid.
13 First Marine Division Commander's report on Guadalcanal Operations, Phases I–IV, with appendices.

Chapter 4

1   Davis, *The Story of Ray Davis*, 46.
2   Davis Oral History transcript, 116–117.
3   Samuel B. Griffin, *The Battle for Guadalcanal* (Philadelphia, PA: J.B. Lippincott, 1963), 23.
4   Davis Oral History transcript.
5   First Marine Division Commander's final report on the Guadalcanal Operations, dated 24 May 1943.
6   Luckey interview.
7   General A. A. Vandegrift, USMC (Retired). Oral History interview (Quantico, VA: Oral History Collection, Marine Corps Historical Center). Hereafter Vandegrift interview.
8   General Gerald C. Thomas, USMC (Retired). Oral History interview (Quantico, VA: Oral History Collection, Marine Corps Historical Center, 1966). Hereafter Thomas interview.
9   First Marine Division Commander's final report on the Guadalcanal Operation, dated 24 May 1943.
10 General Merrill B. Twining, USMC (Retired). Oral History interview (Quantico, VA: Oral History Collection, Marine Corps Historical Center, 1967). Hereafter Twining interview.
11 Ibid; Griffin, *The Battle for Guadalcanal*, 22.
12 Twining interview.
13 Davis, *The Story of Ray Davis*, 49.

Chapter 5

1   First Marine Division Commander's final report on the Guadalcanal Operations, dated 24 May 1943.
2   Ibid.
3   Ibid.
4   Davis Oral History transcript, 116.
5   Ibid.
6   Vandegrift interview.
7   Luckey interview.

8   Davis Oral History transcript, 119.
9   First Marine Division Commander's Final Report of the Guadalcanal Operation, dated 24 May 1943.
10   Thomas interview.
11   *Solomon Islands Campaign I: The Landing in the Solomons 7–8 August 1942, World War II 75th Anniversary Commemorative Series,* Combat Narratives, Naval History and Heritage Command.
12   Vandegrift interview.
13   Luckey interview.
14   Vandegrift interview.
15   George W. Garand and Truman R. Strobridge, *History of Marine Corps Operations in World War II, Western Pacific: Western Pacific Operations* (Washington, D.C.: Historical Division, Headquarters, U.S. Marine Corps, 1971), 243.
16   John Miller, *U.S. Army in World War II, The War in the Pacific, Guadalcanal: The First Offensive* (Center of Military History, U.S. Army, Washington, D.C., 1995).
17   Twining interview.
18   Vandegrift interview.
19   First Marine Division Commander's Final Report of the Guadalcanal Operation, dated 24 May 1943.
20   Allan R. Millett, *In Many a Strife, General Gerald C. Thomas and the U.S. Marine Corps 1917–1956* (Annapolis, MD: Naval Institute Press, 1993), 167.
21   Thomas interview.
22   First Marine Division Commander's Final Report of the Guadalcanal Operation, dated 24 May 1943.
23   Davis, *The Story of Ray Davis*, 51.
24   Thomas interview.
25   Twining interview.
26   Davis Oral History transcript, 120.
27   Vandegrift interview.
28   Ibid.
29   Twining interview.
30   Thomas interview.
31   Vandegrift interview.
32   Commanding General, First Marine Division, WATCHTOWER operation, Ser 00204, Phases I–IV, Final Report.
33   E. B. Potter, *Nimitz* (Annapolis, MD: Naval Institute Press, 1976), 177–178.
34   Vandegrift interview.
35   *Solomon Islands Campaign I: The Landing in the Solomons 7–8 August 1942, World War II 75th Anniversary Commemorative Series,* Combat Narratives, Naval History and Heritage Command, 24.
36   Report of Action, 7–9 August, Commander, Task Group 62, 1, 3.
37   Major John L. Zimmerman, *The Guadalcanal Campaign* (Washington, D.C.: Historical Division, Headquarters, U.S. Marine Corps, 1949), 25.

Chapter 6

1   *Solomon Islands Campaign I: The Landing in the Solomons 7–8 August 1942, World War II 75th Anniversary Commemorative Series,* Combat Narratives, Naval History and Heritage Command, 23.

2   Richard B. Frank, *Guadalcanal: The Definitive Account of the Landmark Battle* (New York, NY: Random House of Canada, Limited, Toronto, 1990).

3   Twining interview.

4   Major John L. Zimmerman, *The Guadalcanal Campaign*, 26.

5   Ibid, 44.

6   Davis, *The Story of Ray Davis*, 53.

7   Davis Oral History transcript, 120.

8   Ibid.

9   Davis interview.

10   Lieutenant General Richard C. Mangrum, USMC (Retired). Oral History interview (Quantico, VA: Oral History Collection, Marine Corps Historical Center).

11   Lieutenant General Louis E. Woods, USMC (Retired). Oral History interview (Quantico, VA: Oral History Collection, Marine Corps Historical Center). Hereafter Woods interview.

12   Tatsuhi Saito, "Battle for Guadalcanal: As Viewed from the Perspective of the Concentration of Forces," *International Forum on War History Proceedings,* 2013.

13   Davis, *Protector of Freedom*, 8–3.

14   Davis interview.

15   Davis, *The Story of Ray Davis*, 53.

16   Thomas interview.

17   Ibid.

18   Miller, *United States Army in World War II: The War in the Pacific. Guadalcanal: The First Offensive.*

19   *Fortitudine*, Historical Bulletin Volume XXII, Fall 1992, no. 2.

20   Thomas interview.

21   Vandegrift interview.

22   Ibid.

23   A. A. Vandegrift, *Once a Marine: The memoirs of General A.A. Vandegrift, Commandant of the U.S. Marines in World War II* (New York, NY: Ballantine Books, 1964), 131.

24   Vandegrift interview.

25   Woods interview.

26   Davis, *Protector of Freedom*, 9–1.

27   First Marine Division Commander's Final Report of the Guadalcanal Operation, dated 24 May 1943.

28   Ibid.

29   Ibid.

Chapter 7

1   Mangrum interview.

2   Vandegrift interview.

3   Ibid.

4   Merillat, *Guadalcanal Remembered* (New York, NY: Dodd, Mead and Company, 1982), 102.

5   Robert L. Ferguson, *Guadalcanal—the Island of Fire: Reflections of the 347th Fighter Group* (Fallbrook, CA: Aero Publishers, 1987), 62.

6   Zimmerman, *The Guadalcanal Campaign*, 67.

7   Ibid.

Chapter 8

1   Zimmerman, *The Guadalcanal Campaign*, 67.
2   Ibid.
3   Ibid.
4   Eric Hammel, *Guadalcanal: Starvation Island* (New York, NY: Crown Publishers, Inc. 1981), 171–172.
5   Ibid.
6   Davis interview.
7   Vandegrift interview.
8   First Marine Division Commander's Final Report of the Guadalcanal Operation, dated 24 May 1943.
9   Davis interview.
10   Ibid.
11   Davis, *The Story of Ray Davis*, 56.
12   Ibid, 121.
13   Davis interview.
14   Lieutenant General Charles H. Hayes, USMC (Retired). Oral History Transcript (Washington, D.C.: History and Museums Division, Headquarters, U.S. Marine Corps), 70.
15   Davis interview.
16   Twining interview.
17   John B. Lundstrom, *First Team and the Guadalcanal Campaign: Naval Fighter Combat from August to November 1942* (Maryland: Naval Institute Press, 1994).
18   Davis, *The Story of Ray Davis,* 56.
19   Vandegrift interview.
20   First Marine Division Commander's Final Report of the Guadalcanal Operation, dated 24 May 1943.
21   George McMillian, *The Old Breed, A History of the 1st Marine Division in World War II* (Washington: Infantry Journal Press, 1949).
22   Twining interview.
23   Davis interview.
24   Ibid.
25   Davis, *Protector of Freedom,* 9–2.
26   Davis interview.

Chapter 9

1   Frank O. Hough and John A. Crown, *The Campaign on New Britain* (Washington, D.C.: Historical Branch, Headquarters, U.S. Marine Corps, 1952), 12.
2   Davis, *Protector of Freedom,* 9–3.
3   George McMillan, *The Old Breed, A History of the First Marine Division in World War II* (Washington, D.C.: Infantry Journal Press 1949), and Hough and Crown, *The Campaign for New Britain.*
4   Luckey interview.
5   Davis Oral History transcript, 126.
6   Luckey interview.
7   Hough and Crown, *The Campaign on New Britain.*
8   Special Action Report, Cape Gloucester Operation, First Marine Division, 1943–1944.
9   Ibid.

10 Davis interview.

11 Davis, *Protector of Freedom*, 9–4.

12 Davis interview; Special Action Report, Cape Gloucester Operation, First Marine Division, 1943–1944.

13 Davis interview.

14 Davis, *The Story of Ray Davis*, 127.

15 Ibid, 62.

16 Ibid.

Chapter 10

1 Lieutenant General Lewis Fields, USMC (Retired). Oral History interview (Quantico, VA: Oral History Collection, Marine Corps Historical Center).

2 Davis interview.

3 Vandegrift interview.

4 Selden interview.

5 General Oliver P. Smith, USMC (Retired). Oral History interview (Quantico, VA: Oral History Collection, Marine Corps Historical Center).

6 Unknown.

7 Peleliu: 1st Marine Division, Special Action Report, Palau Operation, 6; Honsowetz interview.

8 Peleliu: 1st Marine Division, Special Action Report, Palau Operation, 7; Honsowetz interview.

9 Davis, *Protector of Freedom*, 10–5.

10 Ibid.

11 Davis Oral History transcript, 129.

12 Davis, *The Story of Ray Davis*, 67.

13 Ibid.

14 Smith interview.

15 McMillan, *The Old Breed, A History of the First Marine Division in World War II*.

16 Peleliu: 1st Battalion, 1st Marines, Historical Report.

Chapter 11

1 McMillan, *The Old Breed, A History of the First Marine Division in World War II*.

2 Gayle interview.

3 Honsowetz interview; Davis interview.

4 Gayle interview.

5 Peleliu: 1st Battalion, 1st Marines, Historical Report, 6.

6 Garand and Strobridge, *History of Marine Corps Operations in World War II, Western Pacific: Western Pacific Operations*, 78.

7 Lieutenant General Merwin H. Silverthorn, USMC (Retired). Oral History interview (Quantico, VA: Oral, History Collection, Marine Corps Historical Center); Smith interview.

8 Davis interview.

9 Silverthorn interview.

10 Davis interview.

11 Peleliu, 1st Marine Division, Special Action Report, Palau Operation.

12 Garand and Strobridge, *History of Marine Corps Operations in World War II, Western Pacific: Western Pacific Operations*, 102.

13 Ibid, 104.

14 Ibid.

15 Robert Ross Smith, *U.S. Army in World War II, the War in the Pacific, The Approach to the Philippines*, (Washington, D.C.: Center of Military History, 1984), 495.

16 Garand and Strobridge, *History of Marine Corps Operations in World War II, Western Pacific: Western Pacific Operations*, 103.

17 Don Moore, "Corsair Fighter Pilot recalls, World War II," *Englewood Sun*, Englewood Florida, 19 November 2002.

18 Jeter A. Isely and Philip A. Crowl, *The U.S. Marines and Amphibious Warfare, Its Theory, and Its Practice in the Pacific* (Princeton, NJ: Princeton University Press, 1951).

Chapter 12

1   Lieutenant Robert W. Fisher's unpublished memoir, Maryland State Archives.

2   Peleliu: 1st Battalion, 1st Marines, Historical Report, 4–5.

3   Ibid, 5.

4   Smith interview.

5   Peleliu: 1st Battalion, 1st Marines, Historical Report, 5.

6   Ibid.

7   Gordon D. Gayle, *Bloody Beaches: The Marines on Peleliu, Marines in World War II Commemorative Series* (CreateSpace, 2013).

8   In General O. P. Smith's oral history, he stated 38 amtracs had burned.

9   Peleliu: 1st Battalion, 1st Marines, Historical Report, 5.

10 Ibid.

11 Davis interview.

12 Davis, *The Story of Ray Davis*, 10–8.

13 Peleliu: 1st Battalion, 1st Marines, Historical Report, 5.

14 Lieutenant Robert W. Fisher's unpublished memoir, Maryland State Archives.

15 Davis interview.

16 Smith interview.

17 Davis Oral History transcript, 132.

18 Peleliu: 1st Battalion, 1st Marines, Historical Report, 7.

19 Davis interview.

20 Peleliu: 1st Battalion, 1st Marines, Historical Report, 8.

21 Ibid.

22 Ibid.

23 Lieutenant Robert W. Fisher's unpublished memoir, Maryland State Archives.

24 Peleliu: 1st Battalion, 1st Marines, Historical Report, 9.

25 Ibid, 13.

26 Smith interview.

27 Peleliu: 1st Battalion, 1st Marines, Historical Report, 9–10.

28 Ibid.

29 Gayle, *Bloody Beaches: The Marines on Peleliu*.

30 Peleliu: 1st Marine Division, Special Action Report, Palau Operation, 67.

31 Ibid, 68.

32 Ibid.

33 Ibid.

Chapter 13

1   Benis M. Frank, General Raymond G. Davis U.S. Marine Corps (Retired). Oral History transcript (Washington, D.C.: History and Museums Division, Headquarters, U.S. Marine Corps, 1978), 133.
2   Peleliu: 1st Battalion, 1st Marines, Historical Report, 12.
3   Ibid, 11.
4   Ibid.
5   Davis interview.
6   McMillan, *The Old Breed, A History of the First Marine Division in World War II*, 304.
7   Major General O. P. Smith Memorandum: Action Report of Amphibious Operation to Capture Peleliu and Angaur dated 9 May 1945, 24.
8   McMillan, *The Old Breed: A History of the First Marine Division in World War II*, 306.
9   Davis interview.
10 McMillan, *The Old Breed: A History of the First Marine Division in World War II*, 306.
11 Dick Camp, *Last Man Standing, The 1st Marine Regiment on Peleliu, September 15–21, 1944* (Minneapolis, MN: Zenith Press, 2008), 220–221.
12 Peleliu: 1st Battalion, 1st Marines, Historical Report, 11.
13 Ibid.
14 Ibid.
15 Ibid.

Chapter 14

1   Davis interview.
2   Peleliu: 1st Battalion, 1st Marines, Historical Report, 20.
3   Ibid, 17.
4   Camp, *Last Man Standing, The 1st Marine Regiment on Peleliu, September 15–21, 1944*, 226–227.
5   Major General O. P. Smith Memorandum: Action Report of Amphibious Operation to Capture Peleliu and Angaur dated 9 May 1945, 39.
6   Peleliu: 1st Marine Division Special Action Report Palau Operation, 67.
7   McMillan, *The Old Breed, A History of the 1st Marine Division in World War II*, 54.
8   Camp, *Last Man Standing, The 1st Marine Regiment on Peleliu, September 15–21, 1944*, 214.
9   Jeter A. Isely and Philip A. Crowl, *The U.S. Marines and Amphibious Warfare, Its Theory, and Its Practice in the Pacific*, 402.
10 Camp, *Last Man Standing, The 1st Marine Regiment on Peleliu, September 15–21, 1944*, 215–216.
11 Ibid.
12 Lieutenant Robert W. Fisher's unpublished memoir, Maryland State Archives.
13 1st Battalion, 1st Marines, Historical Report, 19.
14 Camp, *Last Man Standing, The 1st Marine Regiment on Peleliu, September 15–21, 1944*, 284.
15 Burke Davis, *Marine, The Life of Lt. Gen Lewis B (Chesty) Puller, USMC (Ret)* (Boston, MA: Little Brown and Company, 1962), 222.
16 Peleliu: 1st Marine Division, Special Action Report, Palau Operation, 67.
17 Ibid, 100.
18 Ibid, 101.
19 Ibid, 97.
20 Ibid, 92.
21 Camp, *Last Man Standing, The 1st Marine Regiment on Peleliu, September 15–21, 1944*, 237.

22 Ibid, 238.
23 Ibid, 244.
24 Ibid.
25 Ibid, 241.
26 Ibid, 249.

Chapter 15

1   Peleliu: 1st Marine Division, Special Action Report, Palau Operation, 92.
2   Camp, *Last Man Standing, The 1st Marine Regiment on Peleliu, September 15–21, 1944*, 269.

Chapter 16

1   Camp, *Last Man Standing, The 1st Marine Regiment on Peleliu, September 15–21, 1944*, 271.
2   Ibid, 275.
3   Ibid.
4   Ibid.
5   Ibid, 280.
6   Ibid, 281.
7   Ibid, 285.
8   Ibid, 274.
9   Silverthorn interview.
10 Davis interview with author.
11 Harry Gailey, *Peleliu: 1944* (Mt Pleasant, SC: Nautical & Aviation Publishing Co. of America, 1983).

Chapter 17

1   Davis interview.
2   Ibid.
3   Davis, *Protector of Freedom*, 11–8.
4   Ibid, 11–4.
5   Ibid, 11–6.
6   Ibid.
7   Ibid, 11–5.
8   Ibid, 11–9.

Chapter 18

1   Edward Craig, *Incidents of Service, 1917–1951* (Unpublished manuscript), 148.
2   Davis, *Protector of Freedom*, 12–1.
3   Craig, *Incidents of Service, 1917–1951*, 147.
4   Davis, *Protector of Freedom*, 12–3.
5   Ibid, 12–4.
6   Ibid.
7   Craig, *Incidents of Service 1917–1951*, 149.
8   Davis, *Protector of Freedom*, 12–1.

9   Davis, *The story of Ray Davis*, 85.
10   Craig, *Incidents of Service*, 1917–1951.
11   Davis, *The Story of Ray Davis*, 85.
12   The gallows site is located on what is now the Federal Aviation Administration complex adjacent to the Navy Computer and Telecommunications Area Master Station, according to Captain Joseph Commette, U.S. Navy. Davis, *Protector of Freedom*, 12–5.
13   Tony Palomo and Paul J. Borja, *Liberation—Guam Remembers: A Golden Salute for the 50th Anniversary of the Liberation of Guam* (Guam: Golden Salute Commemorative Committee).
14   Davis interview with author.

Chapter 19

1   Davis, *Protector of Freedom*, 12–8.
2   Ibid, 13–1.
3   Ibid, 13–2.
4   Ibid, 13–3.

Chapter 20

1   Camp, *Leatherneck Legends, Conversations with the Marine Corps' Old Breed* (Minneapolis, MN: Zenith Press, 2006), 195.
2   Ibid, 196.
3   Ibid.
4   Ibid, 197.
5   Ibid.

Chapter 21

1   Camp, *Leatherneck Legends*, 198.
2   Ibid, 199.
3   Craig, *Incidents of Service 1917–1951*, 153.
4   Smith interview.
5   Camp, *Leatherneck Legends*, 205.

Chapter 22

1   Camp, *Leatherneck Legends*, 204.
2   Ibid, 205.
3   Ibid.
4   Ibid.
5   Davis interview with author.
6   Davis interview.
7   Davis, *Protector of Freedom*, 13-5.
8   Ibid.
9   Davis, *The Story of Ray Davis*, 96.
10   Davis Oral History transcript, 151.

11 Andrew Greer, *The New Breed, The Story of the U.S. Marines in Korea* (New York, NY: Harper & Bros, 1952), 105.

12 Litzenberg interview, 27–30 April and 10 July 1951, 30.

13 Davis, *Protector of Freedom*, 14–1.

14 Davis, *The Story of Ray Davis*, 98.

15 Davis Oral History transcript, 154.

16 Davis, *The Story of Ray Davis*, 97.

17 Smith interview.

18 Davis Oral History transcript, 153.

Chapter 23

1 Davis, *Protector of Freedom*, 14–3.

2 Don Knox, *The Korean War, An Oral History, Pusan to Chosin* (New York: Harcourt Brace Jovanovich, Publishers, 1985), 303.

3 Ibid.

4 Davis Oral History transcript, 156.

5 Litzenberg interview 27–30 April 1951, 30.

6 Joseph R. Owen, *Colder than Hell: A Marine Rifle Company at the Chosin Reservoir* (Annapolis: Naval Institute Press, 2012).

7 Shelby L. Stanton, *America's Tenth Legion, X Corps in Korea*, 1950 (Navato: Presido Press, 1989).

8 Davis, *The Story of Ray Davis*, 98.

Chapter 24

1 Camp, *Leatherneck Legends*, 257.

2 Ibid, 255.

3 Lynn Montross and Nicholas A. Canzona, *U.S. Marine Operations in Korea, Chosin Reservoir Campaign Vol 3*, (Washington: Historical Branch, G-3, Headquarters U.S. Marine Corps, 1957), 7.

4 Ibid.

5 Roy E. Appleman, *South to the Naktong, North to the Yalu, June–November 1950* (Washington, D.C.: Center of Military History, 1992), 609.

6 James Bamford, *Body of Secrets, Anatomy of the Ultra-Secret National Security Agency from the Cold War Through the Dawn of a New Century* (New York, NY: Doubleday, 2002), 28–29.

7 Camp, *Leatherneck Legends*, 254; Smith transcript, 223.

8 Camp, *Leatherneck Legends*, 254.

9 Stanton, *America's Tenth Legion*, 160–161.

10 Smith transcript, 227.

11 Litzenberg interview, 27–30 April 1951.

12 Davis Oral History transcript, 157.

13 Montross and Canzona, *U.S. Marine Operations in Korea, Vol 3*, 82.

14 Stanton, *America's Tenth Legion*, 160–161.

15 Edwin H. Simmons, *Frozen Chosin, U.S. Marines at the Changjin Reservoir*. Korean War Commemorative Series (Washington, D.C.: Government Printing Office, 2002).

16 Davis transcript, 157.

17 Ibid.

18 Davis, *Protector of Freedom*, 14–4.

19   Simmons, *Frozen Chosin, U.S. Marine at the Changjin Reservoir.*

20   Davis Oral History transcript, 157–158.

21   Raymond G. Davis Collection (AFC/2001/001/22816), 2005 and (AFC/2001/001/89653), 2013. Veterans History Project, American Folklife Center, Library of Congress. Hereafter, Raymond G. Davis Collection, Veterans History Project.

22   Ibid.

23   Stanton, *America's Tenth Legion*, 163.

24   James Bamford, *Body of Secrets* (New York, NY: Doubleday, 2009), 29.

25   Montross and Canzona, *US Marine Operations in Korea*, 103.

26   Camp, *Leatherneck Legends*, 258.

27   Montross and Canzona, *US Marine Operations in Korea*, 103.

28   Camp, *Leatherneck Legends*, 258.

29   Ibid.

30   Ibid.

31   Davis Oral History transcript, 259.

32   Camp, *Leatherneck Legends*, 259.

33   Appleman, *South to the Naktong*, 609.

34   Ibid.

35   Prisoners reported that 70% of the *124th CCF Division* were former members of the Chinese Nationalist Army who had been captured by the Communists during the Chinese Civil War and subsequently inducted into the Communists units.

36   Camp, *Leatherneck Legends*, 259.

37   Bowser Oral History interview, National Museum of the Pacific War, OH00859.

38   Davis Oral History transcript, 162.

39   Davis, *The Story of Ray Davis*, 102.

40   Staff Sergeant Twohey and Corporal McDermott each received the Silver Star for destroying the North Korean tank.

41   Camp, *Leatherneck Legends*, 260.

42   Montross and Canzona, *US Marine Operations in Korea*, 103.

43   Davis Oral History transcript, 160.

44   Interview with General Ray Davis, by Charles Stone, 29 November 1979, McDonough, GA.

Chapter 25

1   Camp, *Leatherneck Legends*, 262.

2   Ibid, 260.

3   Ibid.

4   Ibid, 262–263.

Chapter 26

1   Clay Blair, *The Forgotten War* (New York, NY: Times Books, 1987), 572.

2   Chosin Resevoir was the Japanese name for Changjin Reservoir. These Japanese names were derived from maps produced by the Japanese Imperial Land Survey of 1933–1943 and used by X Corps in 1950. Stanton, *America's Tenth Legion*, 155.

3   Smith interview, 227.

4   Davis Oral History transcript, 163; Litzenberg interview 27–30 April and 10 July 1951, 37.

5   Raymond G. Davis Collection, Veterans History Project.
6   1st MarDiv after-action report, 47.
7   Ibid, 49.
8   Davis Oral History transcript, 163.
9   Camp, *Leatherneck Legends*, 263.
10 Ibid.
11 Ibid.
12 Smith transcript, 227.
13 Montross and Canzona, *US Marine Operations in Korea*, 133; Stanton, *America's Tenth Legion*, 193.
14 Camp, *Leatherneck Legends*, 265.
15 Smith transcript, 229.
16 Camp, *Leatherneck Legends*, 265.
17 Knox, *The Korean War, Pusan to Chosin, An Oral History*.
18 Camp, *Leatherneck Legends*, 266.
19 Ibid.
20 Ibid.
21 Ibid.
22 Ibid, 267.
23 Ibid.
24 Ibid.
25 Ibid, 268.
26 Ibid.
27 Raymond G. Davis Collection, Veterans History Project.
28 Ibid.
29 Smith transcript, 230.
30 Ibid.
31 Camp, *Leatherneck Legends*, 269.
32 Ibid.
33 Ibid.

Chapter 27

1   Camp, *Leatherneck Legends*, 270.
2   Litzenberg interview, 27–30 April and 10 July 1951, 32.
3   Camp, *Leatherneck Legends*, 269.
4   Roach statement.
5   Davis, *The Story of Ray Davis*, 111.
6   Raymond G. Davis Collection, Veterans History Project.
7   Ibid.
8   Camp, *Leatherneck Legends*, 270.
9   Ibid, 269.
10 Camp, *Leatherneck Legends*, 270.
11 Raymond G. Davis Collection, Veterans History Project.
12 Ibid.
13 Camp, *Leatherneck Legends*, 270–271.
14 Raymond G. Davis Collection, Veterans History Project.
15 Major Tighe statement.

16 Raymond G. Davis Collection, Veterans History Project.
17 Hovatter statement.
18 Ibid.
19 Ibid.
20 Raymond G. Davis Collection, Veterans History Project.
21 Camp, *Leatherneck Legends*, 271.
22 Ibid, 271–272.
23 Ibid, 272.
24 Ibid.
25 Ibid.
26 Tighe statement.
27 Ibid.
28 Camp *Leatherneck Legends*, 273.
29 Tighe statement.
30 Davis, *The Story of Ray Davis*, 114.
31 Raymond G. Davis Collection, Veterans History Project.
32 Camp, *Leatherneck Legends*, 273; Tighe statement.
33 Camp, *Leatherneck Legends*, 273.
34 Raymond G. Davis Collection, Veterans History Project.
35 Tighe statement.
36 Camp, *Leatherneck Legends*, 273–274.
37 Ibid.
38 Raymond G. Davis Collection, Veterans History Project.
39 Camp, *Leatherneck Legends*, 274.
40 Hovatter statement.
41 Litzenberg interview, 27–30 April and 10 July 1951, 33.
42 Simmons, *Frozen Chosin, U.S. Marines at the Changjin Reservoir*.
43 Tighe statement.
44 Ibid.
45 Camp, *Leatherneck Legends*, 275.
46 Raymond G. Davis Collection, Veterans History Project.
47 Ibid.
48 Joseph Owen, "Chosin Reservoir Remembered," *Marine Corps Gazette*, December 1980, 52–55; Camp, *Leatherneck Legends*, 276.
49 Owen, "Chosin Reservoir Remembered," 52–55.

Chapter 28

1 Litzenberg interview.
2 A unit of fire is a prescribed quantity of ammunition for a given organization or weapon based on the number of rounds that on the average are expected to be used in one day.
3 Smith transcript, 226–227.
4 Stanton, *America's Tenth Legion*, 245.
5 Raymond G. Davis Collection, Veterans History Project.
6 Owen, "Chosin Reservoir Remembered," 52–55.
7 Dowsett interview.
8 Davis, *Protector of Freedom*, 14–24.
9 Ibid.

10   Davis Oral History transcript, 173.
11   Davis, *Protector of Freedom*, 14–25.
12   Owen, "Chosin Reservoir Remembered," 52–55.
13   Camp, *Leatherneck Legends*, 275.
14   Davis, *The Story of Ray Davis*, 126.
15   Litzenberg interview.
16   Ibid.
17   Smith transcript, 249.
18   John Toland, *In Mortal Combat, Korea, 1950–1953* (New York, NY: William, Morrow and Company, Inc, 1991), 363.
19   Chosin, Heroic Ordeal of the Korean War, 390–391.
20   Protector of Freedom, Ray Davis, MOH, 14–26.
21   John Toland, *In Mortal Combat, Korea, 1950–1953*, 364.
22   Raymond G. Davis Collection, Veterans History Project.
23   Davis Oral History transcript, 178.
24   Davis, *Protector of Freedom*, 14–27.
25   Davis Oral History transcript, 182.
26   Smith interview.
27   Davis Oral History transcript, 182.
28   Smith interview.
29   Davis, *The Story of Ray Davis*, 130.
30   Davis Oral History transcript, 184.
31   Ibid.
32   Ibid, 186.

Chapter 29

1   Raymond G. Davis Collection, Veterans History Project; Litzenberg interview; Smith interview.
2   Davis interview.
3   Ibid.
4   Ibid.
5   Ibid.
6   Ibid.
7   Davis, *The Story of Ray Davis*, 135.
8   Davis, *Protector of Freedom*, 14–31.
9   Davis, *The Story of Ray Davis*, 135.

Chapter 30

1   Davis, *The Story of Ray Davis*, 135.
2   Ibid.
3   Ibid.
4   Ibid, 136.
5   Ibid.
6   Ibid.
7   Ibid, 136–137.

Chapter 31

1   Davis, *The Story of Ray Davis*, 138.
2   Davis Oral History transcript, 198.
3   Ibid, 139.
4   Ibid, 140.
5   Ibid.
6   Ibid, 146.
7   Ibid, 142.
8   Ibid.
9   Ibid. 144.
10 Ibid, 153.
11 Ibid, 154.
12 Ibid, 156.
13 Ibid.
14 Ibid, 161.
15 Ibid.
16 Ibid.
17 Ibid, 163.
18 Ibid, 176.
19 Ibid, 178.
20 Ibid.
21 Davis interview.
22 Ibid.
23 Davis, *The Story of Ray Davis*, 184–185.
24 Ibid, 185.
25 Ibid.
26 Davis interview.

Chapter 32

1   Camp, *Leatherneck Legends*, 286.
2   Ibid.
3   Ibid, 287.
4   Davis interview.
5   Charles Smith, *U.S. Marines in Vietnam, High Mobility and Standdown, 1969* (Washington, D.C.: History and Museums Division, Headquarters, U.S. Marine Corps, 1988), 16.
6   Camp, *Leatherneck Legends*, 290.
7   Ibid, 291.
8   Ibid, 290.
9   Davis, *Protector of Freedom*, 22–4.
10 Ibid.
11 Davis, *The Story of Ray Davis*, 190.
12 Ibid.
13 Davis, *Protector of Freedom*, 22–3.
14 Camp, *Leatherneck Legends*, 293.
15 Ibid.

Chapter 33

1   Davis interview.
2   Davis Oral History transcript, 269.
3   Camp, *Leatherneck Legends*, 294.
4   Davis interview.
5   9th Marines Command Chronology.
6   Davis, *The Story of Ray Davis*, 192; Smith, *U.S. Marines in Vietnam, High Mobility and Standdown, 1969*, 16.
7   LtCol Albert T. Conord USMC, *General Raymond Davis and the Principles of War* (Quantico, VA: Masters of Military Studies, Command and Staff College, 2001).
8   Davis, *The Story of Ray Davis*, 195.
9   Davis Oral History transcript, 239.
10 Davis, *The Story of Ray Davis*, 195.
11 Camp, *Leatherneck Legends*, 297.
12 Smith, *U.S. Marines in Vietnam, High Mobility and Standdown, 1969*, 16.

Chapter 34

1   Davis, *Protector of Freedom*, 23–2.
2   Camp, *Leatherneck Legends*, 298.
3   Camp, *Leatherneck Legends*, 299.
4   Ibid, 300.
5   Ibid.
6   Ibid.
7   Ibid.
8   Davis Oral History transcript, 242.
9   Camp, *Leatherneck Legends*, 303.
10 Ibid, 301.
11 High Mobility in Northern I Corps Tactical Zone, Davis brief to Amphibious Warfare School and Command and Staff College, Quantico, 1968–1970.
12 Camp, *Leatherneck Legends*, 302.
13 Ibid.

Chapter 35

1   Camp, *Leatherneck Legends*, 297.
2   Ibid, 305.
3   Ibid, 303.
4   Ibid, 305.
5   Ibid, 306.
6   Ibid.
7   Ibid, 307.
8   Ibid.
9   Ibid.
10 Ibid, 308.

11   Ibid, 309.

12   Ibid.

13   Ibid.

14   Ibid, 310.

15   Ibid.

16   Ibid, 311.

17   Smith, *U.S. Marines in Vietnam, High Mobility and Standdown, 1969*, 41.

18   Camp, *Leatherneck Legends*, 311–312.

19   Davis' son, Miles, was assigned to the 3rd Marine Division after graduating from The Basic School. He was further assigned to the 9th Marine Regiment as a platoon commander. He was wounded in action while on Operation *Dewey Canyon*. General Davis flew into a hilltop landing zone just as a CH-46 helicopter made an emergency landing. His son came out of the bird to greet his father.

20   Ibid, 312.

21   Ibid.

22   Ibid.

23   Ibid, 313.

24   Ibid, 314.

25   Ibid.

Chapter 36

1   General Raymond G. Davis' presentation to Amphibious Warfare School and Command and Staff College, 1968–1970.

2   Ibid.

3   Ibid.

Epilogue

1   Davis, *The Story of Ray Davis*, 231–232.

2   Ibid.

3   Ibid, 252.

4   Davis, *Protector of Freedom*, 25–1.

5   Davis, *The Story of Ray Davis*, 246–247.

6   Davis, *Protector of Freedom*, 26–8.

7   Ibid, 26–6.

Index